DATE DUE			

NEW FRENCH IMPERIALISM
1880—1910

LIBRARY OF POLITICS AND SOCIETY

General Editor Michael Hurst

Church Embattled: Religious Controversy in Mid-Victorian England by M. A. Crowther

The Politics of Government Growth: Early Victorian Attitudes Towards State Intervention 1833–1848 by William C. Lubenow

The Origins of Franco's Spain: The Right, the Republic and Revolutions 1931–1936 by Richard A. H. Robinson

The Peelites and the Party System 1846–1852 by J. B. Conacher

Unionists Divided: Arthur Balfour, Joseph Chamberlain and the Unionist Free Traders by Richard A. Rempel

Political Change and Continuity 1780–1885: A Buckinghamshire Study by Richard W. Davis

IN PREPARATION

The Countess of Huntingdon's Connexion by Alan Harding

Portuguese Society 1680–1756 by John Villiers

The Pastoral Profession by Brian Heeney

ASSOCIATED VOLUMES

Quisling by Paul M. Hayes

Key Treaties of the Great Powers 1814–1914 selected and edited by Michael Hurst

NEW FRENCH IMPERIALISM 1880—1910: THE THIRD REPUBLIC AND COLONIAL EXPANSION

James J. Cooke

DAVID & CHARLES : *Newton Abbot*
ARCHON BOOKS : *Hamden, Connecticut*
1973

This edition first published in 1973 in Great Britain by
David & Charles (Holdings) Limited Newton Abbot Devon,
and in the United States by Archon Books Hamden Connecticut

0 7153 5808 1 (Great Britain)
0 208 01320 2 (United States)

Set in eleven on twelve point Imprint
and printed in Great Britain
by Latimer Trend & Company Ltd Plymouth

Contents

TO JOSEPHINE

Foreword

WRITTEN IN the old style of African history, Professor James J. Cooke's study of France's new imperialism between 1880 and 1910 is excellent. It describes effectively a chapter of European history that is a necessary background for recent African history. Although Professor Cooke touches on Asian topics, his book is essentially about Europeans in Africa and about policy-makers in France who made decisions that affected the course of African history. At his best, Cooke effectively describes the relationship between officials in the field and civil servants, government officials and other shapers of public opinion back in France. In short, he offers a study of policy formation in diplomacy and imperialism during the most intense phases of the scramble for Africa. The author also manages to elucidate more clearly than any of his predecessors the fascinating work of lobbying groups in France which usually managed to ignore the normal party squabbling of French politics in their pursuit of further conquests and more glory. *New French Imperialism 1880–1910* clearly shows what may be gained from a careful reading of archives in France and in Great Britain—a deepened understanding of an important chapter of European history. Best of all, perhaps, the study never loses sight of the individuals involved. It does not deal with abstract ideas in a void, but always in the context of very real people.

As already noted, Cooke's study offers particularly lucid explanations of how and why men on the spot and key leaders in Paris were able to co-operate so effectively. Three men, Théophile Delcassé, Eugène Etienne and Gabriel Hanotaux, dominated the colonial policies of the French Third Republic in the late nineteenth and early twentieth century. None was as determined an imperialist as Etienne, and Cooke quite rightly concentrates on this *colon* who represented the Algerian province

7

of Oran and was in and out of government throughout the period from 1880 to World War I. The three leaders, Delcassé, Etienne and Hanotaux, were all second-generation colonialists—they all claimed to be the heirs of Jules Ferry and Léon Gambetta. They were supported by a cast that included such men-on-the-spot as Hubert Lyautey and publicists of the rank of Joseph Chailley-Bert and Auguste Terrier. In recreating the story of such men, of their conflicts and successes, Cooke fills in an important gap in the history of the Third Republic. He gives new depth to the understanding of imperialism that might be gained from more theoretical studies such as Henri Brunschwig's *French Colonialism 1871–1914: Myths and Realities* and Raymond F. Betts' *Assimilation and Association in French Colonial Theory, 1890–1914.*

Perhaps Cooke's *New French Imperialism 1880–1910* will gain well-deserved success and this will encourage him to write a biography of Eugène Etienne on the model of Christopher Andrew's excellent book entitled *Théophile Delcassé and the Making of the Entente Cordiale.* This suggested contribution would help keep alive a fascinating area of historical investigation, 'old line' African history, that has been recently neglected because of new approaches—perhaps only a fashion—of African histories. There are still many valid questions to be asked and answers to be offered in this imperialist school of historical interpretation. *New French Imperialism 1880–1910* is a prime example of the value of this kind of study.

Alf Andrew Heggoy
The University of Georgia
Summer 1972

Introduction

IN THE long history of France, the era of New French Imperialism was relatively short. It lasted from 1880, a decade after the crushing defeat in the Franco-Prussian War, to 1910, only four years away from the outbreak of World War I. During that brief thirty years three men dominated colonial affairs. Gabriel Hanotaux, Théophile Delcassé, and Eugène Etienne formed the triumvirate who watched, at differing times, over the fortunes of the French empire. All three were servants of the French people: Hanotaux and Delcassé were foreign ministers, while Etienne was a deputy from Oran, Algeria, and for twenty years was the Vice-President of the French Chamber. Differing in backgrounds and personalities, these three men were allies in the imperialistic cause, and they could be called militants. However, the alliance between these men broke down as first Hanotaux and then Delcassé had to contend with the overall problems of French diplomacy while Etienne, remaining free of such responsibilities, tended to interpret all issues in the light of colonial expansion. None of the three could have been successful in expanding the empire had they not been staunchly supported by a host of dedicated colonial activists. In fact, without the vocal and influential members of the Colonial Party in the French Chamber and the *Comité de l'Afrique française*, colonial expansion would have quickly died for lack of support.

Hanotaux began his career as an historian, famous for his multi-volume history of modern France. Journalism was the vehicle for Delcassé, and Etienne started his mature life as a businessman. All three men were the colonial heirs of Jules Ferry, and all three were the political sons of the burly, one-eyed Republican, Léon Gambetta. However, other imperialists shared different backgrounds and other social allegiances. Hubert Lyautey was a convinced aristocrat and a staunch Roman

Catholic. Jean Baptiste Marchand, a simple soldier, appeared seemingly free of social or religious prejudices. The Baron de Rothschild was a Jew, while other colonialists were anti-clericals or atheists. New French imperialists were a coalition of men with various types of political philosophies and professional positions united behind one common goal—the planting of the tricolour on to the unclaimed portions of Africa and Asia. The imperialist alliance was tenuous at best, but it came together after 1880 with such force that it altered the course of French politics and history. New Imperialism was predicated on a simple patriotism and on a reaction to the shame of 1870—the defeat of France by Bismarck's Germany.

The War of 1870 left France prostrate. Her humiliation at the hands of Prussia was a shock to Europe. Reacting to her military disgrace, France searched for new areas in which to regain national prestige and glory. With a large portion of her industrial land seemingly under permanent German occupation, new areas of trade, commerce, and industrial growth had to be found. The French in 1880 were no strangers to colonialism. Once a mighty French empire had existed in the New World, but after a century of wars and European peace settlements, France held only scattered overseas colonies. In Africa the older colonies of Senegal and Algeria were good foundations on which to build a new empire, while Tonkin could serve as a springboard for further Asian conquest. Unfortunately for the colonial dreamers, Mexico, the great imperial disaster of the Second Empire, had soured the French people. The occupation of Tunis in 1882 and the steps towards the consolidation of Indochina were greeted, as a result, with indifference and hostility in France. The work of Jules Ferry, the first master New Imperialist, went unappreciated by the people and, more importantly, by the French Chamber. Ferry, an imposing and austere Protestant from the Vosges, served France during that very critical decade following the fall of the Second Empire. He recognised the absolute folly of the cry for an immediate war of revenge against Germany. Bismarck was the master of continental Europe and Ferry knew it. The demands of the *revanchards* like Georges Clemenceau, the young Paris deputy, would be met in the future, but not in the 1880s.

France had to reforge her prestige in the community of European nations. This, according to Jules Ferry, would have to be done, not on the Rhine, but in Africa. The imperialists never forgot 1870. Acting on Jules Ferry's wise lead, the colonialists began the *revanche* with the struggle for the unclaimed portions of the non-Western world. For advocating such policies, Ferry was sent into early retirement by the Chamber of Deputies. But he left behind a number of disciples who would carry on his imperial work. Activists such as Gabriel Hanotaux, Théophile Delcassé, Charles Jonnart, Paul and Jules Cambon, Eugène Etienne, and others, all called Ferry their master. Building on his foundation, these men constructed a vast empire. With diverse personalities and differing approaches to republicanism, the New Imperialists contributed energy, intelligence, and passion to their cause. The French colonialists claimed that they were men of action, and they were. Few of them were philosophers, and they served French colonialism in many ways, as propagandists, as explorers, or as authors. Many men such as Joseph Chailley-Bert were famous as colonial theorists, and others, like Joseph Galliéni or Jean Baptiste Marchand, explored Africa and Asia. When the struggle for colonialism had to be joined in the Chamber, Eugène Etienne led.

Etienne was born in Oran, Algeria, in 1844. Of French and Corsican peasant stock, Etienne's early life was one of bitter struggle. Instilling in him a Republican equalitarianism, the harsh frontier environment of Algeria coloured Etienne's outlook on life and gave to him a driving ambition to succeed and a ruthlessness which so typified the business community of the late nineteenth century. The Algerian spokesman was well suited for the role he was to play in the colonial movement, since he was a man of action. Like most Frenchmen, he was affected deeply by the disaster of 1870. Finding his outlet in imperial expansion, Etienne devoted his energy to that cause. He entered the Chamber in 1881, an avowed Republican follower of Léon Gambetta and Jules Ferry.

The Chamber, and in fact all of France, was on the verge of the era of New French Imperialism. Tunisia had been annexed into the empire and the Egyptian Crisis of 1882 was only a year away. These two events would shape the decade of the 1880s, as Tunisia showed that colonial acquisition was possible without great bloodshed and expenditure of money. The Suez Crisis of 1882 revealed how delicate was France's situation in the European world. The hesitation of the de Freycinet cabinet to act in concert with Gladstone's England lost for France a position in Egypt. Embarrassing France at a moment when she could least afford to be hurt as far as prestige was concerned, Egypt, as will be seen later, added to the colonial movement an air of competition with Great Britain over African territory. While the English could afford to be reflective on the colonial issues, France could not. Any territory lost would be interpreted as another blot, a stain on the already sullied honour of France.

With this in mind, the small group of colonialists began their work in the 1880s. Paris, the political, social, and economic hub of France, was a brilliant city enjoying her glorious period of art, music, and literature. The colonialists came to the City of Lights determined to restore French glory and prestige: they were to be found in Africa, on the Chad, the Niger, the Congo.

Chapter 1 PRELUDE TO NEW IMPERIALISM 1880-7

In 1880 France could look back over a tumultuous decade of disgrace and partial recovery. In 1870 she was a defeated nation, torn apart by bloody civil war and ideological conflict. By the end of that ten-year period France had recovered to a remarkable degree. However, the French soul still bore scars from the bitter, humiliating defeat by Germany, and many deputies in the Chamber were determined to wipe away that stain. Any offence to the national honour of the Third Republic simply could not be tolerated by patriotic Frenchmen. But there were many roads to revitalisation: Clemenceau preached a gospel of revenge, while Jules Ferry cautioned against rash action. Many deputies sided with Ferry, a late convert to the cause of imperial expansion, who envisioned new imperialism as based mainly on national and on economic needs. Many capitalist-oriented deputies and annexationists, it is true, saw colonialism as a vehicle for economic expansion, but Ferry saw it essentially as a way to refurbish national prestige. Of course, economic considerations were still present in his colonial ideology. In the past, however, colonialism, regardless of its reasons, had proven to be disastrous in regard to national pride and honour.

Louis Philippe had used Algeria as a lever in France's diplomatic dealings with Britain in the 1840s, and the absorption of all of Algeria into the French empire was carried on with little governmental planning, public knowledge, or actual support. The liberals of 1848 who toppled the Orleanist monarchy did not have a clear-cut policy in respect to the colonies, let alone further colonial expansion, and consequently during the hectic days of 1848 northern Algeria was divided into three departments and granted representation in the Chamber. On the other hand, the demands by the revolutionaries to abolish black slavery damaged sugar production in the West Indies, and placed a financial burden on the Caribbean colonies as well as on the homeland. The hostile attitude of the Martinique sugar planters in regard to the ending of slavery did not endear colonialism to the liberals of 1848, who tended to see imperial expansion, at least in the Caribbean, as oppressive and counter to their basic humanitarian ideals.

Imperialism consequently emerged from 1848 as a tarnished institution, and under the reign of Napoleon III the situation deteriorated as Napoleon's policy lead to a further series of setbacks for France overseas. The French intervention in Indochina in 1859 raised a storm of protest in Paris over the cost, and this prompted Napoleon III to consider a complete withdrawal from the area. When the Mexican adventure began to deteriorate seriously, the emperor contemplated bringing French troops home from south-east Asia; he was dissuaded by a powerful combination of clergymen, Bordeaux shipping magnates, and the Ministry of the Marine. Despite the rising protests France would stay in Indochina.

Also damaging to the prestige of colonialism was the fact that many soldiers and administrators in the colonies acted on their own, and in disregarding the advice and often the wishes of the Paris government they incurred the wrath of many anti-Bonapartist deputies. Interesting to note, Jules Ferry was one who criticised the government for its colonial policies and obvious weaknesses in dealing with men such as the headstrong Louis Léon Faidherbe in western Africa.

When the empire fell in 1870, imperialism was clearly in disrepute, as many regarded colonial adventures as the partial cause of the collapse. The troops kept in Algeria, Senegal, and Indochina, they argued, could have helped turn the tide in France in 1870. As doubtful as this seems, it was still true that during the 1870s there were few vocal imperial adherents in France, but by 1880 the picture had changed a great deal. By 1881 a number of activist deputies had been elected to the Chamber, especially from the colonies. François de Mahy of Réunion, Gaston Thompson of Constantine and Eugène Etienne of Oran were examples of three such politicians who were avowed annexationists. As Gambettist republicans they were dedicated to making imperialism popular in their respective districts and in France as a whole, and in the long run they also enjoyed a position of respect within the colonialist ranks. Etienne, for example, was a personal friend of Gambetta and Ferry. In fact, the deputy from Oran was known as a protégé of Gambetta, and was a constant visitor to his home. When Gambetta died in 1882 Etienne was requested by the dying man to remain alone with him until the end came. His colleagues in the Chamber, especially Ferry and the imperialists, detected in the bull-necked Etienne a man of dedication and great energy. Gifted with a deep voice and persuasive manner, he was quickly singled out by the Republican leadership as a man with a future in French politics.[1]

An embryonic imperialist movement, which was slowly taking on some form and substance in the 1880s, was not a monolith, nor could it have been. Each colonialist came to Paris with his own political philosophy. It so happened that these men shared a concern for empire and the expansion of France overseas. Those who were from the colonies expressed an immediacy which other expansionists from metropolitan France did not have; however, certain basic concepts were held in common by the colonialists. Eugène Etienne, who acted as the annexationists' spokesman for many years, denounced the concept of a strict imperialist political party as being harmful to the cause. The colonialist vote, in so far as a block existed, had to be courted by all sides, and Etienne believed that concessions would have to be made to expansionist sentiment in order to obtain their votes for or against legislation.[2]

Etienne's attitude toward the colonies could be summarised in one sentence: 'Every colonial enterprise is a business which must be prudently and practically conducted',[3] and he voiced the colonialists' utilitarian approach to colonialism by saying, 'We are not philosophers; we are men of action. . . . We want our colonies to strengthen, extend, and enrich France; we must act and act practically.'[4] The drive to make the empire show some tangible value for France was necessary because there always remained in the Chamber forces antagonistic to colonialism. The *revanchards* continually questioned the value of Tunis and Tonkin when Alsace-Lorraine remained under German control. By the turn of the century the Socialists, under the formidable Jean Jaurès, questioned both the cost and the morality of imperialism.

But many expansionists were not concerned with the lofty concepts of morality. Agreeing with Lenin's later thesis that imperialism was the highest state of capitalism, they would have added that without a doubt it was the finest endeavour. Aspiring to a colonialism that would be productive for France, they had little time for the ideal of assimilation, which was '. . . a spontaneous collaboration and cordiality [between France and the natives]'.[5] The native, the anti-assimilationists believed, was the least important element in the French colonial system. The *colon*, a European settler in a hostile, non-white land, was like the western pioneer in the United States; he became the keystone of French control in the colony. If the French tricolour was to wave continually over a colony, it would have to be supported by the *colons* and a strong, nearly independent colonial army.[6] Indifferent to the needs and aspirations of the subject peoples, the annexationists considered the white settlers as the producers of raw materials necessary for French industry, and as buyers of French manufactured finished products: the base of neo-mercantilism, as the colonialists saw it, had to be the European colonist.[7] For example, the 200,000 Frenchmen in Algeria living in the midst of over 2 million Muslims became for Eugène Etienne a special *cause célèbre* in the Chamber, and he never tired of telling the Chamber that the *colons* of Algeria, facing great dangers, were the solid foundation of France's Maghribi empire.[8]

Despite the Algerian deputies' concern for the safety of the *colons* in that North African colony, the remainder of the Chamber was at that time uncommitted to action. Actually, the emergence of the *colon* in Algeria, as far as the Chamber was concerned, would be in another century and as a result of another crisis. In the 1880s, however, the arguments surrounding the position of the colonial settler as a participant in the industrial expansion of France played a more important role. This certainly appealed to Jules Ferry, who was more inclined to accentuate the position of the colony and the settler vis-à-vis industrialism than the pioneers' possible role in extending the population of Frenchmen in the overseas possessions. Jules Ferry was the leader of the

'Opportunist' block within the Chamber, and, in the colonial sphere, Ferry's policy was simple: temporarily forget the *revanche* and concentrate on the expansion of empire. For the stone-faced Protestant with imposing mutton-chop whiskers the motto was: 'Colonial policy is a son of industrial policy.'[9] Psychologically, colonies would help France forget about the humiliation of 1870. They would provide industrial France with necessary raw materials and eager markets. Many annexationists believed that the loss of Strasbourg could have its compensation in Tunis or Tonkin and the acquisition of Tunisia, Indochina, and other areas would go far in making the *revanche* a policy of national redemption which would eventually be realised.[10] While the colonialists could never forget Alsace-Lorraine, they realised that hasty military action to recover them would cause a disaster far worse than 1870. Ferry's concepts of imperialism and his opposition to a strict policy of revenge before France had reforged a strong nation became the imperialists' philosophy.

One of the first steps toward the reforging of France by imperial expansion came during Ferry's first ministry, in 1881. Ironically, Ferry was not dedicated to the cause of annexation, but because of the actions of expansionists in the Quai d'Orsay and the colonial military he was forced by their deeds to move toward the occupation of Tunisia. In many respects the Premier was the victim of scheming undersecretaries and colonels, but once involved in Tunisia he slowly became aware of the potential of the empire. This hesitation was in striking contrast to the second Ferry ministry, from 1883 to 1885, when colonial acquisition became the order of the day with activities in the Congo, Madagascar, Somaliland, and Tonkin.

The Tunisian expedition, protested by many deputies, paved the way for future expansion, and many aspects of the annexation of Tunisia became lessons for future colonial officials and administrators. All of the anti-assimilationist tendencies of new French imperialism were present when French troops moved into Tunis and its hinterlands. The treaty between France and the Bey of Tunis, signed on 12 May 1881, was ostensibly meant to restore internal order and to overhaul the chaotic Tunisian financial system; however, the actual, on the spot, implementation of the treaty by the French military forces was quite different. The

commanding general of the occupying forces ordered his sub-
ordinates to discover the 'political news circulating in their areas
and send it without delay to their superior . . .'.[11] This was done
first to insure the safety and mission of the French forces, then
to establish military authority in Tunisia.

On 10 June 1882, the commanding general issued another
order permitting the local French commanders to administer
justice and to punish Muslims (despite Islamic law) who committed any offence against the occupying authority.[12] Kept from
metropolitan public view, the military administration was following a colonial policy advocated by the Parisian colonialist minority.
The slow increase of French authority at the expense of the
Tunisian Bey was one which reflected the times and the violation
of Islamic law clearly showed a basic unconcern with native
customs or institutions. The residency system served a propaganda purpose, but the colonialist deputies, including Etienne,
preferred direct control of a colony by a governor general because
they considered the natives unfit to govern themselves, the
European presence being the only stable element in the colony.
Although they felt that the residency system, with an administra-
tor in theory acting with the Muslim chief, was a weak way to
add colonies to the empire, most annexationists never openly
attacked the Tunisian residency system as such. One occupied
colony was much better than none at all, but generally the
colonialists preferred a more centralised administration of the
colonies because they feared any weakening of imperial influence.
Since they distrusted the natives, the expansionists wanted tight
control of the overseas areas, and centralisation of administration,
they hoped, would bring an imperialist continuity to colonial
affairs both within the colonies and in Paris. Even where centralised administration existed, such as in Algeria, the colonial
deputies pushed for more concentration of authority both in
Algiers and in Paris.

The deputies from Algeria, with Etienne as their spokesman,
suggested in 1882 that the Chamber establish an advisory
commission on Algerian internal, administrative development,
to make recommendations for future laws about the executive
organisation of Algeria.[13] Waldeck-Rousseau, a man openly
friendly to imperial expansion, was suggested as the man to head

such a commission. The Chamber, the colonialist feared, without the right guidance, might not be able to administer the colonies properly. The Chamber had never clashed with the Under-secretary of State for Colonies, who was officially subordinate to the Ministry of Marine. But to avoid a confrontation of any sort, the block of colonial-minded deputies pushed for what they considered to be proper colonial legislation and administration.[14] For the expansionists the problem of irritation between the Chamber and the Undersecretariat was lessened when Félix Faure, a future president of the Republic, took the portfolio for the position in 1882. Faure, Etienne, and the colonialist deputies shared many of the same concepts about the colonies and their administration, and Etienne had been instrumental in convincing Faure to take over the colonial portfolio.[15] Suggesting that Faure had an excellent reputation in the Chamber, the deputy from Oran insisted that his colleagues would respect and follow him.[16] Among the colonial-minded members of the Chamber, Faure was the choice for the post because he was considered to be a staunch imperialist.[17] His position was enhanced when Jules Ferry actively supported his administration of the office in regard to imperial questions.

By early 1883 the colonial group began to take shape within the Chamber. At first, the colonial group in the Chamber was composed of Gaston Thompson of Constantine, François de Mahy of Réunion, Etienne, and a few dozen metropolitan Frenchmen dedicated to colonialism.[18] The colonialists never had any intention of forming a political party in the strict sense of the word, but they were determined to shape France's colonial future to suit themselves. The colonial group included from its genesis members from almost every political group. Because most colonialists were Republicans, however, the Monarchists and Bonapartists seldom found any basis of agreement which would permit them to associate with the colonial group. Many of the rightists were avid *revanchards*, and colonialism conflicted with their principles.

Even Jean Jaurès, the future socialist giant of early twentieth-century France, praised the efforts of colonialists. He felt that imperialism was an agent for spreading French culture and ideas. At a conference of the *Alliance française* held in Albi, France, in

1884, the idealistic Jaurès claimed that colonialism could only bring the goals of assimilation to fruition. Jaurès believed that France's mission was to spread the gospel of French culture, liberalism, and egalitarianism: the principles of 1789.[19]

The natives, Jaurès believed, would be aided '. . . when by intelligence and heart they have learned a little French'.[20] Jaurès practised the politics of emotion, while Etienne practised the politics of pragmatism. The two men were never on good terms, and as imperialism became more aggressive and threatened to lead to war over Africa, Jaurès withdrew all support from annexationism. Etienne was a man of business, a capitalist, and as Jaurès became more wedded to socialism, the two clashed bitterly in the Chamber. By 1904, with Etienne submerged in the preparations for Moroccan penetration, the two became irreconcilable enemies. As the French ideals of assimilation became secondary to territorial acquisition and to commercial profits, Jaurès grew more antagonistic to colonialism, and long before his death in 1914, Jean Jaurès had become the leading anti-colonialist voice.

The majority of the colonialists, however, had little time for assimilation or for worrying about the linguistic aspects of colonialism. The same year that Jaurès addressed the conference of Albi, Etienne told the Chamber that the *colons* of Algeria were vastly outnumbered by the hostile Muslims, and that there were many Spanish workers in Oran who were involved in pro-Spanish agitation against French authority.[21] Etienne demanded more troops for the protection of the *colons*. He stated that France had sent soldiers for a short tour in Algeria, but 'it is not a year of service which we ask of our young men [in Algeria], service [there] . . . is permanent . . . every hour, every minute.'[22]

The work of the *colons* of Algeria, Etienne stated, would be of little value unless the area were developed with the financial and legislative help of the Paris government. The ideas of public works to build up Algeria became the key to success in the mind of Etienne. Speaking to the Chamber, he called for the construction of a railroad into isolated southern Algeria, and for the improvement of the ports of Oran, Bone, Algiers, and Phillippeville. The harbour of Mers-el-Kebir should be enlarged as a part of the general public works to benefit the French navy.[23]

The majority of the imperialists rejected assimilation as an impractical ideal. France, like the rest of the European world, became aware of the then current scientific attitudes towards racial differences. The theories of Charles Darwin filtered into France at the same time colonialism was growing in respectability. Darwin's concept of the development of the species was applied to the races, and in the social transition the European whites became regarded as the best of all the world's racial groups. This Social Darwinism influenced the thought of many of the leading colonialists, Etienne included, and changed the course of imperialism.[24] The new imperialists were certain that there were vast cultural and intellectual differences between the races. One anti-assimilationist deputy told the Chamber, 'The natives do not regiment themselves well or submit to our discipline: the nomadic life suits them better.'[25] In their minds the entire question could be boiled down to a simple formula: the hard-working, thrifty French *colons* as opposed to a lazy, improvident Muslims or blacks. When the Chamber considered raising several regiments of native troops, a colonialist spokesman exploded, asking why the deputies would consider native formations when they already had '. . . intrepid Zouaves, Foreign Legionnaires, and *Chasseurs d'Afrique*'.[26]

The imperialist deputies in the Chamber were not alone in their white supremacist attitudes; the idea that the subject peoples were inferior to the French was widespread among colonial officials. Jules Cambon, when governor general of Algeria, stated: '[France] has shown her generosity; she has wanted to upraise . . . [the Muslim Algerians'] moral and intellectual standards, and raise the condition of their persons . . .'[27] Cambon's paternalistic attitude was typical of the period's flirtation with racism and Social Darwinism. General Joseph Galliéni's concept of the *politique des races*, which was successfully practised in the colony of Madagascar, also reflected the belief that races were inherently different. Galliéni exploited the natives' customs and rivalries to divide the non-European population of the island. Once the native population ceased to have any unity, the French could rule without fear of a massive rebellion. By using the divisions among the natives and superior French technology, the colonial administrators could mould the area into the type of colony that France wanted. The idea of divide and conquer was put into practice in 1882 in Tunisia, when orders were given to local military commanders to '. . . Learn the currents of all political news circulating in the area . . .', and to 'Study the politics and [local] administration of the native population living in their area . . .'.[28] Etienne, for example, warned the Chamber, '. . . we do not hope to obtain the assimilation of the native races in one day. We [colonialists] have shown that for a long time we will have to contend with the customs of the [natives].'[29] Like the western United States, the French empire was wild and untamed. The Muslims, he believed, were like little children, but their capability for rebellion and violence was a ghost that continually haunted the annexationists, spurring them to demand, on every occasion, expanded military protection for the European settlers.[30]

A new colonial philosophy began to shape as the expansionists rejected assimilation. 'Association', as the new concept was called, simply tried to ignore the natives of the empire. The natives, in the minds of the imperialists, were present in the colonies, and were unable to comprehend the values of French technology or assimilate the glories of French culture. As Jules Cambon stated, they were, as far as the imperialists were concerned, little children who had to be treated as such. Local, native political and social systems would not be altered, and the colonialists would encourage the natives to continue to exist within their own systems. Equality, or the hope of first-class French citizenship, was simply not a part of the associationists' concept of the empire. Hospitals, roads, and a few schools would be built as humanitarianism and propaganda demanded, but this would be about all that would be done. As Etienne had indicated, the imperialists' first concern was the *colons*, not the natives.

In 1885 the colonial question erupted in the Chamber in a series of bitter debates which placed the reputation of Jules Ferry and the colonialists in jeopardy. The Ferry Ministry in 1884 and 1885 had intervened often in Indochina and in Madagascar, and each step toward further occupation lead to hostile clashes in the Chamber. Believing that stronger action was necessary in the colonies, Ferry, Admiral Peyron, the Minister of the Marine and Colonies, and Faure, the Undersecretary of State for Colonies, had removed a number of weak or argumentative officials in Indochina and replaced them with stronger imperialists.[31] This irritated the anti-colonial forces within the Chamber even more. However, Ferry, who was President of the Council of Ministers, continued to push for continued penetration and reorganisation of Indochina.[32]

In the spring of 1885 the Ferry Ministry was replaced by one lead by Henri Brisson. Brisson maintained a colonialist administration at the Ministry of the Marine and Colonies by appointing Admiral Galiber as its chief. Galiber, conspicious in the naval action in Madagascan waters in 1883 and 1884, asked Félix Faure to retain the colonial portfolio.[33] One of the major problems facing the Brisson cabinet as well as Ferry's colonialists in the Chamber was the forthcoming debates on the budget for Indochina which would be held in late 1885. Already, many members of the Chamber were openly upset over French moves in Madagascar, and when Charles de Freycinet, the Minister of Foreign Affairs in late 1885, announced to the Chamber that a peaceful accord had been reached with the sovereigns of Madagascar, deputies from the left and monarchist right demanded to know why such a solution could not be found in Indochina.[34]

The debates on the budget for Indochina were heated and long, with the deputies lining up according to political persuasion. Jules Ferry, Faure, de Freycinet, Etienne, and others defended the Bill against the attacks from the left and the monarchist right, and despite the surprising defection of one deputy from Algeria the budget carried. The debates had been as much a defence of colonial policy as it had been a post-mortem judgement on the expansionist attitude of the Ferry ministry. It appeared that the Opportunists would support colonialism as a part of their policy, even though some did so weakly.[35]

The Indochinese debates of 1885 marked something of a milestone for the cause of French colonial expansion because it brought to the front the small number of deputies who would form the nucleus for the French colonial party by 1892. In 1885 they were influential in urging the Chamber to support France's actions in Indochina, and after bitter debate funds were allocated for the administration of the region. More importantly, however, was the fact that the annexationists had emerged as a vocal force tied basically to republican ideology. Colonialism transcended party lines and labels and was yet to be properly evaluated, but the imperialists such as Eugène Etienne and Félix Faure could see that expansionism was gaining some respectability despite its tarnished image. The conflict between the republicans and the monarchists aided in the acceptance of colonialism because republicans, despite their personal feelings, tended to support anything the monarchists stood against. Certainly the personal friendship between Ferry, Etienne and Faure did not hurt the imperialist cause.

The administration of Félix Faure at the colonial undersecretariat came, for the expansionists, at a fortunate time. Faure was respected as a man with a great insight into governmental as well as colonial affairs, and as such he enjoyed the confidence of most of the Republicans. The tenure of Faure at the undersecretariat was not a militant one; in the long run, however, it was an activist one. Enjoying the respect and support of Ferry, Etienne, and most of the imperialist deputies, Faure showed that his office would interest itself, with ever increasing intensity, in the affairs of the overseas possessions. He set a basic tone for his successor, Eugène Etienne, who would add a militant threat to the position. By 1887, the imperialists were prepared to push their expansionist concepts and to try to enlarge France's empire.

Notes to Chapter 1 will be found on pages 175–6.

Chapter 2 ANNEXATION AND EXPANSION 1887-90

In May 1887, Maurice Rouvier formed his first cabinet; he chose Eugène Etienne, an old political comrade from Marseilles, to serve as Undersecretary of State for Colonies. While a minor post in the cabinet, the undersecretariat did control the far-flung empire. Félix Faure, chosen by Jules Ferry to head the department in 1883, left to his successor a well-run organisation, but more important was the fact that Faure had maintained excellent relations with the Chamber and with various ministries of the government. Jules Ferry trusted him implicitly with the fate of the empire,[1] as did many other officials. While not a spectacular man, Faure prepared the way for Etienne, and he aided in making the position of Undersecretary of State for Colonies a respected and consulted member of the government.

The most pressing problem facing the undersecretary was that of a serious reorganisation of the empire into some sort of functioning system. France had acquired new colonial holdings over a period of three decades, but the task of giving form and substance had not been fully undertaken. Joseph Galliéni, some ten years before his policy of the *tache d'huile* became famous, warned colonialists that, 'I continue to believe in the future of our growing, far-flung empire, and [that] its abandonment would be a gigantic wrong for our country.'[2] The neglect of an empire by France was an absurdity to Galliéni and his imperial allies. The British had found that an empire could drift away, as in North America in 1776. Etienne, to avoid the same fate for French colonies, issued reform decrees on 2 and 5 September 1887, which set the tone for his five years as colonial undersecretary. His directive of 2 September placed many lieutenant-governors, commandants, and residents into a unique category called *les administrateurs coloniaux*.[3] The decree of 5 September created governors for the colonies of Mayotte, Obock, Saint Pierre and Miquelon, and Diego Suarez.[4] This decree upgraded the executive and administrative status of each colony, and it was clear that even the smallest colony was of interest to Etienne. The reform decrees did a great deal to raise the status of all colonial governors by adding them to the important *classes personelles*. This meant that the French government, usually through the colonial secretariat, paid for certain expenses such as trips back to France and made financial allowances for a portion of the maintenance of the governor and his staff of secretaries and assistants.[5]

By adding the colonial executives to the *classes personelles*, it was possible for men of any social and economic standing to become high officials in the imperial administrative apparatus. These decrees, applauded by the imperialists, made it clear that wealth would no longer be the prerequisite for the appointment of a man to executive position in the colonies. As a bourgeois Republican, the undersecretary had little regard for the noble born. He felt that the imperial administration should be staffed by men dedicated to colonial expansion. However, these reforms were opposed by some colonial agents in Indochina who felt that the undersecretariat would use the measures to oust them from their jobs. This so-called 'injustice' was viewed as a threat to the older administrators in the area.[6]

Unfortunately for annexationists, France was in the midst of a serious political crisis in late 1887, and as a cabinet official Etienne was swept along with the tide of political misfortune. To complicate France's political misfortunes the Wilson Affair became known in the Paris press in the autumn of 1887 and further seriously upset the French equilibrium. Daniel Wilson, a senator and son-in-law of Jules Grévy, the French president, was accused of taking advantage of his influence with the Elysée Palace by peddling positions and decorations, including the Legion of Honour, to the highest bidders.[7] The Wilson scandal, used by Clemenceau in the Chamber,[8] rocked the French state. The Opportunists, led by Jules Ferry and other Republicans, bitterly attacked Grévy and the Rouvier government and they toppled it from power in the autumn of 1887.

The deputies then turned on Grévy and demanded his resignation as well. Ferry harboured a desire to run for the presidency, and therefore led the attack against Rouvier and Grévy, but his attempts to return to power were fruitless. As American ambassador Robert McLane reported to Washington, 'No words can describe the excitement of the [Paris political] community when this fraud was exposed. . . . The Chamber of Deputies manifested the same rage as all the press.'[9] Because of Rouvier's resignation, the imperialists' most able exponent was temporarily forced out of administrative office.

McLane, concerned about the Wilson crisis and the possibility of a Boulangist coup, informed the State Department that the political situation was serious as the Chamber refused to support any government until Grévy was gone. Grévy had recommended several new premiers, but the Chamber opposition led by Ferry and Clemenceau refused even to consider them. In late November Grévy surrendered and tendered his resignation, but on 1 December there were noisy demonstrations in Paris against any move by Jules Ferry to take the premiership or presidency.[10] The austere Ferry, unable to inspire public enthusiasm, knew that the populace were infected with the Boulanger fever. The political crisis ended any chance Ferry had for power for ever. However, the undersecretariat continued to function under Félix Faure.

Félix Faure, a man who was not fully trusted by the more militant imperialists, returned to the undersecretariat to take up residence as its chief. Galliéni wrote that, as ordered, he was leaving the Sudan for his new post in Indochina, but he feared that his successor would not be as staunch an imperialist as he would desire.[11] He also advised Paris that France needed to be especially aware of British influence in western Africa. The English, whom Galliéni called 'our adversaries', continued to penetrate the hinterlands of the Niger River. To counter British subversion in West Africa, the colonel believed that the natives of the empire should be taught in French schools by French instructors. They should be guided into a strict loyalty to France.[12]

While Faure and Etienne were concerned with the growing friction in West Africa, they were also involved with Indochina. Both men had extensive dealings with the area. The problems of south-east Asia were acute also, and during the period between his terms as colonial undersecretary, Etienne continued his interest in the area. Faure had worked on the problem of a sensible governmental structure for Cambodia and Indochina during his term as undersecretary, and Etienne had signed two decrees on 17 and 20 October 1887, which set the reorganisation in motion. The decree of 17 October centralised the administration of Cochin China, Tonkin, and Cambodia under a *Gouverneur General civil de l'Indo-chine*. The executive apparatus of Annam and Tonkin was also transferred from the Ministry of Foreign Affairs to the Ministry of the Marine and Colonies. The confusing dual authority had caused a slowdown in decision-making. Etienne tried to reorganise by centralising the whole of Indochina into a single administrative unit, thus eliminating the dual responsibility for the executive apparatus.[13] Three days later a second decree was issued recognising some dual control of Indochina's defensive forces because the colonial troops were under the authority of the War Ministry. The Colonial Marines, however, were subject to the Ministry of the Marine and Colonies.[14]

On 12 December 1887, the undersecretariat issued a third decree concerning the Indochinese organisation. This decree gave to the governor general the power to appoint civil employees other than those directly named by the ministers of foreign affairs and the marine. It indirectly deprived the president of the republic of some direct authority with regard to the appointment of officials to south-east Asia. The governor also received the right to place certain areas of Indochina under martial law without prior consultation with Paris.[15] The modification of the executive system in French south-east Asia marked the high point in Etienne's first tenure as undersecretary. The energetic action taken by him and the three key decrees issued in the autumn of 1887 marked him as a man of action and foresight. Warning Etienne that the Chamber would think a lot less of his work than did the more knowledgeable colonialists, Ferry stated that the undersecretariat would have to do more toward unifying all of the Asian colonies.[16]

Colonial annexation had a number of detractors and antagonists in the Chamber. In the political confusion which followed the

Wilson Affair and in the wake of Boulanger's rise to prominence, many deputies, especially the rightists and the *revanchards* who followed Clemenceau, questioned the soundness of a policy of colonial expansion while the humiliation of 1870 remained unavenged. Ferry and the colonialists clung to imperialism as a keystone of foreign policy, but the Chamber remained sceptical if not hostile. The growing number of colonialists watched as Félix Faure again took the portfolio of colonies in the newly formed Tirard government.

However, Faure, well known to the imperialists, was as dedicated to the annexationist cause as his predecessor. An energetic exponent of colonial expansion, he tried to carry on his predecessor's work in a spirit of continuity in the administration of the colonies. During the debate on the colonial budget on 13 February 1888, Faure went before the Chamber to ask for more funds to continue the reorganisation of Indochina. Since the budget had been drawn up by Etienne, Faure was unfamiliar with it. Attacked by the *revanchards* for spending vast sums of money and for sending troops to south-east Asia when, as they claimed, the work of France was on the Franco-German frontier, Faure seemed bewildered as he was forced to defend a policy which was essentially Etienne's. The former undersecretary asked if he might address the Chamber to justify his own Indochina policy.

While Indochina had not been one of Etienne's primary imperial concerns, he defended the colony during the bitter debates of 1888. Because of his staunch belief in colonialism as a necessity for France and out of his longstanding friendship for Jules Ferry, the deputy from Oran was vocal in his attacks on the anti-imperialist delegates. His most emotional response occurred when a deputy demanded that France withdraw all French soldiers and administrators from Indochina. Seeing this as a possible major defeat for imperial France, Thompson of Constantine, de Mahy of Réunion, and Etienne joined together in denouncing the plan for a withdrawal from the south-east Asian colony.[17] At one point the imperialist deputies even accused some members of the Chamber of supporting colonialism simply as a means of securing lucrative appointments as governors and administrators for political friends and supporters. Regarding the colonies as a place where social standing and family heritage meant nothing, most annexationists decried such a situation despite loud hoots and jeers from the right.[18]

Etienne continued to defend his actions in respect to the Asian colony by asking why the Chamber believed that he sought to unify Indochina. Etienne answered his own question saying, 'I must tell you that even before being charged with the administration of colonies, I was imbued with that conviction that it was absolutely necessary to realise that vital work.'[19] The unification was necessary because of the forces of anarchy which disrupted the life of Indochina. Because of bandits and terrorists, Indochina, from Hanoi to Saigon, needed security and authority. Prosperity, if it were ever to come to Indochina, rested first on internal peace and security.[20] The union of the provinces, claimed Etienne, was necessary, '. . . in administration as well as finances. In policy, [we must] proceed with great prudence, and we must, step by step, influence [the natives] by a calm, dignified, but firm attitude. . . .'[21]

In the course of the defence, the imperialist deputies crossed swords with the mighty Clemenceau. Etienne, acting as their spokesman, claimed that there were about 36,000 troops engaged in various peace-keeping activities in Indochina. Suddenly a *revanchard* deputy shouted, 'It would be better that those 36,000 troops be in France [on the eastern frontier].' Quickly, Etienne replied that of that large number of soldiers, 22,000 were native troops. The remaining 14,000 were metropolitan troops, Algerians, and Foreign Legionnaires. Clemenceau, glaring, jumped up, and told Etienne that there were 10,000 more metropolitan troops employed in Indochina than the former undersecretary had indicated. Stunned into silence, and evidently caught in a misinterpretation of the facts, Etienne did not respond. Clemenceau, sensing a brief victory over the enemy, again informed the deputy from Oran that those soldiers would find better work in the Vosges line.[22] The two enemies glared at each other, and amid shouts from the right and *revanchards*, the Chamber adjourned for the day.

The clash between Clemenceau and Etienne was typical of the former's dislike for the colonial militants and of his growing irritation with imperialism. These bitter exchanges, which filled the Chamber until both sides fully united in opposition to Germany in 1914, revealed the basic division in French political opinion over colonialism. For Clemenceau the most important thing was the *revanche*; for the expansionists it was colonial annexation. The antagonism toward colonial acquisition was well founded. The costs were very high, and despite attempts during the 1890s to exploit the colonies, there were recurring, large financial deficits. Indochina alone cost France over 30½ million francs in 1888. Despite the obvious yearly expenditure, the colonialists believed that one day Indochina would be like Senegal, '. . . the only colony which gives us compensation'.[23] There were also some less apparent advantages. The imperialists believed, for example, that the colonies could help France's naval forces. Galliéni, staunchly loyal to the annexationist cause, constantly wrote to point out the potential use of the colonies for military purposes. He advised that the excellent colonial harbours could be developed for naval use. The colonies of St Pierre and Miquelon, Martinique, and the ports of Dakar, Diego-Suarez, Saigon and Haiphong, Galliéni suggested, should be enlarged and fortified while European soldiers and marines should also be sent to reinforce Guadaloupe, Guyana, and Réunion.[24]

Galliéni already influenced Etienne's colonial career and his advice became a guide to practical action for the deputy from Oran. Etienne, for his part, realised that colonialism per se would never be very popular in France: for support of imperial adventures, the colonialist would have to turn to the army. Men like Galliéni and his young subordinate Hubert Lyautey were lifelong supporters of colonialism, and the military became the primary supporters of militant colonial policies outside the colonial group in the Chamber and the activist colonial organisations such as the *Comité de l'Afrique française*.

Despite the gains made by the expansionists in 1888, colonialism was overshadowed in the Chamber as the French Republicans had to cope with the seriousness of the rise of General Georges Boulanger. As Robert McLane reported to Washington, Ferry and the Opportunists attacked Boulanger to try to shore up the Republican government,[25] and during 1888 Boulanger was investigated by the army and his name was removed from the active list because of his political activities. Inflamed rightists attacked the Republic over the Wilson Affair and Boulanger's demotion, and they assaulted the democratic processes of the Third Republic. During the confusion over Boulanger, the colonialists succeeded in removing the administration of the colonies from the Ministry of Marine to the Ministry of Commerce and Industry. The imperialists feared that the Navy was a bastion of rightists, and that the colonies could be damaged by the antagonism of the Monarchists. The move to Commerce and Industry was also designed to give the colonial undersecretary more authority. On 17 March 1889, Etienne was appointed to that position by Louis de Freycinet, who headed a new government.

Etienne had a new spacious office on Rue Saint Florentin and the position he was to hold and manage for the next three years began to take on importance as France's empire grew in size. The great penetration of Africa was beginning in earnest, and explorers, under orders from Etienne, began to open up the 'dark continent'. New colonies such as Dahomey were added to French Africa, and a prime example of Etienne's interest in new colonies in Africa was his executive decree which founded the colony of Guinée. The undersecretariat created the colony, on 1 August 1889, for two reasons. Primarily there was an interest in the growing imperial competition between England and France. The colonialists believed that the creation of the colony provided a presence which would serve as a challenge to the British in the Niger region. Hoping to increase and consolidate the French African empire, they wished to give an immediate form, structure, and government to the area.[26]

The undersecretariat had to deal with the problem of contracting penal labour for the mines of New Caledonia, a practice which many deputies criticised as harsh and inhuman. In this first opportunity to appear before the Chamber as undersecretary, Etienne was determined that the office would be represented with determination and force. Defending the convict labour system, Etienne claimed that New Caledonia could be a rich colony, but an extensive public works system was necessary to make the colony yield a profit. The penal law, he pointed out, was put in force for the entire empire in 1864, and since that time convicts had built roads, dams, and gendarmerie stations and barracks. The system had worked so well for New Caledonia that common sense and good economics demanded its continuance. In New Caledonia, Etienne claimed, convict labour had reduced the building and construction costs by a million francs.[27]

In 1889, however, the New Caledonian question took on more meaning: the rich nickel mines were producing a very vital raw material for France, penal labour was used in the exploitation of the mines, and also the colonialists envisioned using the Pacific colony as a source of meat for the French army. France lacked adequate beef sources, and suppliers had to be contacted in the western United States. This foreign import and dependence on the cattle of the American plains would be stopped when New Caledonia began to function as a supplier of beef.[28]

The colonialists were practical men, and they realised and displayed during the interpellation on New Caledonia the necessity for a colony to have some sort of raison d'être. No true imperialist could ever point to the empire without mentioning the financial or strategic benefits to France. To make a colony work for the mother country, two things were necessary: trained personnel and loyal, 'pacified' natives. To ensure the accomplishment of those two goals, two decrees were issued by the government establishing the *école coloniale*, thus assuring the empire of a continuing supply of loyal colonials and native administrators. These decrees dealt with the financial backing for the school and with the course of study to be offered in the school.[29]

One of the decrees dealt with the status of native students at the *école coloniale* since the loyalty of the subject peoples in the empire was of great concern to colonialists. To assure that the natives remained loyal to France, they would be trained in the metropolitan country. Not acting out of any assimilationist or humanitarian impulses, the annexationists theorised that the main purpose of the school was a pragmatic one of keeping the empire free of rebellion from the top down. The first students admitted from the empire were Indochinese who were recommended by Galliéni.[30]

All students, regardless of national origin, had to have '[moral training], excellent health, and a sufficient [educational] background'.[31] The *école coloniale* was controlled by Etienne and a

c

council of administration which assured permanent colonialist control of the admittance and curriculum. Over three decades the school functioned as a reservoir for colonial executive talent. While not concerned with colonial philosophy or theoretical issues, the school became the keystone for the new wave of imperialists which poured out of France for the next half-century.

The colonialist effort was also bolstered by the *Comité de l'Afrique française*, founded in 1890 by a number of influential imperialists who saw the need for a concerted effort in Africa, where France was threatened by British advances. France, the colonialists believed, had lost too much to Britain by default or inaction in Africa, especially Egypt. The founders of the *Comité* wanted to insure that this would not happen again. The French imperialists had reason to fear the efforts of the British in western Africa. Great Britain, though the Royal Niger Company, a commercial organisation founded by the imperialist George Taubman Goldie in July 1886, tried to claim all the Niger River region for England.[32]

In 1890, Théophile Delcassé, who held a post at the Quai d' Orsay, tried to counter this action by establishing French commercial trading companies which had been advocated earlier by Etienne. Delcassé, committed to action in Africa, urged an apathetic Chamber to vote credits for the enterprise. The deputies refused to tender large sums of money for a project which they believed to be a waste. Delcassé, an undersecretary in the Quai d'Orsay, was fully convinced of the value of such a project for commercial enterprise to challenge the English. When, in 1893, Delcassé became chief of the colonial office in the Ministry of Marine he established a number of commercial concessions by decree.

Theoretically, France and England settled some of their African problems, especially that of a definition of borders between the Niger River and Lake Chad. In August 1890 a line was drawn from the southern tip of the lake to the town of Say on the west bank of the Niger River. All the area above the line was supposed to be French and all land below it was destined to be British. This rather hazy definition of the French and English territory only led to more serious problems. Four years later, in 1894,

Captain Frederick Lugard explored the Niger region; he was warned by Goldie that since 1890 the French had made a large number of treaties with the natives in the British region. Lugard's orders were to contest those agreements.[33] Goldie's information about the French attitude was correct, because as soon as the Niger agreement was signed Etienne began to order explorers into the area. By the time Lugard arrived in Nigeria in 1894 there were over five French explorative missions operating in the area.[34]

The colonialists reacted to the growing friction in western Africa by dispatching several missions and by founding the *Comité de l'Afrique française*. Thirty colonialists, determined to convince a reluctant public and an apathetic Chamber of the value of colonialism, met together to form the new, vocal African committee. Numbered among the ranks were well-known men such as the Prince d'Arenberg, Robert de Caix, and Hippolite Percher.[35] Percher, because of his fanatical devotion to colonialism, was appointed editor of the *Comité*'s monthly magazine, the *Bulletin*. With the open support of Delcassé, d'Arenberg, Etienne, and de Caix, the new editor became the voice of the colonial movement. He wrote under the name of Harry Alis until his death in 1895 as a result of a duel with an outraged deputy. Percher, or Alis, became the symbol of colonialism, a major imperial author,[36] and his favour was eagerly sought by many of the European colonial powers. In fact, he was showered with gifts by agents of the Belgian King Leopold II because the monarch wanted Alis to champion his cause in the Congo through the editorial columns in the *Bulletin*. While Leopold's men in Paris tried to influence every deputy and important figure, they were especially interested in Harry Alis.[37] However, it appeared from the letters written by Leopold's representatives in the French capital that Eugène Etienne was one man the Belgians could not bribe. They feared the creation of an independent colonial ministry, and they especially did not want Etienne to become its chief. The undersecretary refused to be a party to any act which might endanger French imperial interests, and he repeatedly urged the Chamber to grant commercial concessions in French West Africa and the Congo. Etienne had become a man to be feared as well as respected.[38]

Soon after the founding of the *Comité*, men like Galliéni and Lyautey joined. The years from 1887 to 1890 had been a time of organisation for the colonialists, a prelude to the great years of activity from 1890 to 1910. The establishment of the colonial group in the Chamber aided in the founding of such important annexationist institutions as the *école coloniale*, and the *Comité de l'Afrique française*. They had placed their stamp on French colonialism, and by their efforts the concept of empire was implanted in France, preparing the way for the colonial work of the 1890s.

Notes to Chapter 2 will be found on pages 176–8.

Chapter 3 THE OPENING OF AFRICA 1890-2

THE LAST two years of Etienne's rule at the Rue Saint Florentin were busy and productive ones filled with great work which realised dreams for the empire. The years from 1890 to 1892 were unsettling for France. The Panama Canal scandal broke on the political scene, but like so many affairs at which the French feign so much outrage, it had little real effect on the Chamber. Georges Clemenceau, somewhat tarnished by the Boulanger Affair, was implicated in the Panama incident and lost his Chamber seat for a time.[1] The *Comité de l'Afrique française* was growing faster than any other colonialist-oriented group in France, and in 1891, a year after its founding, it reported 942 members and a working capital of over 187,000 francs.[2] Baron Alphonse de Rothschild of the Paris branch of the famous banking family contributed 10,000 francs to the *Comité* in 1891 and the influential publishing firm, Maison Hachette, gave 5,000 francs.[3] With the backing of the Rothschilds and with the presses of Hachette at its disposal, the *Comité* felt it necessary to work as quickly as possible to consolidate France's holdings in western Africa.

The situation in West Africa had grown into a serious problem for the French colonialists. Britain continued to make territorial gains around the Lagos area and threatened to move deep into the hinterland toward Lake Chad which the French claimed. These rival claims from the coast to Lake Chad were mainly paper claims because neither the French nor the British had actually sent missions to take personal charge of the region. Both countries had excellent beachheads in the area—France at Dakar and the British at Lagos. It was a matter of who could act first and with stronger resolve. Etienne was also under pressure from a number of powerful colonialists to establish as quickly as possible a French presence in the vast hinterland of central

37

Africa toward Lake Chad. Eugène-Melchoir de Vogüé, a conservative spokesman and famous literary figure, wrote in the
November 1890 issue of the *Revue des Deux Mondes* that France
was inviting a disaster by not pushing rapidly into the central
African interior. De Vogüé warned that there were three European powers in competition for that region. England, France,
and Germany had an equal chance of reaching the interior and
claiming it for their African empire. Seeing this as a threat to
France's colonial expansion, de Vogüé urged militant action.[4]
This was a voice that the leadership of the colonial party could
not ignore, and they hastened to send as many missions as possible
into the region. Sympathetic with the position taken by de Vogüé
and other imperialist authors, the undersecretariat was convinced
that the time was right for an aggressive exploration of the interior
of Africa to Lake Chad.

A mission under Captain Monteil had been officially dispatched
in 1890 at the same time as the Royal Niger Company began
pushing into the interior toward Lake Chad.[5] Since 1889,
Britain and France were in competition all over western Africa,
and to try to avoid bloodshed the two nations signed an agreement on 5 August 1890 to define the region between the Niger
and Lake Chad. The agreement, signed by England's Lord
Salisbury and France's Ambassador Waddington, recognised
the British protectorate over Zanzibar as *fait accompli*. Then
the two negotiators drew a vague, unenforceable line from the
southern tip of Lake Chad to the town of Say on the bend of the
Niger River.[6]

The colonial leadership, upset over the confusing decision in
western Africa, urged in 1889 the organisation of the mission of
Paul Crampel to explore the vast region from southern Algeria
to the Chad and to the French Congo. Speaking before the *Comité*
in 1890, Crampel, who was already well known for his work with
de Brazza in the French Congo, said, 'One dies not have to have
a passion for complicated theories. . . . The union of the shores
of Chad to those of our possessions of Algeria and of the Congo
and of the [French] Sudan will be a formula, and my voyage will
be the symbolic deed.'[7] Crampel left France with official blessings on 10 March 1890, never to return. Later that year, the
survivors of the mission staggered into Brazzaville in the French

Congo, with the news of their leader's death. The demise of Crampel was surrounded with mystery, and the full details of his death never came to light.[8] However, it appeared that the Crampel mission, even before its departure, caused some irritation in the imperialist ranks. The great French explorer Savorgnan de Brazza had been offered the position as chief of the expedition to the Chad, but he refused because of his great interest in the French Congo. Etienne then hand-picked Crampel, who was known to be very intelligent and intrepid, but somewhat headstrong. Evidently, de Brazza, who had vast experience in African exploration, made some suggestions concerning the course and attitude of the mission, but Crampel refused to consider any suggestions made by de Brazza.[9] This situation prompted a series of letters between Etienne and the angered de Brazza concerning the incident over a two-year period after Crampel's death, and to make matters even worse Harry Alis strongly praised the dead Crampel's deeds and memory. The first edition of the *Bulletin* which appeared in 1891 was devoted to the ill-fated Crampel mission. However, the imperial activists had committed France to a specific course of action by exploration, and intrepid explorers prepared the groundwork for the opening of French Africa.

At a meeting of the *Comité de l'Afrique française* on 31 August 1891, there was general gloom over the failure of the Crampel mission to accomplish great things. The acting president, Prince d'Arenberg, was pressured by Harry Alis to issue a statement of deep regret and to reiterate the *Comité*'s support for active exploration. It was at that meeting that Jean Dybowski's name was mentioned, probably by Alis, as a possible successor to Paul Crampel.[10] Alis immediately championed Dybowski, and he placed pressure on Etienne to accept Jean Dybowski as the new explorer of central Africa. Not satisfied with this victory, Alis began an active campaign to staff the new mission with his friends. Charles de Maistre was proposed to the Dybowski mission with the active support of Alis, and when the mission departed from Bordeaux in late 1891 de Maistre was a member.[11]

The unfortunate death of Paul Crampel was overshadowed by the fact that the area from the Chad to Say was still unexplored. To remedy this situation, which the colonialists felt to be critical, new missions were formed to explore the area. Etienne approved of Captain Jean Dybowski, a man familiar with Africa, to lead a new group, and Dybowski, well aware of Crampel's death, was more than ready to undertake the task. Etienne stressed to Dybowski that his mission to the Chad had to be conducted peacefully and with a minimum of friction with the natives. The Crampel party had some nasty encounters in the region where Dybowski was to go but Crampel had sent back to Paris a vast amount of information concerning that region of central Africa. De Brazza, who was the Commissioner General of the French Congo, tried to warn Etienne and especially Crampel that in gathering important geographical and tribal data concerning central Africa there might be serious and violent encounters with the tribes.[12] Despite the power of Etienne in such matters as official orders to the missions, the *Comité de l'Afrique française* could exert great pressure. In a letter to Dybowski, Prince d'Arenberg stated that the *Comité* expected great things from him, and basically he was to follow in the footsteps of Crampel. Perhaps as a counterweight to the growing influence of Alis, d'Arenberg warned that de Brazza was not to be ignored and that he was to be consulted while the mission was in the Congo region.[13] Certainly, the Undersecretariat for Colonies was also determined not to suffer another disaster such as the one which befell Paul Crampel's mission. To make sure that this was carried out, Etienne instructed his explorer to '[have] no recourse to arms until the last extremity, and never to use force against the natives and . . . accentuate the peaceful nature [of the mission]'.[14] Despite the instructions given by Etienne, the Dybowski mission ended in failure when its chief, becoming seriously ill in the Congo, was forced to return to France.[15] Despite the obvious failures of the Crampel and Dybowski missions, Etienne had committed France to an active policy of African exploration, and, logically, annexation. Never fully certain of public or official approval, Etienne continued his policy of penetration, drawing France into Africa.

The initiative for the penetration of Africa passed from Rue Saint Florentin to the Chamber, and in early March Etienne was called before the deputies to defend his work in western Africa. Of great interest to the Chamber were the continual reports of disorder and anarchy in Dahomey. The Dahomey situation occupied a great deal of the Chamber's time because the small enclave, situated near Senegal and the Ivory Coast, formed an important part of French West Africa. The harbour of Porto Novo, in 1890 not too impressive, could be improved as a naval base which would serve as a link in the chain of French maritime ports.

Etienne informed the Chamber that in 1851 a treaty between French representatives and the king of Dahomey gave to France the exclusive right to trade in the Porto Novo region. By that treaty, the French gained the right to build Fort Whyda. Etienne added that the French representatives in Dahomey '. . . are forced to attend certain [tribal] ceremonies, and when one speaks of rituals in that country he means human sacrifice'.[16] The astounded and silent Chamber gazed at the undersecretary, and some gasped in horror. With this reaction in mind, he then said that the king of Dahomey was contesting sections of the 1851 treaty, saying that it was never intended that huge tracts of land be permanently given to France. Porto Novo fell within the lands reclaimed by the king. To complicate matters, enraged warriors of the monarch had attacked and burned a section of Porto Novo, and Etienne claimed that these new actions endangered European lives and property. The Chamber was reminded that France had a detachment of Legionnaires in Dahomey, and if the situation did not stabilise itself, 'It will be necessary to take more energetic measures.'[17] To this calculated bellicosity the Chamber responded with cheers. Etienne's speech on the crisis which was brewing in Dahomey was a masterstroke. The tales of human sacrifice upset the Chamber; it was uncivilised and not very French. It prepared the minds of the deputies for the 'more energetic action' which Etienne wanted. The Chamber was convinced by Etienne's dramatic revelations that any action to pacify Dahomey would be a real step forward for civilisation in Africa.

On 10 May 1890, the deputies called the undersecretary back to the Chamber to discuss the progress of the Dahomey situation. He told the deputies that the king of Dahomey had been informed that the French government insisted on the enforcement of all the articles of the 1851 treaty. But, Etienne warned, as long as France showed any hesitation, trouble was going to spread to the

French Sudan or to Senegal. France had the duty to protect British nationals as well as French citizens and he asked, 'Must we expose our nationals as well as foreigners to a massacre?'[18]

There was danger, the imperialists believed, in not taking swift action in Dahomey, because a withdrawal or a defeat in the area would menace all of France's African empire.[19] The fear of losing West Africa caused Etienne to formulate several decrees concerning the area, revealing his concern over the turmoil. He turned his attention to the French Sudan, and on 18 August 1890 the master of the colonial ministry issued a directive giving greater executive powers to the governor general of the colony. His office became almost totally separate from the governor general of Senegal. A decree promulgated on 6 September 1890 created a military *commandant superieur* for the Sudan. While nominally dependent on the governor of Senegal for military reinforcements, he could take independent military action.[20] Etienne's whole approach to Africa was one of greater freedom of action for the local commanders. Believing that an overcentralised colonial administration would only hurt colonialism because of the time element involved in decisions and because of the possibility of eventual interference from an unfriendly government in France, Etienne emphasised that final authority must rest with the man on the spot.[21]

The problem of one colony dependent on another for decisions was a serious one. In the case of Senegal and the Sudan, both areas had slowly grown in terms of the white population and its needs. One governor could not administer both areas efficiently. It was no longer practical to burden Dakar with the problems of the Sudan. On 18 August 1890, Etienne gave the Sudanese commandant the executive powers 'to regulate the political and administrative organisation of the French Sudan'.[22] All civilian and military personnel in the Sudan, by the 18 August decree, came under the authority of the governor, and his financial and executive offices were fixed at Kayes. But, most important, the budget for the Sudan was separated from the budget for Senegal. The responsibility for the budget was given to the Sudanese governor.[23]

The creation of the independent administration had a very practical reason because French explorers used the Sudan as a base of operations. They needed a secure position from which to operate. These explorers leaving the Sudan traversed the whole of central Africa, but Lugard, the British explorer, seriously doubted that the French had ever accomplished as much as they claimed.[24] But if the French did penetrate from the Chad to the Niger and to the Congo, it was because of a base of operations in the French Sudan.

The resistance to European penetration in Africa was determined, and both the English and the French governments had to enlarge the military forces engaged in pacification of the region once they were committed to expansion and exploration.[25] This was one of the main considerations for the creation of the separate authority for the Sudan where African resistance was staunchly resolved to keep European intruders out. The British were not much better off with their natives in Nigeria. Sir George Goldie told Lord Lugard that many Englishmen felt that the penetration of Africa, for both England and France, was impossible and economically not very practical.[26] However, in both England and France the imperialists felt that they were playing a deadly game for gains in prestige and territory with extraordinarily high stakes.

To lessen the possibility of a lengthy, costly resistance to French penetration in the Sudan, Gabon, and the French Congo,[27] Etienne issued two decrees in November and December 1890. On 18 November he signed a decree establishing a tariff policy for Gabon and the Congo. Included in this decree was a definite prohibition of the sale of liquor and modern rapid-firing rifles to the natives.[28] Etienne signed still another decree on 30 December 1890, which prohibited the importation of liquor and modern rifles for resale to the natives in the remainder of French West Africa. Both these decrees followed the guide-lines which were established by the Brussels Convention of 1890. This convention bound the signatories to refrain from the sale of modern firearms and liquor to the Africans. By the second decree, the only weapons the natives could buy were old flintlock muskets for hunting. The reasoning behind these decrees was simple. The prohibition of modern firearms meant, in theory, that only European troops would have modern, rapid-firing rifles, and would thus have complete firing superiority over the natives.[29]

Early in 1891, the Chamber called on the undersecretary during

an interpellation on the West African situation. He informed it
that a crisis level had been reached in Dahomey with heavy
attacks on French forces in the Porto Novo area. The Foreign
Legion had been dispatched to aid troops in the region. Etienne
warned that a direct attack on the hinterland of Dahomey would
be necessary because France had the duty to protect her nationals
and commerce.[30] For the colonialists, the use of force had two
drawbacks. There was always the chance that the fighting could
spill over into British Nigeria and involve Great Britain in the
conflict. The use of extensive force also brought confusion as to
the ministerial responsibility for the troops involved. According
to a law of the Republic signed 15 July 1889, the Minister of
Marine was responsible for infantry and artillery of the Marine.
The Minister of War furnished units of the regular army and
Foreign Legion. The colonial gendarmes were also under the
authority of the War Ministry.[31] The seeds for an interdepart-
mental conflict over military responsibility were planted if and
when the colonial undersecretariat was forced to call for large
numbers of troops for Dahomean operations.

For long-term pacification, most imperialists preferred the
idea of a colonial gendarmerie, under the control of the Minister
of War. On 6 June 1891 the War Ministry, prompted by the
colonialists, issued a joint decree reorganising the colonial gendarmes. The War Ministry controlled the policies of arms,
ammunition, and tables of organisation.[32] The military aspects
of colonial penetration became one of the expansionists' most
constant interests, and through their friends Galliéni and Lyautey
they retained great influence within the army, even though many
of the imperialists supported Dreyfus during that period of
spectacular confusion. The Dreyfus Affair would reveal a great
deal about the overall philosophical make-up of the colonialists.
Since the cause of colonial expansion was supported so generously
by Baron Rothschild and many members of the Jewish business
community, the imperialists could not afford to be anti-Dreyfus.
Also, many colonial advocates simply did not care what faith a
man professed as long as he defended the cause of territorial
acquisition. While these tendencies were very evident in the
early 1890s, they did not come into full public view until
Dreyfus became a *cause célèbre* in France.

While the advocates of expansion were involved with the situation in Dahomey, they were also concerned with problems relating to the French Congo. The undersecretary made no secret of his desire to exploit immediately the economic possibilities of the African colonies. Since a colony had to show an immediate profit, Etienne was determined to bring commercial investors into the area, and he referred to the progress of this movement as rapid and 'splendid'. Etienne might call it splendid but the Chamber was unconvinced, and in 1891 that legislative body refused to increase the budget for the Congo. They preferred to allow the Congo to develop by private investments. This pleased Etienne, who reminded the deputies that the Congo had been added to the empire without great bloodshed and that the explorers—de Brazza, Alexandre Mizon, and others—had secured the region for a reasonable cost.[33] Why not now allow other Frenchmen to develop it for France? A colony on the banks of the Congo River, he reasoned, would not only bring economic benefits to France, but would also add great prestige to the French nation, and another drop of the stain of 1870 would be eradicated. Patriotism could and would go hand in hand with capital and industry.

Etienne wanted the Chamber to agree to the immediate concession of a large tract of territory to a private company headed by Célèstin Daumas.[34] Supported by his staunch ally Théophile Delcassé, the undersecretary argued that only through such commercial concessions could the French Congo develop properly. Despite eloquent arguments by Etienne, Delcassé, and others, the Chamber refused to grant, by law, the tract of land to Daumas. Disappointed by the Chamber's actions, Etienne tried to give as much support as possible to the concession theory, which had become known as the 'Etienne Project'. The undersecretary decided to reintroduce the project at the Superior Council of the Colonies, scheduled to meet in late 1891.[35]

The situation in Africa was not the only concern at the colonial ministry. During a speech on the budget for Indochina in the Chamber on 27 November 1890, the undersecretary outlined the continual problems facing the French colonial administration in that area of south-east Asia. The major problem in Tonkin was 'endemic Malady', piracy or terrorism. Like a cancer, the unrest had spread, unchecked, from Tonkin to Hanoi and then into all of Indochina. The French had committed many metropolitan and native troops to the battle against it, but nothing seemed to stop the growing military involvement.[36] The economy-minded Chamber was informed that Indochina did not need more Legionnaires or French regular troops. What was asked for were credits to build an Indochinese national guard and immediate funds to begin a massive plan of public works to help in the work of pacification. The undersecretariat had created a native national guard force by decree on 3 February 1890. The orders were quite explicit: 'The governor general of Indochina . . ., under the direct authority of the Minister charged with colonies, is responsible for the guarding and . . . the defence of the territories placed under [his] orders.'[37]

The Indochinese confusion plagued the colonial administrations in Hanoi as well as Paris. Hanoi was becoming the executive and social hub of French south-east Asia. Young French officers like Hubert Lyautey graced the salons of Hanoi's social élite, but Hanoi was only a brief respite from the constant battles in the rice paddies and steaming jungles.[38] Outside the gaily lighted hub, Algerian sharpshooters, African infantry from Senegal, and German-speaking Legionnaires died in perfect equality with St Cyr dandies. It was not a matter of public works or civil guards for French Indochina. The major error of Galliéni and the Paris colonialists was that they did not realise nor admit the magnitude of the struggle. Indochina remained a festering sore which continued to cause France serious trouble. Etienne, never feeling the passion for Indochina that he did for Algeria, came to realise that south-east Asia was not a premier member of the French empire. In Algeria he had opposed native troops because he wanted to keep Algeria totally French. In Indochina he had created a large native civil guard, but in Algeria only the European could bear arms. Etienne's love was Algeria, and that Algeria was French. Indochina remained on the periphery of Etienne's colonial concern. Africa had become by 1890 the great area of expansion for the French colonialists, and that continent had to be protected for French commercial and military expansion. Little real value, they believed, would come quickly from Indochina. But Africa was another matter entirely.

Reports had reached Paris that caravans, loaded with goods from the Sudan, were being attacked and looted in the South Oranais, the southern area of Oran Province. Etienne became involved in the issue because of the connection with the Sudan, and also because, as an Algerian *colon*, he was greatly interested in anything which affected the relationship between France and Algeria, especially the lucrative caravan trade. The colonialists realised that the pacification of the Oranais and the Saharan oases would be the first step toward the penetration of Morocco. Caravans from the Sudan destined for Oran or Algiers were attacked in southern Algeria by Morocco-based bandits. The French military had demanded the occupation of the oasis of Tuat near the Algero-Moroccan frontier as the first step in the pacification of the region,[39] but this was sure to bring France into conflict with Morocco.

The border of Algeria and Morocco south of the Moroccan oasis town of Figuig was undefined, and no one was quite certain what constituted French or Moroccan territory. The military and the colonialists wanted to occupy slowly the oases, starting with Tuat, as a staging area toward Morocco.[40] The imperialists' interest in the South Oranais grew in intensity until they openly demanded the annexation of Morocco in 1898. In 1891, the border problems in the South Oranais attracted little attention outside of the colonialist-military circles. The situation there was mainly a problem for the Minister of the Interior, who ruled over Algeria, and for the Quai d'Orsay, which had to deal on a diplomatic level with the Cheriffian Empire of Morocco.

Any overt interference at that point by France would have been unjustified, and in 1891 Etienne, the prime mover in colonial adventures, had more pressing problems in Indochina. He considered a plan to help relieve some of the pressure on the government of Indochina. In January 1891, Etienne announced that he was going to call a meeting of the *Conseil superieur des colonies* to discuss some reform measures for all the colonies, and to propose aid for Indochina.[41] The Superior Council of the Colonies, created in May 1883, had the duty of advising the Undersecretary of State for Colonies. Etienne enlarged the number of members by a decree signed on 29 May 1890, because he felt the growing size of the empire called for more representation,

The council included senators and deputies from the colonies, special delegates sent from each colony, and representatives from colonial groups such as the *Comité* and the Paris Geographical Society.[42]

Etienne called the council for two specific reasons. He wanted to introduce two proposals affecting the older colonies of Martinique, Guadaloupe, and Réunion. These colonies, he felt, should be classified as 'assimilated' colonies which would make them equal to the mother country. They would be equal in rights with France, and they would '. . . [participate] in the benefits of the social state which comes close to that [practised in] the Metropole'.[43] The second item on Etienne's agenda concerned Indochina. There Etienne wanted to create a special superior council to advise and assist the governor. The special problem of anarchy in that south-east Asian colony, Etienne felt, merited the extraordinary measure.[44]

The Indochinese proposal was a product of the growing involvement of Rue Saint Florentin with the situation in the south-east Asian area. Etienne knew that Indochina was a real problem area in the empire, and next to that area of south-east Asia he felt that Dahomey was also a trouble spot. As long as Dahomey continued to fester, the important work of opening West Africa could not continue. The two areas of Indochina and Dahomey represented the same problems of resistance to pacification, and the imperialists felt that they had to be quieted before exploitation could begin.

Etienne was concerned about exploitation because he felt that the French people would never accept colonialism until it showed a profit, and to be certain that the colonies did, he restated his belief in the 'Etienne project'. The project was brought up again at the meeting of the Superior Council of Colonies in 1891. Etienne told the delegates that it was necessary to follow the lead of the British who permitted the Royal Niger Company and the British East Africa Company to exploit their areas. First, France had to grant large tracts of land to the commercial companies in the colonies. In turn, once these companies began to produce raw materials in the colonies, they would improve rivers, build roads, and establish schools.[45] But this was no more than a restatement of his earlier position, and the Superior Council of the Colonies already agreed with him. Each council member pledged to lobby for the passage of commercial concessions when the Bill was reintroduced in the summer of 1891.

Proposals were introduced into the Chamber on 19 July 1891 to establish regulations for the granting of the concessions in the colonies. The proposed laws remained in the Chamber, and because of apathy and anti-imperial hostility, they died there, stillborn. Few of the non-colonialist deputies actually understood the concessions, and only the dedicated imperialists supported them.[46] Théophile Delcassé defended the project before the Chamber, but to no avail. Etienne and Delcassé were the two most vocal exponents of the 'Etienne project', and when Delcassé became Minister of Colonies in 1894, he set the project in motion by decree. Thus the colonialists got their revenge.

The failure of the commercial concessions to capture the imagination of the Chamber showed the growing antagonism between the colonialist and anti-colonialist deputies. During the debate for the colonial budget for 1892, Etienne and Clemenceau crossed swords again. Clemenceau complained that Etienne was wasting French troops and he shouted at Etienne, 'Do not forget that Germany still holds Alsace-Lorraine as a colony.' Etienne fired back, 'You will find on the west coast of Africa an expanse of land as large as Germany herself; on the east coast we have just [begun] to create an immense empire. . . .'[47] Clemenceau doubted that Africa could possibly be equal to Germany, but Etienne fired back that because of Clemenceau's rejection of French colonialism, 'You have betrayed our fatherland.'[48] The centre and left broke into loud applause at the stinging rebuff to the 'Tiger'; Clemenceau was stunned into silence.

A *revanchard* deputy asked if it were true that almost every mission sent into Africa, Crampel and Dybowski included, had failed, and whether these continual failures were costing great sums of money. Etienne responded in the affirmative that it did cost money and he promised that all missions made at government expense would be reported to the Chamber.[49] He realised that the colonialists were planning to send their own missions to bypass the miserly Chamber. The directors of the *Comité de l'Afrique française* decided, in the wake of the Crampel and Dybowski failures, to organise its own expedition to explore the

D

Chad-Sudan region. For some time the *Comité* had debated the possibility of getting involved in central African exploration. The funds for such an expedition were available in the *Comité*'s treasury.[50] Harry Alis, the outspoken advocate of such an action, wrote:

> The *Comité de l'Afrique française* has, in effect, played in that vast national enterprise [of exploration] a role more important still by the popularity which it has given to French expansion in Africa, by the precise direction that it has imprinted on our colonial policy by the considerable effort that it has directly undertaken.[51]

The *Comité* dispatched the mission of Captain de Maistre to explore the region from southern Algeria to Lake Chad and down to the French Congo. Unlike the preceding missions, the de Maistre expedition completed its work, and this was a boost to the prestige of the *Comité* and for Etienne. But, while Etienne was enjoying the success of the de Maistre mission, trouble again flared up in Dahomey. The king of Dahomey opened attacks on Porto Novo and demanded a revision of the 1851 treaty to enlarge his share of the import duties.[52]

During the debate on the budget for 1892, Etienne was asked by anti-expansionist deputies about the growing conflict in Dahomey. He responded by demanding that more troops be sent to the West African region to hold down the level of violence in Dahomey. The master of Rue Saint Florentin asked the Chamber to reconsider the stillborn 'Etienne project' when he told the deputies, '. . . Let us say to the [capitalists] go to Africa, take your capital and establish a commercial link with the Metropole. . . . Collective efforts are necessary.'[53] In the Belgian Congo, with commercial concessions, companies made over 65 million francs in one year, but in the French Congo, without concessions, the exploitation amounted to only $2\frac{1}{2}$ million francs per year. Etienne told the Chamber that France had to 'imitate the other [powers]', and establish commercial concessions.[54] The Chamber remained unmoved, and the project was not revived for consideration.

Until the Dahomean situation calmed down there could be no possible thought of any commercial exploitation. The attacks on Porto Novo grew in intensity and Europeans were killed.

On 6 April 1892 Etienne, much to his distaste, was forced to transfer the responsibility of Dahomean pacification to the Ministry of Marine. General Dodds, stationed in Senegal, moved his command, including a battalion of Foreign Legionnaires, to Porto Novo to protect European lives and properties. The summer heat and ever-present disease took a frightful toll of the troops; but a Legion detachment of two hundred men fought into the hinterlands and inflicted a decisive defeat on the Dahomean natives. Dodds could then inform Paris that he believed that the final conquest of Dahomey was entering its final phase.

The last stage of the Dahomean penetration came at the end of Etienne's term at Rue Saint Florentin. Under his control the French empire began to change complexion; it was no longer a hodge-podge of small disconnected colonies. While Etienne was mainly concerned with Africa, he did a great deal to consolidate Indochina. The numerous decrees which set out governmental policy in Africa and in Indochina, and the continual process of exploration marked Etienne's policies as a success. For Etienne, the five years as undersecretary assured him a place as the leader of the colonial party. He would exploit this position while in the Chamber, but not in the government, during the years that followed. The term as undersecretary had also revealed the growing rift between expansionist and non-expansionist sentiment in the French Chamber. The defeat of the 'Etienne' project was simply a reflection of the distaste which many deputies had for imperialism in Africa. It appeared to them that Africa was a bottomless pit which might very well drain France's fragile recovery after 1870. That 'terrible year', the anti-colonialists felt, had to be washed away. Certainly, the imperialists would agree with this, but their emphasis on the revitalisation of France was quite different. However, after Etienne's term at the colonial undersecretariat, imperialism for the Third Republic would never be the same. A colonial part had emerged in France, as had spokesmen for the colonialist cause. Etienne, Delcassé, Alis, and others would continue to have a lasting impact on the future course of French government vis-à-vis the colonial movement, especially in Africa.

Notes to Chapter 3 will be found on pages 178–80.

Chapter 4 THE EMERGENCE OF THE COLONIALISTS 1892-6

AFTER A long period of hostility, Pope Leo XIII urged the Catholics of France to accept the authority of the Third Republic. The moderate Republicans began to work with the less doctrinaire members of the Monarchist-Catholic right. This brought on bitter fights within the Chamber over the influence of the Catholic Church in France. The dogmatic anti-Catholic forces were led by Georges Clemenceau who saw the Catholic *Ralliement*, or acceptance of the Republic, as a plot instigated in Rome by the Jesuits and Leo XIII. Clemenceau attacked the ministry of Charles de Freycinet for working with the moderate right, and in February 1892 the Cabinet fell.[1] However, this did not signal a change in the militant colonialists' prestige, since the *Comité* was strong, Gabriel Hanotaux and Théophile Delcassé retained posts in the government, and a powerful colonial party emerged in the Chamber.[2] The African empire was expanding, while the friction between Britain and France had been growing since both countries entered the race for Africa. Besides the continual heat generated by the colonial conflicts, France began to move toward the penetration of Morocco.

As soon as Etienne returned to the Chamber he gathered around himself almost a hundred imperialists and formalised the colonial party. Not a political party in the strict sense of the word, it was made up of deputies from the entire spectrum of French political thought, with only a concern for the empire in common.[3] Bolstered outside of the Chamber by the activities of the *Comité de l'Afrique française*, the articulate colonial party undertook the work of popularising the empire.[4] Because of growing imperial antagonism with Britain, the colonialists continued to urge a stronger, more militant action in regard to France's African policy.[5]

The power and authority of the colonial party within the Chamber became quite apparent when they were able to elect Etienne as vice-president of that body in 1893. The position of vice-president was a powerful one, and the colonialists' victory reflected the respect and authority which they were enjoying. The vice-presidency was vital to their cause since it guided the Chamber in its deliberations on laws and on general policy. Etienne as vice-president was one of the most powerful men in French politics, and in this influential position he could exert pressure on the Chamber to accept his own special proposals. The governments of France depended on the Chamber for their very survival, consequently the imperialists and their leader held a large amount of power.

To continue propaganda for the colonial cause, the imperialist leadership helped to found the *Dépêche coloniale* to supplement the *Bulletin* of the French Africa Committee, and colonial causes needed as much propaganda as possible. The Chamber asked Etienne to defend his colonial work in the Sudan and Dahomey, and on 11 April 1892, the former undersecretary said that 'The Sudan is an immense territory which will one day, still far off . . . be joined to our holdings in Algeria.'[6] The gigantic mass of central Africa was a primitive frontier area, and it would take time to develop, but '. . . it is certainly destined for a [brilliant] future'.[7] The richness and prosperity for the Sudan was yet to come. This speech by Etienne was intended to impress the anti-colonial deputies. The great danger to France in Africa, Etienne warned his fellow-representatives, was from the British, especially on the Niger River. Unless France acted with dispatch, France would have no future in western or central Africa. The cost in lives and money of opening West Africa was considerable, and despite the expenditure the results were not especially rewarding. Attacked by the *revanchards* for the use of combat forces so far from France, Etienne and the colonialists would have to produce a very real profit for the home country.

The income from France's colonial adventures might have been more promising had not the French allowed Britain such a large lead in the race for East Africa. The colonialists harboured a smouldering resentment against England for the Suez occupation of 1881 and 1882, and for the Anglo-German agreement in East

Africa of 1890. France could only look at the Red Sea and Persian Gulf for her small bases in Obock, Djibouti, Diego-Suarez, and later Madagascar. Perhaps some day the tricolour might fly over Khartoum and Addis Ababa, but in 1893 the Union Jack seemed to rule most of the eastern skies from Suez to India and the militant Lord Rosebery, Foreign Secretary in Gladstone's cabinet, appeared determined that Britain should remain the dominant power in East Africa.

The French colonialists were willing to see the Germans gain some foothold in eastern Africa rather than have the entire area go to the British by default. Sir Arthur Hardinge, sent to eastern Africa by the Foreign Office, wrote, 'The French consuls in Eastern Africa were generally more unfriendly to British interests than the Germans, and whenever these conflicted they usually sided with the latter.'[8] Labosse, the French consul in Zanzibar, was in constant contact with the Quai d'Orsay and worked against British interests in Zanzibar and East Africa. His office became the leading centre of anglophobe intrigue in the region.[9]

Competition in East Africa took many forms. When the French government applied for the right to hire native porters from Zanzibar for service in Madagascar, for example, Kimberley, who became Foreign Secretary in Rosebery's cabinet in early 1894, informed Lord Dufferin, the British ambassador in Paris, that the British could not allow it. Kimberley said that their porters were needed for the transportation of supplies within British territory.[10] While Kimberley told Dufferin to express the Foreign Office's official regrets, he recalled that the French had done the same thing to the English in the Ivory Coast.[11] The possibility of co-operation between Britain and France over such a minor point was difficult. This did not seem to be a serious matter on the surface, but the refusal of Kimberley, who represented Rosebery's opinions, represented a deep and basic antagonism between the two nations in Africa.

Even French religious missionaries in East Africa caused trouble for the British officials there. Hardinge recalled, '. . . the French priests were anxious to place Uganda [and other areas in East Africa] under German protection.'[12] The French fathers aggravated the situation by their open anglophobia. In 1894, Hanotaux was informed that the British, to counter the activities of the fathers, stopped payments on the annual donations which the Sultan of Zanzibar had given to them in the early 1880s. The British East Africa Company refused to permit the religious orders the right to import goods into the hinterlands.[13] France and England had agreed to this in the African agreement of 5 August 1890.

The Christian missionary to Africa simply could not divorce himself from the patriotic and nationalist European milieu. The English missionaries and the French missionaries were products of their societies, with all their goals and prejudices, and nowhere was this more apparent than in the colonial conflicts in eastern Africa where Anglo-French competition was brisk.[14] George Pilkington, famous English missionary to Uganda, wrote that what that area demanded was 'Cambridge men—Experience has convinced [me] that educated gentlemen are absolutely needed for Africa'.[15] It was difficult for these men to separate themselves from their homelands, and despite the fact that their goal was the Christianisation of Africa, they played at colonial politics. In eastern Africa, the British missionary helped form the *wa-Inglesa*, the Protestant, English-speaking party which was dedicated to the British cause in Africa. The Catholics also formed a French-speaking, Roman Catholic party called the *wa-Fransa*, which in turn espoused the cause of French colonial expansion in the area.[16] The founding of these two political organisations were obviously not part of the missionary's religious duties, and it did ferment tensions in the area. In some cases members of the two parties engaged in combat, and atrocities did occur on both sides. In turn, both London and Paris supported the activities of the various church groups, since it fitted in with colonial policies. The French White Fathers received active verbal support from the colonial activists in the Chamber and in the *Comité de l'Afrique française*, even though some of those members were openly and vocally anti-clerical.

Hardinge believed that the fathers were trying to 'cut asunder the continuous red line connecting Cairo to the [South African] cape'.[17] In 1894, in response to this, Hanotaux went before the Chamber to demand religious toleration for all groups in eastern Africa, and he was supported by Etienne. Lord Dufferin informed Kimberley that Hanotaux had told Sir Eric Phipps, the British chargé in Paris, that France would offer to Britain a trade deal on

Zanzibar and Madagascar. Kimberley, however, believed Hanotaux's offer had to be viewed with great care and caution.[18] Sauzier, the British chargé d'affaires in Madagascar, warned Kimberley that French officials on the island were doing all that was possible to block the flow of British trade despite the offer made by Hanotaux to Phipps.[19]

Kimberley countered this obstruction to British trade by imposing a very heavy import tax on goods imported by the French fathers in Zanzibar. Blanchon, the French consul in Zanzibar, informed Hanotaux that this was a great hardship on the small resources of the fathers. In fact, Sir Arthur Hardinge had refused to aid the group.[20] To complicate matters, the British officials in East Africa were sympathetic to English Protestant missionaries who were in competition with the Roman Catholics. These British officials took steps to expel many of the French Catholic missionaries, and the Quai d'Orsay had to order its representatives in Aden to secure passage to Alexandria, Egypt, for sixteen expelled French clerics.[21] The religious problems in eastern Africa reflected a hostile attitude both in London and Paris, and small issues were blown out of proportion. A small crate of arms imported for use by the French fathers in the hinterlands of Zanzibar caused considerable friction between the Quai d'Orsay and the Foreign Office.[22]

According to the 1890 Brussels Protocol the European nations were pledged to see that the work of colonisation had as a goal the civilising of Africa. The International Anti-Slavery Society was formed as a result of paternalistic concern. Dedicated to the eradication of slavery in the Middle East and Africa, the society was made up of British, French, and German consuls. However, in eastern Africa national interests and colonial policy became mixed with the operation of the society. Hardinge, a champion of abolition, recalled with some bitterness that in Zanzibar Lucien Labosse was the representative of the society, and Labosse saw to it that neither Hardinge nor '. . . any other Englishman was asked to act as his successor or substitute'.[23] Hardinge believed that the French and German consuls were acting in concert to keep '. . . perfidious Albion from becoming mistress of the [society] as well as the seas'.[24]

The irritations in eastern Africa were great, but most of the

French colonialists preferred to act in western Africa because it bordered the territories of North Africa. As long as western Africa remained available for colonisation, the imperialists wished for more definite action there. Etienne believed that any realistic programme for Africa had to begin with Algeria. Algeria served as the starting point for the penetration of Africa. On 6 February 1894, Etienne addressed the Chamber on the subject of Algeria. Some anti-colonialist deputies stated that they had proof that the Muslims of Algeria had been cheated in dealing with the *colons* over land. Etienne, realising that the Muslims had not been treated fairly in land deals, told the Chamber that if this be the case, then they should protect the Algerians by instituting strict segregation —create new population centres for the Europeans and separate them from the Muslims.[25]

Etienne, reflecting the European paternalistic attitudes, told the sceptical Chamber that in reality a bond of affection existed between the *colons* and the Algerians which those who did not reside in Algeria could never comprehend. The European settlers understood the Muslim better than any metropolitan deputy, Etienne said, and understood why the Berbers and Arabs could never be given the vote. The Muslims, Etienne believed, were simple and ignorant people who preferred the carefree life which was free of political conflict and duty. Etienne warned that if the Chamber gave the Maghribi natives the vote, 'It would be necessary to end official colonisation.'[26]

Delcassé and the leadership of the colonial party had asked the Chamber to settle once and for all the question of Muslim control in Algeria by a clarification of the duties and spheres of responsibility of the governor general. Joined by Charles Jonnart, a future governor general, Delcassé and Etienne called for more centralised authority in the chief executive. While admitting that they were striving for 'a very centralised colonial government', Delcassé and his supporters in the Chamber who understood the implications of the proposal failed to mention that more control by a governor general would certainly mean more control by the *colon* element,[27] which would eliminate emphasis on the civilising aspects of colonisation.

The problem of control seemed to occupy much of the time of the colonial party in the Chamber. In May 1893 the deputies debated the question of creating a separate ministry for the colonies. As a former undersecretary, Etienne was strongly in favour of such a cabinet post because of the expanding size of the empire. The addition of new land made a more centralised administration necessary if not vital. Most of the members of the colonial party called the undersecretariat a 'bastard situation'. There was too much competition between the ministries of Marine, Commerce, and Foreign Affairs over the direction and protection of the colonies. A solution was proposed in 1893: the concept of an independent ministry for the colonies. This appealed to the deputies, and on 20 March 1894 they created the cabinet post, naming Théophile Delcassé as its first chief. Delcassé, an ex-journalist turned politician, had gained a reputation as a colonial activist, which did not endear him to the anti-expansionists in the Chamber. His elevation to the rank of minister, however, clearly showed how much strength the colonial party had gained within the Chamber of deputies.

It became apparent that the colonialists were turning their attention toward Morocco as a logical area for French expansion. The addition of Morocco to the empire was important for Etienne and the colonial party. French sovereignty over Tunisia and Algeria gave them a gateway to, and special rights in, the western Maghrib. The desire to fuse the entire Maghrib into a French possession was a great factor in the plans for Morocco. Morocco could not be annexed into the French empire quickly because it was an independent nation with a long history of self-administration. The nations of Europe, especially Spain and Britain, would be less than willing to see the Cheriffian empire fall under France's control. Etienne believed that France's special relationship to Morocco was founded in the fact that the French flag flew over Algeria and Tunisia.[28] He wrote, 'The enormous sacrifices which we have made in . . . [the Maghrib] will prove to be for nothing if the solution . . . [to the Moroccan question] does not conform to our rights and interests.'[29] Etienne's 'interests' were the commercial ventures in Morocco and the Oranais border, which was undefined. The southern frontier between French Algeria and Morocco had been especially bothersome as the two nations could never agree on a delimitation. The French continually complained that caravans coming from the Sudan to Algeria

were usually attacked by Moroccan tribes.[30] The depredations
could not be stopped until both nations agreed to police powers
and border locations in the Oranais, the western province of
Algeria. The colonialists, however, seemed unwilling to settle a
problem which, if troublesome, could lead France into taking
military action inside Morocco itself.

The Cheriffian court could do little to guard the unsettled
boundary. The death of the strong Sultan Moulay Hassan in
1894 did very little to help the situation because his son Abdel
Aziz was far too young to exert his authority along the 400km
frontier, much of which was not determined. The French decided
that it would be best to place a career diplomat as a consul in the
Muslim Holy City of Fez. In Fez, the Quai d'Orsay had employed
an Algerian Muslim to watch over and negotiate French interests
in Morocco, but the minister believed that a Frenchman would
speak with more determination and authority.[31] Maximilien de
la Martinière, a member of the French consulate in Tangier,
warned that the placing of a Christian in Fez was difficult,
because a Muslim had the advantage of language and religion
and could blend into the population. There would be great
danger to a French Christian because the Moroccan population
of Fez was suspicious of foreigners and non-Muslims.[32]

The *Bulletin*, the militant journal of the *Comité de l'Afrique
française*, reported that placing a French consul at Fez would be
a great victory for proponents of annexation, and that the prestige
of France would be enhanced by the addition of the consulate;
but the *Comité* also warned that it would lead to the demand for
such a right by the British and others.[33] To complicate matters
for the colonialists, trouble often flared at the disputed oases
complex of Tuat in the southern region of Oran Province. A
number of Moroccan tribal leaders had been killed in raids on
French outposts in the region. Moroccan tribes terrorised the
Algerian and Moroccan oases in the Sahara, and the *Bulletin*
announced that it believed that the late Sultan Moulay Hassan
had commissioned several leaders to keep the French in a state
of confusion. The Moroccan situation, the *Comité* believed, had
made the entire border from Figuig, the southern tip of the
defined border, to the trackless Sahara unsafe. It would be best
for the French to take unilateral action and occupy Figuig and

Tuat. The problem for the imperialists was one of proper timing and preparation.[34] Etienne, de la Martinière, and Sevin-Desplaces, a writer for the influential *Nouvelle Revue*, were all interested in adding Morocco to the French empire. Etienne, because of his Algerian background, made the penetration of Morocco a pet project, and after 1904, with the founding of the *Comité de Maroc*, it became his primary colonial objective. In 1895-6 the French nation could not be forced into a Moroccan venture; she would have to be seduced.

Early in 1894 Delcassé revived the 'Etienne project' for commercial concessions in western Africa by ministerial decrees authorising two concessions to private firms in France. Delcassé seemed determined to push the concessions through the Chamber of deputies and the Senate as quickly as possible. Backed by the Minister of Commerce, the new Minister of Colonies argued that such concessions would pacify the region and enable the colonies, especially the French Congo, to prosper.[35] The secretive Delcassé tried to keep the concession made to Célèstin Daumas from open, public view as much as possible, and, in fact, there were few public announcements until Joseph Chailley-Bert, a leading imperialist and editor of the *La Quinzaine Coloniale*, the voice of the *Union Coloniale*, who vehemently disagreed with the whole concept of concessions, forced a debate in the Chamber on the issue in early 1895. Over 3 million hectares of land in the Ivory Coast were transferred to a private company headed by a Monsieur Verdier. The largest grant was the 'concession Daumas' for 11 million hectares in the French Congo.[36] These first concessions were followed by more, as Etienne had foreseen. Concessions were decreed in Dahomey, as well as others in the Ivory Coast and the Congo. The remainder of the Chamber was not as pleased with the revival of the project as were most of the colonialist deputies, and in June 1894 supporters of the commercial concept had to defend the generous grants to a hostile Chamber. Claiming that the idea of concessions had been a part of Colbert's colonial policy which had served France quite well, Etienne asked why not, then, recreate commercial companies in Africa? It was to the best interest of the French nation to exploit as quickly as possible the vast riches in Dahomey, the Congo, and elsewhere.[37]

The deputies, not fully convinced, allowed Delcassé's concessions to stand, and they were not requested to vote credits for private enterprises in Africa, since the defenders of the concession system desired no undue publicity and did not wish to risk another defeat in the Chamber. In this manner, the colonialists sincerely believed, France would have colonial acquisition without contracting a huge debt, and the improvements to rivers and roads would be of vast benefit to the region. The parliamentary victory of the 'Etienne project' was a sign that colonialism was at least becoming more acceptable to a larger number of deputies.

Joseph Chailley-Bert, one of the imperialists' most brilliant theorists and authors, opposed these efforts as the 'weakest means of colonisation'.[38] Warning that in the long run they would mean economic ruin to the African colonies,[39] Chailley-Bert believed that actual colonial prosperity was decades in the future. He said that early exploitative efforts would only drain the colonies. The stimulation of the African colonies could be done in small doses by individual enterprises, but massive efforts were simply premature.[40] 'Success', claimed Chailley-Bert, 'would no longer depend on the faith of the public opinion in the colonial cause.'[41] In fact, it was Chailley-Bert who demanded that a full public debate be held on the concession issue. Risking the displeasure of Delcassé and the imperial chieftains, he sided with left-wing deputies such as Jean Jaurès. Jaurès argued that the manner in which the Chamber gave silent consent to the Daumas concession in 1893 and in 1894 was a blow to liberty, and it damaged the parliamentary system of France. This situation, he warned, 'results in the sacrifice of the Chamber's prerogatives and a substitution of the action of a minister in his cabinet for [the powers] of parliament.'[42] While Chailley-Bert was not in sympathy with Jaurès' concern over an alleged blow to French freedom, he was pleased to see any parliamentary opposition to the concessions in the Congo and West Africa. Delcassé was bitterly assailed by leftist deputies, and one of them asked the Minister of Colonies, 'What will Daumas give in return? Nothing! This is a gift, pure and simple.'[43] The situation became heated and emotions uncontrollable. Harry Alis finally irritated a member of the Chamber when he questioned his honesty over his opposition to concessions. Alis' intemperate remarks, coupled with personal animosities, led to the duel in which Alis was slain in 1895.

Jaurès' forces were determined to halt the concessions, and they proudly attached the label of filibuster to their actions. The left-wing press attacked Etienne and Delcassé as being tools of the 'capitalist monopolies'. The agents of the Belgian king, Leopold II, also pressured against the concessions, but most of the arguments against the granting of huge concessions in the Congo and West Africa were presented by that strange alliance of Joseph Chailley-Bert and Jaurès' Leftists. Certainly, for the imperialists, Chailley-Bert's opposition was a key factor in the final modification of the concessions in the French Congo. The primary goal of making the concessions more responsive to the idea of 'public works . . . in the public interest' was not realised until 1897–8, but the opposition of men like Chailley-Bert had a definite effect toward less reliance on unchecked capitalistic development.

The criticism of Chailley-Bert takes on more importance because he was one of the leading exponents of French colonial expansion. This internal criticism was linked to the fact that neither Etienne nor Delcassé had considered the unsettled frontier conditions in French Africa. The success Chailley-Bert desired depended on the presence of *colons* and trained colonial administrators.[44] He never ruled out the eventual marriage between industry and colonialism, but he did oppose immediate exploitation.[45] Because they were frontier areas, the colonies needed, Chailley-Bert said, solid, effective administration and time to develop.[46] A strong case can be made against Delcassé and Etienne. Their efforts may have been premature in Africa because, in 1894, less than a year after the first commercial concessions were granted in the Congo, Delcassé was still grappling with the problem of a satisfactory administration in that region. On 13 June 1894, Delcassé issued a decree dividing the huge area of the Upper Ubangui River (*Haut Oubangui*) from the French Congo and placing it under the control of a military commandant. Over 3,000km along the Ubangui River was separated from the Congo colony, but this was mainly unexplored and unsettled land. Four months later, Delcassé signed a second decree placing the Upper Ubangui colony under a governmental commission which would aid the commandant in his executive functions.[47] This new decree also committed the French government to spend some money in maintaining the government and its bureaucracy which was bound to come to the Upper Ubangui colony. Delcassé, as usual, tried to keep this fact from the view of the Chamber.

He actively supported the pacification of the Sudan, but his approach was somewhat different from that used by Etienne. Like Etienne, Delcassé maintained a close working relationship with the army, although he did not seem inclined to allow the French military commanders in the area to exercise freely their own judgement.[48] The Ubangui area was treated somewhat like the Sudan, but on a smaller scale. In 1893-4 Delcassé was determined not to allow either the British or the Belgians to gain any sort of foothold on the Upper Ubangui River. One of his standing orders was simply '. . . hold firm on the Upper Ubangui and never give up any of our rights'.[49] Etienne's influence on Delcassé over the Ubangui question was so pronounced that Belgians regarded the deputy from Oran as their personal antagonist in Paris and as a bad influence on the new Minister of Colonies.[50] In the Chamber, for example, Delcassé could always count on the colonialist leadership's aid in asking for financial support for the Ubangui installations.

While Delcassé was concerned with the Ubangui projects, he also had to devote a great deal of time to other African projects. The colonial friction between France and Britain in western Africa had grown to almost crisis proportions. Of particular irritation to the French was the unwillingness of the officials and agents of the British Royal Niger Company to accept as valid the treaties made between the French and native rulers. One such area of contention was the Sultanate of Mouri in the interior of the French Sudan. In 1892 the explorer Alexandre Mizon, financed by the *Comité de l'Afrique française*[51] and the colonial undersecretariat, signed a number of treaties establishing a protectorate over that sultanate. By the terms of the protectorate, France obtained the right to administer the internal affairs of the area. The Royal Niger Company's representatives protested against this. Mizon, who remained in the Sudan, continually informed Joseph Flint, agent general of the English company, that France had exclusive rights in the region and that British protests would have to be made through standard channels.[52]

Mizon sent Delcassé regular reports of the continuing British protests, and he warned Paris that Flint was trying to ruin the prestige of France in the Sudan. France, Mizon stated, had to take forceful action in west Africa or be eclipsed by England.[53] Out of frustration, he wrote numerous letters to the officials of the British company asking if they were even aware of the Franco-Mouri agreement, and he stated that a Royal Niger representative could visit the Sultan of Mouri to see an official copy of the treaty.[54] However, the agents of the company, acting under the orders which were issued by Goldie, declined Mizon's offer of safe passage to Mouri.

Joseph Flint refused to accept Mizon's letters because he used the term 'French Protectorate'. Mizon fired back an angry letter stating, 'I will continue to use the French word "Protectorate" with all the meaning that it has in my language.'[55] Why, Mizon pondered, did not Delcassé and the Quai d'Orsay rush to his support? In a letter to Delcassé, Mizon asked that question, telling the Undersecretary for Colonies that, 'The Niger Company protests as Italy protested against our occupation of Tunisia, as we protested against the occupation of Egypt by England.' But for Mizon there could be no immediate or satisfactory reply since Delcassé had his own opinions about the overall value of the Sudan in relationship to the whole of Africa. Unlike Etienne, Delcassé was not fully committed to total support for the Sudan colony when antagonism with Britain was concerned. Delcassé tended to see issues in the context of the whole African question, and in doing so he supported actions in the Ubangui region, in east central Africa, and even up to the Nile. One area of Africa, like the Sudan, could not be allowed to eclipse the remainder.[56] Delcassé was dedicated to activist expansion, but unlike Etienne he would not push an issue to the brink of an open confrontation with Britain.

The Quai d'Orsay, the Colonial Ministry, and other branches of the government might well protest the confrontation in the Sudan, but they would not allow it to become heated. Many French officials who served in the Sudan in the late 1880s period when Galliéni and Etienne controlled the area simply did not comprehend Delcassé's approach to the Sudanese question. Even when Mizon informed Paris that agents of the Royal Niger Company were telling the chieftains in Mouri that France planned to wage war against them, there was no explosion. Delcassé informed Mizon that he was to hold his ground and insist on the rights given to France by the Franco-Mouri treaty.[57] Delcassé's instructions did not mean, nor did he intend them to mean, that the French were to stand still in the area. The colonial official was too much a militant for that. Mizon and his colleagues were encouraged to enlarge France's holdings in the Sudan with as little irritation as possible. In fact, in the summer of 1893, despite vehement Royal Niger protests, Mizon signed a protectorate treaty with the King of Bassama.[58] Lord Rosebery, in London, went so far as officially to demand the recall of Mizon, but the Quai d'Orsay refused. With this refusal London increased their support of the Royal Niger Company's activities in western Africa.[59] The company ordered their agents to protest continually to Mizon, and the Frenchman replied that Delcassé had not given him any orders to withdraw. He would not, of course, until either the colonial ministry or the Quai d'Orsay ordered him to do so.[60]

Delcassé had shown himself to be an annexationist, but he had also revealed a certain moderation in dealing with colonial affairs. Of course, Delcassé had other interests, such as the Ubangui projects. Delcassé and other colonialists continually asked the Chamber for credits to construct new forts along the Ubangui and the Congo, and to build new telegraphic lines which would link these two regions.[61] A year after the generous Daumas concession in the Congo, the area was still in need of the most basic forts and telegraphic communications. The problem of a simple executive, administrative system was not solved at the time the concession was made, and it could be argued that a grant of millions of hectares was not dependent on settled conditions. But, as Chailley-Bert stated, the government had to secure peace and security first. How could any concession operate without stable internal conditions? Two years after the Ivory Coast grant, the Minister of Colonies was still trying to deal with the problem of satisfactory executive apparatus there. The *Bulletin* announced in March 1895 that a decree had been issued creating a council of

administration comprising the Governor General as president,
and a secretary, an official from the Colonial Ministry, plus two
European *colons*.[62]

About the same time the *Bulletin* reported that the colony of
Dahomey would receive a larger budget for 1896 because of the
extension of the colonial control into the hostile hinterlands.[63]
A writer for the imperialist journal pointed out that the colonial
budget for 1896 provided for a school for the natives in Porto
Novo. The Porto Novo school was to be staffed by European
teachers and a French headmaster, and the writer said, 'It is by
this instruction that we attack the tribes [which] are still in
barbarity.'[64] If the school, the first of its type in Dahomey, was
such an absolute necessity could the territory have been settled
enough for total commercial exploitation? It would seem that
Chailley-Bert was correct and that Etienne and Delcassé placed
the wrong emphasis on immediate exploitation. Chailley-Bert
believed that a colony had to be settled for at least two decades
before commercial development could even be considered. The
ever-increasing cost showed that the colonies were not self-
supporting nor settled enough for commercial expansion. The
impersonal commercial society, Chailley-Bert pointed out, was
interested only in profits, and he warned that large industrial
concerns '. . . are not always the best [friends] at the start of the
colonial period'.[65]

The case of the commercial concessions exposed a paradox in
Etienne's thought; in Algeria he constantly worked for the benefit
of the *colons*, but in western Africa he demanded that industrialisation take precedence over colonisation. Apparently he would have
joined with Chailley-Bert to watch over the *colons'* needs only
as far as Algeria was concerned. Etienne probably believed that
Algeria was the older and more settled colony, but the necessity
to produce large profits was more pressing in western Africa.[66]
Algeria had been a part of the French empire for many decades,
and the French people accepted it as such. Their interest in
western Africa was not great, and consequently they had to be
convinced of the value of imperialism there. Etienne also saw
western Africa as a battleground between Britain and France,
and victory belonged to the nation which settled the area and
made it profitable. He believed that it was not wise to parcel out

mere 600 hectares to refugees from Alsace-Lorraine.[67] The land should be set aside in huge, rich tracts for industrial development. The debate over commercial concessions never really ended. Within the colonialists' ranks the division continued between the 'immediates' led by Delcassé and Etienne and the 'gradualists' who followed Chailley-Bert. The conflict, however, did not split the colonialists enough to slow the process of imperialism. One area of agreement among the colonialists was the development of the 'block' concept of French Africa. French Africa, as the colonialists saw it, should form one unbroken unit of territory from the Atlantic to the Red Sea. If properly used, this block would yield immense prestige and economic benefits to France by providing many military bases and centres for the eventual production of needed raw materials.

The block theory as a formal goal of colonialism appeared in 1893. Louis Sevin-Desplaces, writing in the *Nouvelle Revue*, pointed out to his readers that the many missions to Africa were sent to establish a link between all of France's African possessions.[68] To form the diverse units into a unitary empire, equal attention and equal funds had to be given to each colony. No one colony took precedence over another.[69]

All exploratory missions to Africa set out to unify the French possessions of Algeria to the Sudan and the Congo.[70] Sevin-Desplaces believed that each mission added land to the empire. He wrote:

> . . . the mission Dybowski-de Maistre assured the dominance of French civilisation in central Africa and prepared the grouping . . . of all the [native] people camped between the Ubangui and the Chad consequently the moral and economic junction of our domains [of the Congo] with the territories of the central Sudan [was certain]. . . .[71]

The colonialists who espoused the block concept were courting danger, and the belief that the French empire should extend from Dakar to Djibouti meant a serious challenge to the British in East Africa. The Marchand mission to Fashoda was simply the culmination of this challenge.

Delcassé, Etienne, and Hanotaux, joined by André Lebon, who became colonial minister in April 1894, were determined to forge the French African empire into an instrument of glory for

France. In May 1893, Delcassé, as Undersecretary for Colonies in the cabinet of Charles Dupuy, formulated the plans for an expedition to the Nile. He dispatched Captain Monteil to begin the process of exploration in the area.[72] Hanotaux, later as chief of the Quai d'Orsay, fought against such an obviously dangerous policy, but as the Monteil and later the Marchand mission neared its goal he remained quiet and awaited events.[73] Despite the evident risks, many of the colonialists wanted to take the chance.

Hanotaux, an historian turned diplomat, believed that such a move toward the Nile would bring France very little. In 1895 he was engaged in talks with Eric Phipps, the British ambassador in Paris, hoping that an accord might be reached over the long-standing disputes in Africa. But even though Hanotaux wanted to halt the operations toward the Bar-el-Ghazal and Fashoda, he could not. He feared that the colonialists would call him a traitor and force him from power.[74] Possibly a trade could be worked out involving the Nile and Morocco. The colonialists believed that Morocco was a natural part of the French block in Africa.[75]

The development of the block theory was an important part of the years of propaganda. Delcassé, Etienne, and the colonialists aimed at fusing the French empire in Africa into a unitary structure, but the desire to challenge Britain on the Nile threatened to wipe out all the gains made in Africa since 1870. Those were years of danger because of the friction which developed between England and France over the many African questions. It would be left to the imperialists to find satisfactory solutions to the numerous questions which might possibly lead to an armed conflict.

Notes to Chapter 4 will be found on pages 180–3.

Chapter 5 COLONIAL PROBLEMS IN MOROCCO AND WEST AFRICA 1894-8

THE YEARS from 1894 to 1898 were filled with many colonial problems in Africa. Gabriel Hanotaux became the colonialist-oriented chief of the Quai d'Orsay, and Eugène Etienne was the vice-president of the Chamber. Both men worked together to solve the problems that France faced in North and sub-Sahara Africa. Supported by the *Comité de l'Afrique française*, the two men were able to encourage French colonialism in Africa and to lay the groundwork for the eventual takeover of Morocco. But the most troublesome questions for the French imperialists were the arms problem in western Africa and the long, undefined border between Algeria and Morocco. In western Africa the British and the French clashed over the arms trade which France had tried to limit in 1890.[1] The Moroccan problem was twofold. In 1894 the old Sultan Moulay Hassan died, and the colonialists and the Quai d'Orsay had to decide what action to take in regard to the heir apparent, the fourteen-year-old Abdel Aziz. Also, the Algero-Moroccan border was not defined south of Teniet el Sassi, some 40km from the sea. Beyond that point the frontier was vague, a fact that resulted in a continual state of confusion that often approached a state of war. The Moroccans and the French clashed over exactly what desert territory belonged to either Morocco or Algeria.[2]

Hanotaux had been in the Quai d'Orsay only a few days when Moulay Hassan died on 6 June 1894.[3] Hassan, a respected and strong leader, had successfully kept his nation free from European domination. His son Abdel Aziz was too young to command the respect of many of the older, influential Moroccan tribal leaders. Hanotaux, interested in extending French influence in

Morocco, wanted to make France the leading European power in the western Maghrib. He was determined to withhold recognition from the adolescent heir until he felt France had gained that position as diplomatic leader. After learning that London had dispatched several gunboats to Tangier,[4] Hanotaux decided to go to Algeria to be closer to the centre of activity. He informed d'Aubigny, the French chargé d'affaires in Tangier, that he would arrive at the French naval base at Mers el Kebir to confer with Jules Cambon, Algeria's governor general.[5]

Prior to leaving for Algeria, Hanotaux was assured that he would have the support of the colonial party. On 7 June Etienne addressed the Chamber on France's African policy. The vice-president told his colleagues that the colonialists in the Chamber supported France's imperial policy in Morocco. France, he declared, had to counter England in Africa.[6] When Etienne spoke of Africa, and particularly of Morocco, he warned the Chamber of the serious situation developing along the Algero-Moroccan border. Etienne told the deputies that France had to have a definite policy in North Africa and that because of her predominance in Algeria and Tunisia, France had special rights in the western Maghrib.[7] With the support of the vice-president of the Chamber, the colonial lobby, and the *Comité de l'Afrique française*, the chief of the Quai d'Orsay could act with firmness in regard to the problem of recognition of Abdel Aziz. Hanotaux was determined to have the European powers act in unison in extending recognition to the young sultan. While France led this diplomatic fight, Moroccan internal events would provide the initiative. Lord Dufferin, the British ambassador in Paris, told Hanotaux that London would act in concert with Paris on the Moroccan situation.[8]

The idea that England and France could act together on an African matter was strange to the imperialists. Etienne, trying to challenge the British control of the Niger in western Africa,[9] had demanded positive French steps to insure France's rights and claims in North as well as in sub-Saharan Africa.[10] When Dufferin told Hanotaux that Britain was only interested in preserving her commercial rights in Tangier, the imperialists, including Hanotaux, were sceptical.[11] The British government showed its disinterest when it raised no objections to a French plan to send selected Moroccan children to the *Lycée d'Oran* for an education.[12] London knew that such an education would indoctrinate the children and produce future Moroccan leaders who would be loyal to France.

The co-operative position carried over into the attempts to limit the importation of modern firearms into the kingdom. The influx of contraband rifles and ammunition worried the British and French chargés in Tangier. Both men feared that the recognition controversy would end in a religious war. Such a *jihad* against the Europeans could be bloody, and the British believed it would disrupt their valuable Tangier trade.[13] In this context, and to guard against the smuggling of arms into Morocco, Hanotaux suggested to the British that both states guard the coasts of the western Maghrib. The British felt that such coastal surveillance should be an international project involving Spain as well.[14] D'Aubigny of the French Tangier legation also believed that once the three-power coast guard duty began, the three legations should demand the right to search all incoming cargo for contraband weapons.[15]

In Paris, an increasingly militant Delcassé and the imperialist lobby pressured Hanotaux to strive to extend France's influence in Morocco. In the spring of 1894, the colonialists created still another organisation, the *Union Coloniale française*, which a number of bankers, merchants, and financiers immediately joined.[16] Aided by the *Comité de l'Afrique française*, the Colonial Union promised to be very influential in imperial affairs. Etienne was often a speaker for the union, and the union and *Comité* exchanged officers and drew on much the same membership.[17] Hanotaux could see that at least in financial and governmental circles, colonialism was gaining in popularity. This, no doubt, had great bearing on his resolve to expand France's empire. Since Hanotaux had to answer to the Chamber, he was obliged not to stray far from the colonial path nor for that matter did he want to since he was himself an imperialist and his relations with the numerous expressionist groups remained excellent until the Fashoda affair of 1898.

Hanotaux saw the Moroccan question as one of direct action. Besides withholding recognition from Abdel Aziz and stopping the smuggling of arms into Morocco, the chief of the Quai d'Orsay believed that France would further subvert the standing of the Sultan and *Mahkzen* by forcing a career diplomat into the Holy City of Fez.[18] The British government feared that if the French got their diplomat established in Fez, it would mean that they had won a great advantage over the other European powers. Nevertheless, the British Foreign Office decided to support the French on the issue of the Fez consulate as they had with respect to the recognition of Abdel Aziz. Lord Kimberley asked Sir Eric Phipps, his chargé d'affaires in France, to question Hanotaux about the Fez issue, and to report the reasons behind such a demand. Phipps announced that the Quai d'Orsay demanded such a concession because of the large Muslim Algerian commercial colony in the city. Since there were so many French subjects there, Hanotaux said, France needed an experienced diplomat to handle their problems with the Sultan's government.[19] During the course of other conversations, Hanotaux asked Phipps why Great Britain did not also demand a concession for a later date. Most of the French officials in the Tangier legation believed that such action by England would further weaken the *Mahkzen*, and hasten the eventual French takeover.[20] The British openly acquiesced to French desires over the consulate issue. It was indicative of the role Great Britain chose to play from the Egyptian Crisis of 1882 up to 1904; Her Majesty's Government would never be overly concerned about anything more substantial than England's trade in the western Maghrib.

England's policy of benevolent neutrality became quite obvious when France had trouble with the Moroccans over the oasis complex of Tuat. In the autumn of 1894 the French began to concentrate troops east of Tuat, and the Quai d'Orsay claimed that the military activity was in response to Moroccan depredations which had increased in intensity and frequency. Etienne, pointing to the troubles in the Tuat region for some time, told the Chamber that Hanotaux's diplomacy vis-à-vis Morocco was correct and that France had to act with force and determination at Tuat. In doing so, Etienne claimed, no Moroccan official could ever doubt that France meant to keep order along the border. All of Algeria's European community demanded that France act swiftly along the Oranais frontier.[21]

Etienne's forceful remarks had their desired effect on the Quai d'Orsay. Hanotaux, assured of the powerful Etienne's continued support, informed Phipps that the French government would keep troops on the border to protect Algeria.[22] To insure French predominance along the Moroccan border, Hanotaux exerted pressure on Leon y Castillo, the Spanish ambassador to Paris, to recognise that the Sultan had only religious authority over the Muslims of Tuat, the local police powers belonging to the French.[23] The Spanish agreement with the French position at Tuat was important for the colonialists because Spain had historic claims in Morocco. Etienne, Hanotaux, and other imperialists realised that in the long run Spain could become France's greatest rival in the western Maghrib, and they thought that once Spanish objections were removed Hanotaux could approach Great Britain to discuss the Tuat situation.

In London, de Courcel discussed the Tuat developments with Kimberley. He told the British Foreign Secretary that the Tuat question no longer concerned Spain and the Quai d'Orsay felt that the oasis complex fell within the French sphere of influence. In a personal note to Baron de Reverseaux, the French ambassador to Madrid, de Courcel stated that England agreed to support the French position at Tuat because there was no question of British trade involved. Britain would continue her support of the Quai d'Orsay's policy as long as the French government needed it.[24] De Courcel quite rightly interpreted this as a solid diplomatic step forward toward a French solution to the Moroccan problem.

Early in 1895, Hanotaux again pressed claims for a Christian diplomat for Fez. De Reverseaux informed the Quai d'Orsay that the Spanish foreign minister planned a trip to talk with the Moroccan foreign minister in Tangier. Then the Spanish leader would travel to Rabat to talk directly with Abdel Aziz and the *Mahkzen*. The Spanish government had informed de Reverseaux that they would press France's claims for a Fez consulate. De Reverseaux believed that the Spaniards would also demand the same concession for Madrid,[25] and he warned that while the Spanish and British officials openly supported the French position on the Fez consulate, the members of the Triple Alliance would urge the Sultan to reject it. Already, he learned, the Italian and Austrian chargés d'affaires had told Mohammed

Torres, the Moroccan foreign minister, that their governments disapproved of the Fez project.[26]

Hanotaux wanted to be certain that the British were remaining firm in their support of France. He dispatched Paul Cambon, an old friend, to London to talk with Kimberley about the Fez issue.[27] Cambon informed Hanotaux that Kimberley had restated his support for France, and that the British position was that their only concern was trade in the Tangier area. Finally, Cambon believed Great Britain was determined to maintain her maritime commercial supremacy in Tangier.[28] Hanotaux entered into talks with Dufferin at the same time, and he learned that Mohammed Torres had asked the British Legation to intercede with the representatives of the other European powers to see that they remained in their legations during the time of civil disorders.[29] Hanotaux rejected Mohammed Torres' request, and both the chief of the Quai d'Orsay and Dufferin agreed that such a move would be a restraint to trade in Morocco. Dufferin recognised that Hanotaux wanted to subvert the Sultan's authority, and he aided willingly in the process.

While Hanotaux and Dufferin talked about the basic questions involving the future of Morocco, Etienne continued to demand action in the western Maghrib, but Hanotaux had to face the problem of growing hostilities on the border. Hanotaux did not want to push the frontier problems to the verge of war with Morocco, but Jules Cambon, the governor general of Algeria, was aggressive in his attitudes toward the situation. The governor demanded that Louis Barthou, the Minister of the Interior, allow him to begin a campaign of military pacification in the Tuat region.[30] Jules Cambon knew that he could count on the colonial lobby for support for his Oranais-Tuat policies, and in December 1895 Etienne spoke to the Chamber on the projected Algerian budget for the next year. The situation in the South Oranais, especially near Tuat, continued to hurt Algeria's economy.[31] Etienne watched over the developing conflict in the Department of Oran with great interest. But he could rest assured that the Algerian officials would continue to take action along the frontier.[32]

The long undefined border between Algeria and Morocco was not the only problem that troubled the imperialists. In 1895 West Africa became another trouble spot for both France and

Great Britain. England and France claimed large tracts of land in the area, and the competition between the two European powers was brisk and often dangerous. The British held Nigeria and Sierra Leone, while the French held the Ivory Coast, Dahomey, and Senegal. The vast hinterlands to Lake Chad had been contested in the early 1890s when Etienne was Undersecretary of State for Colonies. France and England had not settled the borders from the Chad to the Say on the Niger, and while they argued over that problem they created others on the western coast of Africa.

The importation of illegal firearms was the other serious problem in western Africa. In the autumn of 1894 Hanotaux was informed by the governor general of the Sudan that modern rifles were reaching rebellious natives from the British colony of Sierra Leone. Delcassé, the Minister of Colonies, passed the note on to Hanotaux. The arms situation immediately became a diplomatic responsibility because Hanotaux had to try to stop the influx of arms by bargaining with the British.[33] The British government also felt quite strongly about the arms situation because they found that rifles had been smuggled into Nigeria and Sierra Leone from French arsenals in the Ivory Coast and Dahomey. Kimberley's response then to France's requests for talks over the limitation of arms trade into the Sudan was cool; he told the French to put their complaint into a formal diplomatic protest.[34] Kimberley did tell Hanotaux that the British colonial officials in Sierra Leone would investigate the French charges that the colony was used as a smugglers' base of operations.[35] In a letter to Hanotaux, Lord Dufferin, the British ambassador, suggested that the French stop all sales of arms in their colonies adjoining Nigeria and Sierra Leone. Hanotaux agreed that all sales would stop in the Ivory Coast only if the English promised to do the same in their colonies.[36]

The colonial party and *Comité* were directly involved with the arms problems, and, as France's leading exponents of colonialism, they generally supported Hanotaux's diplomatic efforts in regard to western Africa. In a speech before the Chamber on France's policy in sub-Saharan Africa, Etienne stated that France had rights and interests in western Africa, and the Chamber should support the efforts of the government to secure those rights. The

British, he stated, had to be shown that France was firmly attached to her African colonies.[37] The backing of the colonial advocates did have its limitations, however, because they would not have wished for a diplomatic break with Britain over the arms problem in western Africa which they viewed as minor in the context of the whole scramble for African territory. In 1898, when France had been humiliated at Fashoda, they carefully refrained from excessive calls for reprisals. Probably Hanotaux knew that the imperialists would not chance the loss of the West African colonies, and he felt that he had to reach some agreement with England.[38]

However, Hanotaux and the colonialists were captives of their own imperial policy in Africa. While Hanotaux pondered the control of arms and the possibility of a Franco-English accord, the governor general of the Sudan informed the Quai d'Orsay that he opposed any limitation on the arms trade because any halt could only benefit the British in Nigeria and Sierra Leone. A pause, the governor general argued, would help the English pacify Nigeria.[39] Despite the warnings of the Sudanese governor general, Hanotaux realised that he had to end the arms trade in all of western Africa. He learned from de Courcel that London was highly irritated by the whole situation. Reports had reached 10 Downing Street from Sierra Leone that the natives were using modern French-made rifles to resist the British. Kimberley felt he had protested the situation enough, and that the possibility of military intervention had to be considered.[40]

Hanotaux tried to reach some accord with the British, but his problem was compounded by the growing friction along the Algero-Moroccan border. For the Quai d'Orsay and the imperialists this problem was more pressing. Etienne, because of the proximity to Algeria, was more concerned with the Moroccan problem; he felt that by adding Morocco to the French empire, France's prestige would be greatly enhanced. Hanotaux's problem was complicated by the actions of Algeria's Governor, Jules Cambon. André Lebon, the Minister of Colonies, warned Hanotaux that Cambon's fears were grounded in the reality of the problems of the South Oranais. Lebon basically agreed with Cambon that the French government had to take forceful steps to guarantee the safety of the settlements along the border.[41]

Jules Cambon, frustrated with the hesitancy of the Paris government to ensure security, wrote a long, bitter letter to Jules Méline,
president of the Council of Ministers.[42]

Cambon told Méline the border incidents were a direct result
of orders issued from the Sultan's court at Fez. Careful not to
cite any specific evidence of the charge, Cambon stated that
Tuat was a centre of anti-French agitation because of those orders.
To prepare for the peaceful penetration of Morocco, Jules
Cambon suggested that France should take and hold Tuat and
other border oases without delay.[43] Cambon, because of his
association with Etienne and because of his position as governor
general of Algeria, became one of the militant Moroccan annexationists. Acting on his own authority, he ordered French colonial
troops to take and hold the oasis of In Salah on the Algerian side
of the frontier near Tuat. Méline was greatly distressed, but at a
meeting of the Council of Ministers he found that Louis Barthou
and André Lebon supported Cambon. Despite the open arguments of Barthou and Lebon, Cambon was officially but weakly
reprimanded for his actions at In Salah.[44]

The official rebuff did not deter Jules Cambon, and in a letter
to General Billot, the Minister of War, he demanded that a
railroad be built from In Salah south into the Sahara. He
believed that such a rail line would enable the rapid dispatch of
troops into trouble spots.[45] Cambon believed, as did Etienne,
in the use of the railroad as a rapid means of penetrating Morocco.
Later, when Etienne was pushing for the conquest of the western
Maghrib, he urged the Chamber to vote credits for an increase
in the number of rail lines south from the fort at Colomb-Bechar
on the border.

Meanwhile, Hanotaux was engaged in preliminary negotiations
with the British over imperial problems in western Africa; he
did not want the southern Algerian question to divide the Méline
cabinet. He quite rightly sensed that there was a certain amount
of antagonism between the two groups: Barthou and Cambon on
one side and General Billot and Méline on the other. Sensing
that he was losing the respect of Jules Cambon,[46] Hanotaux
wrote to Barthou to try to heal the split.[47] He told Barthou that
the Quai d'Orsay informed the Moroccan government that Tuat
was part of Algeria and that he had secured English support for

France's position on the oasis question and in the whole area. Hanotaux also informed Barthou that he would tell the Minister of War about all future diplomatic developments between France and England over Tuat.[48]

In November and December 1896, an irritated Governor General Jules Cambon telegraphed Paris that more depredations had been carried out by Moroccans near the oasis complex of Tuat. Louis Barthou wrote to Méline, president of the Council of Ministers, to demand that the Méline government take steps to end such incursions. These outrages, Barthou stated, could not be allowed to continue because any display of French hesitancy in ending them would lead to the probability of future raids.[49] Jules Cambon, obsessed with the Tuat situation, said in a letter to Méline, '. . . Our objective must be also the northern shores of the Mediterranean. In fact the [anarchical] situation in Morocco will benefit us also in Tuat. . . .'[50] Looking forward to the day when France would occupy all of the border area, Cambon, again on his own authority, ordered elements of the XIXth Army Corps in Algeria to the border to prepare new forts and observation posts.[51]

Méline and General Billot received the news of the troop movements with great distress. In Fez, the Sultan reacted by dispatching an expedition of 1,500 well-armed cavalrymen to the frontier. French mounted troops and Moroccan cavalry faced each other at the unoccupied oasis of Amlet and town of Udjda.[52] However, Cambon's militant orders had their desired effect on the *Mahkzen*. Hanotaux told Barthou that Mohammed Torres had given his personal assurances that Abdel Aziz would see to it that depredations stopped near Tuat and that Moorish troops would be withdrawn.[53] Etienne supported Cambon's actions in the Oranais, saying later that the In Salah operation and the dispatching of troops only enhanced France's position along the frontier. Probably, he believed, other oases along the border would be taken in the same manner.[54]

The Moroccan government was unable to insure peace and tranquillity along the frontier as long as the French continued to show signs of activity in regard to Moroccan territory. Abdel Aziz's authority declined within his own kingdom, and as his personal rule degenerated the tribes along the border refused to respond to his orders. Once free of the Sultan's rule, rebellious tribes raided across the Algerian frontier at will. The young Sultan had an excellent adviser in Ba Ahmed, his Grand Vizier, and as long as Ba Ahmed maintained his authority over the Sultan, the tribes mainly remained loyal to Fez. However, as Abdel Aziz came under the influence of his greedy, pleasure-loving European entourage, the reputation of the whole court declined. Many tribes, feeling no longer bound to a Sultan with self-seeking, non-Islamic advisers, would not obey his commands.[55]

In 1898, the raids became worse and Paris was forced to react. The *Bulletin* delighted in reporting that Abdel Aziz found it impossible to control his own countrymen in south-east Morocco. The *Comité* warned that any harm done to Europeans in the western Maghrib would attract swift retribution.[56] In December 1898, after the Fashoda crisis had toppled Méline and Hanotaux from power, the imperialists spoke out on the Tuat situation and urged Théophile Delcassé, the new Foreign Minister, to conclude a trade with England of the French claims on the Nile for a preponderance in the western Maghrib.[57] Their basic reason for such a trade was the proximity of Algeria and Tunisia to Morocco, and they stated that France had been concerned with the border problem centring around Tuat for a decade. 'France has', Etienne proclaimed, 'rights and obligations which are superior to those of all other [European] powers.'[58] Much to the annexationists' satisfaction, the Tuat oasis complex was occupied by French troops in the summer of 1899. The operation was conducted by a small number of Saharan troops, and the oasis complex, including Tuat, Tidikelt, and Gouara, was fortified by penal companies of the Foreign Legion. The Quai d'Orsay received a vehement protest from Mohammed Torres, who claimed that France had violated Moroccan territory by seizing Tuat. Delcassé countered that, according to his maps and the best geographical authorities, Tuat was 50km from the actual border, well inside Algeria.[59]

While the Quai d'Orsay was dealing with the Moroccan government over the Tuat occupation, pressure was being brought by influential colonial societies to occupy totally the western Maghrib. Savorgnan de Brazza, the president of the imperialist-oriented Geographical Congress meeting in Paris, demanded that

France hold Tuat by force if necessary. Tuat, de Brazza believed, would best serve French interests by being linked to the fort at Ain Sefra by rail, and once these two frontier outposts were joined they would serve as a solid base for future Moroccan penetration.[60] The Moroccan government reacted to the Tuat situation with great rage. As the colonialists had foreseen, many Moors, deeply resenting the blatant imperialist move by France, rose in indignation against the French. Because of growing reports of demonstrations and riots in the major cities of Morocco, the Algerian delegates to the Geographic Congress held in Paris demanded that France take advantage of the confusion to occupy the entire country.[61]

The imperialists in positions of power were not ready, in 1898, to take such action. The Fashoda crisis brought into the limelight a new set of officials, and a new set of international and diplomatic conditions which the colonial leaders had to explore. As the new aspects of European diplomacy became clearer, the colonialists would be able to take steps to exploit the Tuat occupation, and eventually they were able to conquer all of Morocco. But first, Delcassé, the colonial party and the *Comité de l'Afrique française* had to learn the lessons of Fashoda.

Notes to Chapter 5 will be found on pages 183–6.

Chapter 6 THE FRENCH COLONIALISTS AND FASHODA 1894-8

THE FINAL years of the scramble for Africa from 1894 to 1898 brought Britain and France into direct confrontation and often the African conflicts caused sparks in Europe also. The greatest source of irritation in Africa were the constant claims of France to the Nile River. While England and France clashed over the arms situation and territorial claims in western Africa, the major source of confrontation between the two powers was the upper Nile. Foreign ministers on both sides of the Channel had to wrestle with the serious problems facing them in Africa. The French foreign minister, Gabriel Hanotaux, was appointed by Charles Dupuy in May 1894. Delcassé was considered for the position at the Quai d'Orsay, but Dupuy felt that Delcassé was far too militant for the job. Hanotaux was reluctant to take the position, but after Dupuy and President Sadi Carnot promised their full backing and support for his policies, he accepted.[1] However, both Hanotaux and Delcassé were aggressive colonialists and some British diplomats warned that Hanotaux's acceptance of the portfolio of the Foreign Ministry meant a continuation of the colonial conflicts in Africa.[2] While Hanotaux was not an Anglophobe, he intended to press French interests and challenge Britain throughout Africa. Delcassé was as concerned as Hanotaux with the African situation, and often Hanotaux had to try to keep Delcassé's militant colonialism in check.[3] Soon after he assumed the duties as colonial minister, Delcassé dispatched expeditions into the hinterlands of Africa to explore various routes to the Nile,[4] even though Hanotaux was often not informed.

The origins of the French attempt to establish a presence at Fashoda on the upper Nile could be found in their annoyance over the British occupation of Egypt in July 1882. Benjamin

Disraeli, the great exponent of British colonialism, had purchased in the late 1870s the controlling block of stock in the Suez Canal Company. Much to the chagrin of the French, the British were in an excellent position to control the canal. When the London government suggested a joint French-British action to occupy Egypt, the de Freycinet cabinet hesitated. Using as an excuse the fact that such a move might be interpreted as an act of war, the government in Paris procrastinated. On 29 July 1882 the de Freycinet ministry fell, and with its departure any chance of French participation in the Egyptian venture was lost. The British government, fearing for the safety of the canal, ordered the bombardment of Alexandria in July, and by September of that year British troops marched into Cairo. The Quai d'Orsay, realising that it had lost its opportunity, accused the British of perfidy in Egypt. From that point on, the Egyptian question and supposed French rights there became a burning obsession for France.[5] Never recognising that Egypt, for all practical purposes, belonged in the sphere of English colonial interests, the Quai d'Orsay continued to insist throughout the decade of the eighties that France still had rights there. To complicate matters, the Mahdi revolt in the Sudan had driven most Europeans out of the area of the upper Nile. However, by the Anglo-German East African agreement of 1890, all of the upper Nile remained in the British area of control. But still the French entertained dreams of establishing a presence in the reaches of the upper Nile. The vocal demands of the colonial party and the *Comité de l'Afrique française* only added to the desire to attempt something in the area.

The explorative missions sent out by the undersecretariat prepared the groundwork for the Fashoda mission. For example, in August 1892 the undersecretariat allocated 100,000 francs for a mission into central Africa near the Upper Ubangui. The sum given to a Lieutenant de Vaisseau Alexandre Mizon was specifically meant to supply a mapping expedition to the area. In addition to the sum designated by the undersecretariat, the *Comité de l'Afrique française* contributed 15,000 francs, the Chamber of Commerce of Paris added another 5,000 and before the mission departed for Africa, private unnamed contributors donated another 25,000 francs.[6] It was clear that the Mizon mission had almost twice the sum of money which Etienne would officially report to the Chamber. As in the case of other missions such as the ones commanded by Paul Crampel and Jean Dybowski, private contributions from groups such as the *Comité* meant quite probably the difference between success and possible failure. Also, the Chamber was never officially aware of the actual cost of any specific expedition nor, since much of the money came from private sources, would it need to be. Each mission, in the eyes of the imperialists, had a vital purpose, and each explorer pushed the boundaries of French influence and knowledge farther east until by 1892 the map of central Africa became fairly complete.[7] It was not, however, until 1894 that Fashoda was chosen as the place for the attempt to establish a post on the Nile. In May of that year, Delcassé, then guiding the destiny of the colonies, sent Captain Monteil to try to establish 'a French fort in the vicinity of Fashoda'.[8] Delcassé, like Etienne, saw the Nile question in 1894 as primarily one of acquiring as much African territory as possible. The movement west to east was carried on by a number of veterans from the campaigns in the French Sudan.[9] The Sudan and the West African areas of operation had seen periods of confrontation and tension with both the British and the Belgians, and it was quite probable that both Delcassé and Etienne conceived of the mission on the Nile as a simple extension of the competition which was so prevalent in the western portion of the continent.

Distrusting both England and Belgium, Etienne had told Alexandre Ribot, the Minister of Foreign Affairs in 1892, that he fully intended to try to block any colonial movement by the British and the Belgians in the area of the Bar-el-Ghazal. The Undersecretary for Colonies believed firmly that those two states were acting in accord on the whole of the Nile question.[10] This attitude was also assumed by Delcassé when he held detailed discussions concerning the Upper Ubangui and Nile questions with the explorer Monteil in Paris in 1892.[11] Throughout 1893 Delcassé, by decree, reinforced the small missions already in the Upper Ubangui and Bar-el-Ghazal areas, and the colonial party in the Chamber rallied to support the various plans to dispatch missions to the contested regions. With the full power of the Quai d'Orsay behind it, the Fashoda project was born.[12]

The question of the Nile concerned Etienne, and as Vice-President of the Chamber he was in a position to aid his allies at the Quai d'Orsay and Colonial Ministry. In 1894 he told the Chamber that France had historic claims on the Nile, and it was up to the Quai d'Orsay to secure those rights. By throwing his support behind Hanotaux and Delcassé, Etienne assured himself of Chamber support for most French imperial policies in Africa.[13] Etienne, Hanotaux and Delcassé convinced the reluctant Chamber to vote credits for the creation of new posts on the Upper Ubangui River,[14] the back door to control of the upper Nile. Delcassé agreed with Etienne and decided to authorise exploration toward the Nile. During the summer of 1894 French missions claimed the length of the Ubangui River up to the small town of Bar-el-Ghazal which was very close to the upper Nile.[15] The French had not tried to conceal their activities on the Ubangui River or on the Bar-el-Ghazal River.[16] No one, Delcassé wrote to the Quai d'Orsay, could be allowed to block the French march to the Egyptian Sudan.[17] Determined to reach the Nile River with a military force, Delcassé was prepared to risk some alienation between the French and Belgian governments. Hanotaux, in 1894 and 1895, kept the two governments from reaching a point of confrontation over the African question only with great care and tact. The colonial party convinced the Chamber to support Delcassé's and Hanotaux's actions on the Ubangui and Bar-el-Ghazal, and Jaurès and the emerging left, to support the march into east central Africa.[18]

Hanotaux had to deal with great care with the Nile question since Delcassé, Etienne, and the imperialist militants pressured him to be more aggressive. In early May 1894 England and Belgium announced the terms of the Anglo-Congolese Treaty which traded a strip of territory near Lakes Albert-Edward and Tanganyika for a lease on the Bar-el-Ghazal region on the left bank of the Nile. Etienne and the imperialists within the Chamber exploded with rage and correctly interpreted the 12 May treaty as a British effort to block the French from the Nile. Hanotaux, who was new to his office, acted with great care in protesting the agreement, which brought an anguished response from Delcassé who was prepared to dispatch Monteil to Fashoda. The new chief of the Quai d'Orsay, at some risk to his career, calmed the expansionists, and on 14 August 1894 secured a treaty with the Belgians in the Congo which had the effect of nullifying sections of the Ango-Congolese treaty. At the same time Delcassé was forced to divert Monteil from the Bar-el-Ghazal to west Africa, and the situation cooled somewhat. But, the vehement French protests from Etienne in the Chamber Delcassé at the Ministry of Colonies, and Hanotaux at the Quai d'Orsay made it clear to Rosebery, Kimberley, and the British imperialists that France had not given up her dreams of a try at the Nile.

The British were concerned about the obvious French moves toward Bar-el-Ghazal, and Lord Dufferin, the British ambassador to France, warned Hanotaux that London viewed any French presence on or near the Nile as a threat to peace in Africa and in Europe.[19] Hanotaux realised that the English intended to hold the Nile; Dufferin repeated several times that Rosebery and Kimberley might be more than willing to talk about any African problem except the Nile question.[20] The cornerstone of British African policy for Rosebery was total British control of the Nile. While Rosebery and Kimberley instructed Dufferin to stand firm on the Nile issue, the French colonialists planned their coup in the Sudan. Hanotaux and Delcassé had already decided that the French would have to act on the upper Nile, but the chief of the Quai d'Orsay wanted to keep the door open for substantive talks rather than a direct confrontation and this irritated Delcassé who had planned to dispatch Monteil to the area. Therefore he acted as a drag chain on colonialists at home while he instructed Baron de Courcel, the French ambassador to England, to approach Rosebery and Kimberley. But de Courcel, who was devoted to Hanotaux and his policies,[21] reported that Kimberley stated emphatically that any talks between England and France had to be predicated on a French acceptance of a British Nile. Kimberley told Dufferin of his talks with de Courcel, and the British ambassador replied that he doubted if Hanotaux would agree to pre-conditions.[22]

Throughout 1894 the positions of London and Paris remained basically the same. Hanotaux was bound by his alliance with the colonial militants and Delcassé to press the French claims on the Nile. Etienne, repeating his support for the militant policies of Delcassé, presented him with a statue, a gift from the colonial party. The deputy from Oran said that the statue, '[is] a tribute to the services rendered by him to the cause of our colonial expansion. . . .'[23] The open support of the colonial party and the *Comité de l'Afrique française* clearly indicated that at least in imperial policy, France would be tied to the wishes and desires of the colonial lobby. Since the colonial party held such a strong position in the Chamber, it was almost impossible for the Quai d'Orsay to deviate from a militant policy in regard to the Nile, but still Hanotaux seemed inclined to waver somewhat.

The change in the atmosphere of tension, if it came, had to originate in London. In 1895, Lord Salisbury came to 10 Downing Street, and unlike Rosebery and Kimberley, he was vitally interested in finding a mutually satisfactory solution to the African questions. The sixty-five-year-old prime minister, who also took over control of the British Foreign Office, was no jingoist; he wanted simply to find some area of accommodation with France.[24] However, his task was made difficult by bellicose colleagues. Joseph Chamberlain at the British Colonial Office and Lord Cromer of Egypt were opposed to any colonial concessions to France. Reacting to the bitter hostility of these two powerful men, Salisbury was forced to move with great care and caution in reaching a rapprochement with the French. Finding areas of agreement with France was repulsive to Chamberlain who was enraged that Salisbury would consider making any concessions at all to the French anywhere in Africa. In a letter to Salisbury Chamberlain warned, 'We have thrown all of our cards, and they keep all theirs in their hand. In . . . Egypt . . . they are more offensive than ever.' He went on to tell the Prime Minister, 'I firmly believe that if we do not show that we will not be trifled with, we should be driven into a war with disadvantages. . . .'[25] But war with France was exactly what Salisbury wanted to avoid: imperial Germany displayed new naval muscle and this tended to make Salisbury's attitudes more conciliatory toward France.

Salisbury not only had to contend with a belligerent Chamberlain; Lord Cromer in Cairo also showed definite signs of being unwilling to compromise with the French. Cromer wrote to Salisbury that he felt prepared '. . . to grapple with French-

men, Pashas, or any other enemies of my country'.[26] In view of
the friction being generated over the Nile question and the west
African situation, Salisbury would have to muster all of his
moderation and skill to keep the peace in Africa and Europe. He
tried to mollify Chamberlain's Francophobe attitudes because
any humiliation, Salisbury warned '. . . would probably cost the
[French] ministers their offices'. He made it quite clear that the
African questions would '. . . have no justification for war in the
eyes of the English public'.[27]

Salisbury inherited a set of very complex problems from Lord
Rosebery and Kimberley. The slow movement of the French
east, on the Ubangui, meant that they were probably drawing
closer to the Nile. Hanotaux, Delcassé, and Etienne worked to
establish small forts on the Bar-el-Ghazal near the confluence of
the White Nile and the Ubangui rivers. Hanotaux, supported by
the colonial party, asked the Chamber to vote funds for the
building of the posts even though the chief of the Quai d'Orsay
knew that most British diplomats felt that the French presence so
near the Nile was a direct threat to English interests.[28] In this
respect Salisbury was no different, and Hanotaux knew it. But
the historian turned diplomat was in great measure a prisoner of
his affiliation with Etienne's colonial lobby. The entire Bar-el-
Ghazal project was a very expensive one for France, but many
of the colonialists thought it was worth the risks. The Bar-el-
Ghazal posts had to be supplied from the French Congo and the
French garrisons were surrounded by hostile African and Arab
tribes. By 1895, the entire project was consequently reviewed
by the Quai d'Orsay and at the Colonial Ministry; then it was
decided that the build-up on the Bar-el-Ghazal should be
stopped at least temporarily,[29] even though Etienne was certainly
not pleased with this minor turn of events.

The reason for the movement toward the Nile was apparent to
Lord Salisbury, who informed Cromer that the French colonial
party meant to try to unite all of French north and west Africa
with the colony of Obock on the Red Sea, and this plan logically
had to include a military station on the upper Nile.[30] Salisbury
was well aware that the French on the Nile would lead to a clash
between the two states. In late 1896, he received a dispatch from
Francis Plunkett, the British ambassador to Belgium, who was

privy to secret information from the Belgium Foreign Office,[31] which stated that forces had left the French Congo bound for the Nile.[32]

A small force of 200 men under the command of Captain Jean Baptiste Marchand was on the march toward the Nile and Fashoda, which had been the goal of several abortive missions. Delcassé had organised the Monteil mission to explore the upper Ubangui and to try to reach Fashoda;[33] however, the luckless Monteil failed to penetrate the hostile hinterlands of the Ubangui. Much of Monteil's failure can be traced to his own slowness in moving into the Nile region. While he knew the objective of his mission, since Delcassé had made that clear, he seemed quite hesitant, which was not in keeping with his past record or dedication to the Fashoda project. In a letter, after he had given up command of the Fashoda expedition, Monteil explained that he realised that, 'It was therefore logical to assume that Egypt was not in England's hands.' Their official line of reasoning was, in Monteil's opinion, obviously faulty since the British were, since the Suez crisis of 1882, in Egypt and were guarding the area, and the ex-commandant believed that French action would bring a furious response from England, and Britain, he concluded, would never give up her claims on the southern part of the Sudan.[34] In a later letter to Captain Decazes, commandant of a military mission to Upper Ubangui in the summer of 1894, Monteil again indicated his disenchantment with France's militant policy in respect to the Nile area and the Egyptian Sudan. He warned Decazes to avoid any penetration into the Sudan, and if for any reason he had to go into the area, it would be best to first await direct, specific orders from Paris.[35] In no way was Monteil at odds with France's overall imperial policy in Africa, but in regard to the Fashoda operation he saw its great dangers, its glaring weaknesses, and preferred caution.

André Lebon, who replaced Delcassé at the Colonial Office, believed that the small size of the military unit involved was absurd.[36] The entire mission was poorly planned in Paris and Marchand was allotted less than 200 Senegalese infantrymen. However, Marchand did not seem to share Lebon's concern over the size of his mission. In a letter to Victor Liotard, commissioner for the French government in the Upper Ubangui region, the leader of the mission to Fashoda stated that he had nine excellent French officers plus '160 superb Sudanese infantrymen . . . brave and faithful, recruited by [Charles] Mangin and Colonel Trentinean on the Niger. . . '.[37] Marchand knew that he was following in the footsteps of Crampel, Dybowski, and Monteil, but in his letter to Liotard, who had the ultimate responsibility for the supply and passage of the Marchand mission, he did not seem apprehensive. 'I simply want to go to construct a French post at Fashoda',[38] he said, oversimplifying the matter somewhat. Recounting lengthy discussions 'with every minister' (the government), Marchand stated he was more than ready to march to the Nile. This statement, in itself, was quite interesting in that not every minister in the Paris government knew of the Marchand mission to the Nile. Liotard became discouraged over the prospects of the mission, but the overly optimistic Marchand, addressing him as 'my poor Liotard', tried to cheer him by stating that his own enthusiasm was linked with his patriotism.[39] Chiding Liotard for his lack of heart and faith in the imperial future of France, Marchand proceeded with his mission despite great difficulties.

A problem for both Marchand and for Paris was the time required for the exchange of dispatches and consequently Paris, never quite certain where exactly the captain and his command were, had to guess when Marchand might reach his destination;[40] and to complicate matters for the French government, the British knew that Marchand was on the march toward the Nile and the basic element of surprise was lost for the French. The British military intelligence division in Cairo estimated that Marchand must be in command of a force of about 600 well-armed men. Anything smaller, the division speculated, would be absurd, because a small force could not remain in Fashoda in such close proximity to proposed British positions near Omdurman. However, the British realised the seriousness of the mission, and the Cairo intelligence officers added, '[The Division] thinks you will find that before long the French effort to reach the Nile at Fashoda . . . will take a much more tangible form than heretofore. . . .'[41] But official and imperialist ardour for the Fashoda mission waned, and gradually the colonial leadership stopped its violent attacks on Britain in the Chamber, claiming that the prospects of a war with England over any of the African questions was most unlikely. They stated that France did not want a military confrontation with England in Egypt.[42] Slowly changing his position on the entire Nile question, Etienne said the continual friction in Africa threatened all of the French empire. Being an Algerian, the lure of Morocco was very strong, and as events would show, Etienne was more interested in adding the western Maghrib to the French empire than risking a war over the upper Nile which certainly would not be of any benefit to either France or England.

Hanotaux, like Etienne, had come earlier to the realisation that the Nile question was not very likely to yield any great colonial gains for France. Salisbury, believing that Hanotaux was still bound by the demands of Etienne, Delcassé, and the militants of the colonial party to push the Nile question, ascertained that the alternatives for the chief of the Quai d'Orsay were few: a retreat from the Nile without proper compensations would be a serious disaster. Possibly a barter concerning the Nile and Morocco might soothe the tension between the two states. In a letter to Chamberlain, Salisbury reasoned that perhaps a trade between the two states would be in order if Hanotaux and the colonialists would surrender their claims on the Nile for a free hand in Morocco. If this was not satisfactory, Salisbury could possibly offer the Quai d'Orsay the small Caribbean island of Dominica or a complete preponderance in the New Hebrides Islands. Chamberlain was told that in all probability, France would take the free hand in the western Maghrib.[43]

On the other hand, the chief of the Quai d'Orsay was caught in a very serious dilemma. He knew that Marchand would arrive at Fashoda, and this would be a direct challenge to England. Hanotaux had not made nor could make definite preparations to deal with that eventuality.[44] He had argued against the policy that motivated the sending of Marchand to Fashoda, but the mission itself was ordered to proceed in 1895 while Hanotaux was temporarily out of office. When he returned to the Quai d'Orsay, however, Hanotaux did not try to force the recall of the Marchand mission.[45] When Marchand did arrive at Fashoda, Hanotaux wondered how much support he could expect from Etienne and the colonial party,[46] who seemed more attracted to the plan to add Morocco to the empire. When Marchand's presence at Fashoda was public knowledge, Hanotaux's indecision together with Etienne's change of heart on the question of the upper Nile caused the chief of the Quai d'Orsay more difficulties. Now he had to pay for his earlier indecision. He was replaced at the Quai d'Orsay by the ministry that replaced the Méline government, and he would never return to power.

Salisbury, unlike Hanotaux, was not indecisive; he had made concrete plans for the confrontation. England, he reasoned, could afford to appear to be willing to negotiate with the Quai d'Orsay only on the evacuation of Marchand's forces from Fashoda. The Nile question, Salisbury emphatically stated, would never be submitted to international arbitration, and after several stormy conferences with Chamberlain, Salisbury could say that there was a general agreement that the Nile question would be discussed and solved by England and France alone. He told Lord Cromer that England had nothing to gain from a conference. Italy, Austria, and Russia would demand compensation from Great Britain for any support, and the Germans would be excessive in their demands for a *quid pro quo* aid.[47] In a letter to Chamberlain, Salisbury said that England would stand firm on exclusive negotiations between the two states over the Nile. He believed that by asking the other European powers for support, England would create a whole new set of colonial problems. Chamberlain was asked if he thought it wise to set up a defensive committee to prepare for the possibility of an attack by the French on the British in the Sudan; while he felt that the French would not be foolish enough to open hostilities on the upper Nile, it was wise to be ready with a deterrent.[48]

Hanotaux learned that both Salisbury and Chamberlain made their opposition to an international settlement of the Egyptian question well known in England. Chamberlain's menacing tone made a distinct impression on the French diplomats in London and Paris.[49] The small number of troops with Marchand was reported to Salisbury early in 1897, and the Conservative minister knew that Marchand would push on to Fashoda because of his dedication to the colonial cause.[50] The information about the size of the expedition did much to ease the minds of the British officials, and from this intelligence Salisbury reasoned that a full-scale military attack was not about to take place on the upper Nile.

The main question in Salisbury's mind was how far could Hanotaux go in his support of the weak Marchand mission. He knew that the colonial party continued to urge Hanotaux to confront the British in the Nile Valley. Although Etienne exercised a moderating influence in this respect, Hanotaux and Etienne had changed roles since 1895. By 1897, Salisbury feared that hasty action in the area could produce hostilities, and if France had to suffer a diplomatic humiliation over Fashoda it would produce a revolution in Paris.[51] If the moderate Republicans fell from power, what would follow? Salisbury did not want a *revanchist* clique to assume the powers of the government because that could endanger the peace of Europe. Consequently, the British prime minister had to proceed with great caution in order to lessen the chances of a serious political rupture within France.[52]

The possibilities of an upheaval from the side of the colonial activists in Paris were lessened when Etienne wrote a series of articles for the influential newspaper *Le Temps*. Avoiding hostile references to England, Etienne refrained from inflaming the situation any more than it already was. In fact, the leader of the colonial party pointed out that Great Britain had great success in exploiting her colonies by using the commercial company. England's policies were 'full of success', he stated; why then did not France imitate England in Africa?[53] Certainly, Etienne was trying to win favour for the commercial companies which he had advocated since 1890; but more importantly the deputy from Oran sounded a friendly note for the benefit of Great Britain. Praise for Rhodes and Goldie, he hoped, would be interpreted as admiration for the British imperial militants.

Salisbury, also in a conciliatory mood, tried to convince Chamberlain that the danger of a war or a rebellion exceeded the possible advantages which might be gained from disgracing France on the upper Nile. Chamberlain was implored to guard his words and to keep the friction at a minimum because Salisbury knew that time was slowly running out for the British and French: Marchand was nearing Fashoda.[54] Lord Cromer wanted to dispatch several gunboats up the Nile to Fashoda to deal with the French.[55] In June 1898, the news was flashed over Europe that Marchand was near the upper Nile, and the same month the Méline government collapsed under the fire of an irate Chamber. The Méline cabinet, while not fully responsible for the dispatching of Marchand, had to take the blame for what promised to be a nasty international incident.[56]

Hanotaux tried to save the situation by arguing that the Nile question should be submitted to international arbitration. He wrote to Cogordan, the French consul general in Cairo, that he had hoped that once the Anglo-Egyptian armies took Khartoum, the possibilities for multi-national talks would increase. Hanotaux believed that there were international interests in Egypt that all the European powers would be fully committed to preserving.[57] Aware of Salisbury's opposition to any talks over the internationalisation of the Egyptian problem, Hanotaux tried to save face by publicly demanding at least talks over the Nile. The chief of the Quai d'Orsay, under heavy pressure from the *Comité de l'Afrique française* and the colonial party, tried to salvage something for France out of the Fashoda fiasco.

Etienne first urged Hanotaux, then Delcassé, his successor, to demand some compensation for a French withdrawal from Fashoda. Delcassé became Minister of Foreign Affairs in the cabinet of Henri Brisson on 28 June 1898, and was uncertain of what action to take in regard to Fashoda. He received his first dispatch on the Marchand mission on 4 July from Georges Trouillot, the new Minister of Colonies, but this chiefly concerned Marchand's rather serious position at Fashoda.[58] In early August there were many jingoists in England like Chamberlain who would, if necessary, use force to get the French out of the Sudan. Salisbury could be counted on to try to mollify public opinion, but how far could he go against his own people?[59]

In Paris, the colonial party urged Delcassé to make peace with England over the Nile question. While the imperialists disliked losing their long-standing claims to upper Egypt and the Sudan, they knew that Great Britain could not be dislodged from her positions. Edmund Monson told Salisbury that the colonialists were very vocal in their demands for compensation for a retreat from the Nile, and the British Ambassador reported, 'The colonial group is very noisy, and has very able exponents . . . such as M. Etienne.'[60] He told Salisbury that in France the

Fashoda situation had stirred the public, and the volatile French could be raised to a fever pitch by unguarded statements and firebrand newspapers. Monson hoped that an upheaval of that type could be avoided by both governments.

It was obvious that the French military presence at Fashoda could not be maintained. In September the army of Lord Kitchener arrived at Fashoda, and the French realised that they were in an impossible situation. In August 1898 Kitchener took Khartoum, making the French occupation of any part of the Nile impracticable.[61] In London as well as in Paris, the victory of the British army over the forces of the late Mahdi was the key to the holding of the entire Nile Valley. The Paris government had to face the reality of a British victory in the Sudan.[62] In France there was a popular outcry at the humiliation at Fashoda, but Delcassé could not yield to the passions of the moment, nor, for that matter, did he wish to do so. However, the new chief of the Quai d'Orsay did not wish to alienate England and therefore leave France totally isolated and at the mercy of Germany. It was then Delcassé's responsibility to extricate France from her embarrassing situation on the upper Nile. Etienne helped Delcassé in his search for a peaceful solution to the Fashoda incident by leading most of the colonialists to rally behind the Quai d'Orsay in a more forceful fashion than when Hanotaux was struggling with Fashoda. At a monthly meeting of the *Union coloniale* in Paris, Etienne blasted England for her monopoly on the Nile and for the Fashoda humiliation. The French, he warned, expected compensations in the western Maghrib, and '. . . were not always attached to the policy of subordinating [their] interests to British interests'.[63] Etienne had been very vocal in his praise of Marchand and his men, and the captain told the deputy from Oran that he had wanted to rename Fashoda 'l'Etienne' in honour of the colonial leader.[64] Marchand, calling Etienne 'the oldest champion of new French colonialism', thanked him for his staunch support of the mission.[65] The colonial leader, however, refrained from calling for military action against the British and most of the colonialists followed Etienne's example by moderating their attacks on Great Britain's imperial policy on the Nile.

Robert de Caix, writing in the *Bulletin*, reflected Etienne's position when he stated that France had won no glory at Fashoda, and the only honours belonged to Captain Marchand and his small band of Senegalese infantrymen. De Caix observed, 'We arrived at a moment when the British advanced with daring, aided by all the force of *élan* which was enhanced by a victorious campaign. . . . we marched in secret.'[66] Chiding the previous government for its failure on the upper Nile, de Caix called for a total revaluation of France's African policy. It was high time to revise France's policies toward Britain and to try to reach some sort of accord with her in Africa.

The Fashoda crisis had shown that French pretensions on the upper Nile had been an illusion and Delcassé was interested in reaching an accord with England to end the conflict. Ambassador Monson continually visited the Quai d'Orsay to stress to Delcassé that the victory of Kitchener and the subsequent extension of British control over the Sudan was recognised by France as a *fait accompli*.[67] Lord Salisbury sent a telegram to Delcassé which stated that Britain wanted to discuss the African problem with France. However, Her Majesty's Government could not permit any bargaining over the Nile.[68] Delcassé was warned that the jingoists wanted Salisbury to give orders for Kitchener to expel Marchand from Fashoda by force.[69] Also, Delcassé could see that Etienne and the colonial activists had, at their pleasure, withdrawn support for Hanotaux, thereby saving face for themselves. This lesson was not lost on the basically distrustful Delcassé. Delcassé realised that the French could never match the maritime might of Great Britain, and after a detailed study of naval problems, he felt that France could not afford to challenge it.[70]

In an age of seaborne colonialism led by Admiral John Fisher of Britain and Captain Alfred T. Mahan of the United States, the nation with the greatest navy had the lead in imperialism. Auguste Terrier, writing in the *Bulletin*, expressed the growing awareness of the naval might of the United States and Germany. France and Britain, Terrier speculated, would have to join together to redress the imbalance created by the expanding navies of the two nations. To reinstate the seaborne balance of power, he said, 'We [of the *Comité de l'Afrique française*] can say, however, that we desire an understanding with Britain.'[71] Robert de Caix pointed to the crisis of Fashoda and the conciliatory policies of Salisbury as the definite means for a lasting entente between the two imperial powers. Because of the pressing maritime needs of the two countries an alliance would be best for both states.[72]

Echoing this position, Etienne told the Chamber in March 1899 that, '. . . it is necessary to say clearly, especially after the unhappy Fashoda affair that France has [shown] . . . a desire for conciliation and peace.'[73] De Caix noted that Salisbury, Balfour, and Chamberlain declared that Britain did not want a war with France, only peace and understanding. In the *Bulletin*, de Caix wrote, '. . . they have spoken the truth; it at least makes one think of the changing state of the political atmosphere.'[74] From London, de Courcel wrote to Delcassé, '. . . the great majority of the English nation does not desire an argument, let alone a war with France. . . . The natural moderation of Salisbury predisposes him . . . to find a peaceful solution of the Nile question.'[75] From London he learned that the British government led by Salisbury wanted a peaceful settlement to the Marchand mission. Considering that an understanding was important for the future of France, Delcassé appointed the brilliant career diplomat Paul Cambon to replace the retiring de Courcel on 8 December 1898. The haughty Cambon, a friend of Salisbury and Balfour, reasoned that it was time for England and France to join in a period of goodwill.[76] In his first full dispatch to Delcassé, Cambon stated that there was a lot of interest in Britain for better relations.[77]

Salisbury, interested in pushing the growing desire for a *detente*, knew that France could not possibly supply Marchand at Fashoda. The Prime Minister realised that he had the power to order France to withdraw without delay, but his desire for better relations with France prohibited it.[78] In Paris Etienne and the colonialists were convinced that the time was ripe for France to claim Morocco in exchange for which England could have a free hand in Egypt. De Caix, Etienne, Terrier, and the entire *Comité de l'Afrique française* began to urge Delcassé to accept the trade.[79] Paul Cambon and Lord Salisbury signed a convention in March 1899, formally ending the Fashoda crisis; it also opened the way for a meeting of the minds over Egypt and

Morocco. By the end of the Fashoda incident most of the colonialists in Paris realised that the Nile was a closed issue. Delcassé, as the leader of the Quai d'Orsay, thereafter only raised the subject of the Nile as a diplomatic device, fully realising that it was to remain British.

Sir Harry Johnston recalled that for the first time in a decade there were many French diplomats present at his wife's annual New Year's ball given in London,[80] and in May 1899, Delcassé fêted the Prince of Wales in Paris with great pomp and circumstance which delighted the Conservative administration in London.[81] For Etienne and the imperialists, French control in Morocco made much more sense because of the French presence in Algeria and Tunisia. Because of the moderating influence of Lord Salisbury and the changing attitude of Etienne and his colonial allies, the course of the entente ran smoother. The work of conciliation had begun. This task would culminate in the signing of the entente of 1904 and finally in Moroccan annexation in 1912. Also, in many aspects the Fashoda crisis strengthened the hand of the colonial activists since they had emerged from the crisis as the champions of a *detente* between the two imperialist opponents. The ending of support for Hanotaux in 1898 was a clear indication of just how far the imperialists would go to get their way and to maintain their prestige. In the changing political world of the Third Republic each minister and each cabinet had to recognise the vast power of the colonial party and the *Comité de l'Afrique française*. The withdrawal of support could mean political oblivion, and, after 1898, very few ministers, including Delcassé, would be willing to risk it.

Notes to Chapter 6 will be found on pages 186–90.

Chapter 7 THE OCCUPATION OF TUAT 1900-3

WHILE THE colonialists and diplomats were busy seeking a better understanding with Great Britain, the Quai d'Orsay was drawn to a more immediate issue in North Africa. The occupation of the oasis complex of Tuat in 1899 began the policy of deliberate, methodical military penetration of Morocco from the established bases in southern Oran Province. The seizure of Tuat was completed in order to speed the French annexation of the western Maghrib. Jules Cambon, when he was governor general of Algeria in the 1890s, Etienne, and the other colonialists had urged such an action in the Oranais. Now, Delcassé, the chief of the Quai d'Orsay, had to convince the British that the Tuat occupation was the only action France could take to protect the *colons*, commerce and the military posts in Algeria. This operation caused some diplomatic problems for France, and Delcassé had to take the first steps to consolidate the Tuat victory.

The Tuat operation could not have been possible had not France and Britain drawn closer together after the Fashoda crisis. The penetration of Morocco, starting with the Tuat occupation, depended in part on the goodwill of the British government and its representatives in Morocco. The internal situation in Morocco was deteriorating because of her chaotic financial structure, the actions of the Sultan Abdel Aziz, and also a calculated plan formulated by the French colonialists to discredit the Sultan's government in the eyes of the European world. Mohammed Torres, the Moroccan Foreign Minister, tried to find European allies for his nation to help forestall a French takeover, but with little success since most states were hesitant to intervene in what had become a French area of influence. Henri de la Martinière, the French chargé in Tangiers, wrote Delcassé that Mohammed

Torres had visited Sir Arthur Nicolson, the British consul, to protest the Tuat occupation, claiming that the French action violated Moroccan territorial sovereignty. Nicolson told the Moroccan Foreign Minister that England had no interest in problems on Morocco's eastern border, and he advised him to look only to Paris for total satisfaction.[1]

Delcassé watched France's progress at Tuat and in Tangier with some satisfaction, and in a letter to René Waldeck-Rousseau he stated that it was necessary to continue the deliberate policy of slow penetration and subversion in order to keep Muslim resistance at a minimum.[2] Abdel Aziz realised that Morocco was being slowly isolated from the European powers. To try to stop the isolation the Sultan ordered the *Mahkzen* to curb the growing anti-European violence and he also sent a personal order to the tribal leaders at Tuat to submit to French authority.[3] It did not matter what action the Sultan took to stop the rising tide of violence and disorder in the interior of Morocco, since he was basically powerless over his many subjects.[4]

In late December 1900, Delcassé cautioned the militant activists that the pace of penetration had to be slow to keep European complications with the Germans from arising. He hoped to reach a full accord with Spain over the eventual dismemberment of Morocco.[5] Speaking for the imperial activists, Etienne disagreed with Delcassé's policy with regard to Spain, and he claimed, 'Spain can no longer invoke [her] historic claims, respectable without a doubt, but which erect petty barriers to [France's] real interests.'[6] The Geographic Society of Algiers also rejected Spain's claims to Morocco, and the society submitted a list of their own suggestions to the governor general of Algeria to facilitate the penetration of the western Maghrib. The list included the cutting off of all trade with Morocco. By ending all commercial intercourse with the western Maghrib, the society believed, the financial structure of Morocco would collapse faster.[7]

In Tangier, Samuel R. Gummere, the American consul, reported to Washington that the Sultan's government was feeling the effects of the continual subversion by France. In reaction to the Tuat occupation, Mohammed Torres asked the European chargés d'affaires strictly to enforce all sections of their consular treaties. Gummere told Washington that the Moorish government tried to limit the movement and activities of the British and French representatives into the Moroccan hinterland. According to most of the treaties there were strict limits placed on the extent of contacts between Europeans and Muslims. These sections, however, were being openly violated.[8] In the spring of 1900, Gummere informed the American State Department that Mohammed Torres and his staff vehemently insisted that the European consuls restrict their activities to commercial dealings only with Muslims. The American consuls believed that the Moroccan Foreign Minister used diplomacy only when harassment failed,[9] and Mohammed Torres himself endeavoured to get the United States involved with the Tuat problem. On 18 June 1900 he sent a letter to Gummere which attacked the French occupation of the oases. He said, '[You] already know that the Touat [sic] territory since immemorial time forms a part of the Holy Empire of Morocco, as shown in ancient books and geographies. . . .'[10] Gummere commented that, 'The recent operations of the French government which are complained of, have caused great excitement among the Moors. . . .' The American position on Tuat was one of strict neutrality, and Gummere reiterated to the European legation chiefs in Tangier that the United States government took no position on the Tuat or on any Moroccan problem at that time.

The French colonialists, certainly not neutral on the Moroccan question, argued in the Chamber that the occupation of Tuat was vital to French security in the South Oranais. The tribal chieftains near Tuat and In Salah were on the surface loyal to France, or at least loyal to the French military presence, and Etienne believed that their fidelity merited France's full protection from Moroccan reprisals.[11] While the imperialist leaders addressed the Chamber, the situation inside Morocco became worse. In Fez, a mob lynched an American merchant after he had entered a mosque, and Sir Arthur Nicolson informed Gummere that the British and French were trying to ascertain the facts concerning the murder of the American. The American consul warned Washington that the anarchy in Morocco was becoming very serious.[12]

Henri de la Martinière telegraphed the Quai d'Orsay that arms were being smuggled into Morocco at an alarming rate; a battery of new German Krupp cannon were on display in Fez, and the Moroccan army announced that its new equipment included German-made machine guns sent to an infantry regiment in Marrakesh. The French diplomat also warned the Quai d'Orsay that the Sultan had purchased more German machine guns and cannons for other units of the Royal Moroccan Army.[13] To counter the growing influence of the Germans, the French legation offered the service of more French military advisers to instruct the army. But the Moroccan military establishment refused, stating that army briefings and training programmes were closed to foreign military attachés.[14] French officials in Morocco continued to dredge up all sorts of incidents to show that Morocco was close to a state of total anarchy. The constant warnings of massive arms shipments were part of that campaign to discredit Abdel Aziz and the Moroccan government.

Colonel Oscar Burkhardt, the French military attaché in Tangier, continually reported to General André, the Minister of War, that the Moroccan population was in a state of discontent following the Tuat operation. The frivolous social activities of the childish Sultan and his European entourage infuriated devout Muslims who viewed Abdel Aziz's love for European gadgets as a sign of apostasy. Many of the influential and wealthy Muslim merchants of Marrakesh, Burkhardt added, confided to him that an occupation of Morocco by the French would be preferable to civil war and anarchy.[15] The growing discontent prompted Gummere to abandon his neutral position and to act in concert with the other legation chiefs to rebuild the Tangier police force with French-trained officers.[16] Gummere told the State Department that crimes of violence had grown to crisis proportions in the city of Tangier and that the Moroccan police were unable to control the situation. Acting with English, French and Spanish officials, Gummere helped institute the needed reforms, much to the distress of the Moroccan government.

While changes were slowly taking place in Tangier, Delcassé decided to take another important step in the process of Moroccan penetration. He appointed Georges Saint-René Tallandier as the new chargé d'affaires in Tangier. Tallandier was a confidant of the colonial leadership, and a well-known and outspoken advocate of French annexation of Morocco. Arthur Martinsen, the acting American chargé d'affaires, informed Washington that Tallandier arrived in Tangier with a very large escort of three French naval warships. The American remarked that the battleship and two heavy cruisers were, '. . . an unusual display of warships.'[17] The French legation in Tangiers weakly explained that the ships were only coincidental with Tallandier's arrival, although no diplomat could really believe the story.[18]

Tallandier arrived at a time when agents reported that tribal leaders near Marrakesh were obtaining large quantities of modern weapons from the royal arsenals of Abdel Aziz.[19] Ominously, he stated, Abdel Aziz remained in Marrakesh to oversee the distribution of arms, and it was claimed that he had also armed bellicose tribes near Rabat and Fez.[20] However, the military section of the French legation in Tangiers reported that no one except the Sultan's court and his intimate advisers knew the extent of tribal loyalty. Despite the basic inconsistency of Abdel Aziz giving arms to tribes whose loyalty was suspect, the reports were treated as absolute fact in Paris. The French, in truth, were never certain how many weapons had been given to the Muslims to resist the French or how many weapons fell into the hands of Abdel Aziz's enemies, nor, for that matter, did they care.

During a debate in the Chamber in January 1902, a colonialist deputy called attention to the acts of violence near the oasis of Figuig. Etienne rose to speak for the imperialists, and calmly pointed out that France had a very simple policy in Morocco. The main point of France's policy, he claimed, was to supplement the Sultan's authority where Moroccan troops were unable to keep order. In the long run this would have to lead to a seizure of Figuig and other oases, although, as Etienne reminded the Chamber, France had to await events in the western Maghrib and the South Oranais.[21] Etienne had been openly urging a barter of France's claims on the Nile for a preponderant position in Morocco. Behind Etienne's call for prudence was the fact that the Nile-Morocco barter was closer than many deputies realised.[22]

The majority of the members of the *Comité de l'Afrique française* followed their leadership with regard to the policy of waiting in Morocco. Each copy of the monthly organ of the *Comité* carried several horror stories about the treacherous Moroccans or about some alleged outrage. For example, the February edition of the *Bulletin* stated that the Figuig situation was becoming intolerable, but perhaps the French and Moroccan officials could work together to alleviate it.[23] The *Bulletin* pointed out that the opposition to Abdel Aziz was growing because of his taste for European gadgetry. His Islamic subjects believed that the Sultan's addiction to infidel inventions such as tennis and photography brought the entire kingdom to the verge of heresy. Also, many Muslims doubted if the kingdom could long afford such expensive pleasures.[24] The disgust with the Sultan was growing especially in the *Bled es Siba*[25] because of the reports of his love for foreign pleasures. Gummere summed up the state of public opinion when he reported, 'As far as I can ascertain this feeling of [discontent] arises from the conduct of the Sultan in having surrounded himself with Europeans whose customs, such as photography, bicycling [*sic*], playing tennis, etc., he has adopted to a great degree. . . .'[26]

Abdel Aziz, realising that his position within his own country was deteriorating, asked the Quai d'Orsay for a large quantity of modern rifles for his army. A surprised Delcassé informed General André of the request without comment,[27] although like any other imperialist he had little desire to see modern firearms in the hands of the Moroccan army. The Quai d'Orsay had been upset over the number of German weapons that had been added to the arsenals at Marrakesh and Fez. Not surprisingly, Delcassé and André decided not to send any arms to Abdel Aziz which might in the long run hinder the final conquest of Morocco.

Speaking for a majority of the colonial party and *Comité*, Etienne made his position well known in early 1903 when he wrote that the final solution to the Moroccan question was woven into the entire fabric of France's colonial future. France would have to act alone in Morocco because, 'only France, with her Muslim and Berber experiences [in Algeria and Tunisia] can consummate an enterprise of that sort.'[28] The deputy from Oran and Delcassé realised that there had to be a slow policy in regard to Morocco, but the two colonialists differed, however, on the basic approaches to colonial penetration. These differences began to cause serious confusion in the imperialist camp which was misinterpreted by many European diplomats. Prince Hugo von

Radolin, the German ambassador in Paris, detected the two differing attitudes on Morocco and wrote to Baron von Holstein, the Francophobe master of the German Foreign Office, that Delcassé seemed depressed and preoccupied with the growing Moroccan troubles. Von Radolin, misunderstanding Delcassé's deliberate policy, told von Holstein that the French Foreign Minister was trying to avoid military intervention in Morocco.[29]

What concerned Delcassé in the spring of 1903 was the growing leftist opposition to any Moroccan adventure. Jean Jaurès, the Socialist leader, and many of his followers in the Chamber, questioned the value of annexing the western Maghrib. Jaurès and Etienne clashed continually over France's policy toward the Cheriffian Empire. Jaurès condemned military action near Figuig which resulted in the deaths of several French and Moroccan cavalrymen. Etienne, defending Delcassé's policy, told Jaurès that armed action was deemed necessary to protect French commerce and security in southern Algeria. The Chamber, Etienne noted, was divided over the Moroccan issue, but events would prove the government's position to be correct.[30]

The colonial party and the *Comité* hoped that this open split would encourage Abdel Aziz to be bolder in the Oranais, which could hasten French action in respect to Morocco. Charles Jonnart, the new governor general of Algeria, informed Etienne that the entire frontier was in a state of great discontent because of the growing unrest inside Morocco and because of the evident hesitation in Paris.[31] Every indication on the European diplomatic barometer pointed to an acceptance of French takeover by every power except possibly Germany. Prince von Bulow believed that Germany might accept annexation because, '. . . the conquest of Morocco would weaken France militarily.'[32]

Jonnart observed, and told Etienne, that the Algerian Muslim population remained calm in the face of the preparations for action in Morocco, but he also asked Etienne to use his great influence with Premier Combes to get more troops sent into the unoccupied areas of the Oranais. Etienne, probably the most influential politician in the Chamber during the Combes ministry, was asked to put his entire force behind a call for immediate action.[33] Etienne was more than willing to begin the final push in the western Maghrib; he introduced, on 8 June 1903, a project for a railroad from the military base at Beni Ounif to the fort at Ain Sefra. This line would, when finished, link the two posts and push deep into the contested southern area.[34] For the imperialists the one great value of such a line lay in the possibility of rapidly moving troops into the south. The Beni Ounif project was a major step in the evolving French plans for the possible annexation of Morocco.

In a letter from Jonnart to Etienne, the Algerian governor general said, 'I understand perfectly that the Algerian policy and that policy which concerns Morocco, are one and the same with the Quai d'Orsay.'[35] The situation in the South Oranais, Jonnart warned, reached a crisis level with destructive raids from Morocco. The constant rumours of revolt against Abdel Aziz by conservative Islamic elements caused rumblings on the frontier.[36] The imperialists were not displeased with the continual trouble in the Oranais. Tallandier in Tangier wrote to Etienne that the Tangier legation appreciated the work that the deputy from Oran did for the cause of Moroccan penetration. The policy of France in the western Maghrib, he told Etienne, was excellent because each action was deliberate and gauged to show the necessity of French intervention to restore order. If action were taken in Morocco, Tallandier believed, it would have to come in response to Moorish depredations.[37]

In October 1903, Etienne received a letter from Colonel Hubert Lyautey, named with the colonial lobby's support to command the French troops at the oasis post of Ain Sefra, who complained of Delcassé's timidity in pressing the French solution to the Moroccan question. He wrote, 'Despite the promises fixing my authority at least independence [of action] has not come to pass.'[38] Lyautey, a passionate advocate of Moroccan annexation, was impatient to begin the final phase of the takeover. Passion for the colonial cause often was frustrated by the slow processes of European diplomacy, and for the colonialists, 1903 was a setback for the progress of Moroccan penetration. Since 1898 the annexationists had urged the Quai d'Orsay to complete the Egyptian-Moroccan trade, and in 1903 the consummation of the barter seemed close. There was also a growing distrust of Delcassé among the influential imperialists, including Etienne. Etienne did not accept, nor approve of, the slow deliberate approach to the annexation of Morocco.

Agreeing with Lyautey that Delcassé was timid, the colonial leader's affection for the secretive chief of the Quai d'Orsay chilled quite noticeably after 1903. The aggressive colonialists—Tallandier, Etienne, Lyautey, and Jonnart—were irritated with the slow progress of the diplomatic relations and the activities within Morocco which would make the trade a reality. But, the European diplomatic implications were many and complex, and the colonialist militants had to bide their time while the Quai d'Orsay prepared the accords of 1904. The demands of the annexationists for a colonial trade were met in 1904 when Paul Cambon and Lord Lansdowne signed an agreement which eventually grew and became the *entente cordiale*.

Notes to Chapter 7 will be found on pages 190–2.

Chapter 8 THE EUROPEAN IMPLICA-
TIONS OF THE MOROCCAN
PROBLEM 1899-1904

In the wake of the Fashoda crisis, the colonial party and the *Comité de l'Afrique française* grew in power and authority. One of the leading imperialists, Théophile Delcassé, became the chief of the Quai d'Orsay, and in 1899 Etienne was elected again as vice-president of the Chamber. Trying to reverse the hostility toward England, and feeling that an Egyptian and Moroccan diplomatic trade was necessary, the imperialist militants constantly exerted pressure on Delcassé to conclude some sort of accord with Great Britain in order to gain a free hand in the western Maghrib.[1] Lord Salisbury, fearing Britain's isolation from continental affairs, also was urged by many of his own colleagues to reach a firm agreement with France to end the festering African situation.[2]

Ever since the rise of the problems about the recognition of Abdel Aziz and about the Fez consulate issue, the *Comité de l'Afrique française* had shown a growing interest in Morocco. Because of the great border problems, Etienne wanted to annex Morocco to secure Algerian trade and commerce. The French solution to the Moroccan question was made more difficult when in 1900 Lord Salisbury was toppled from power by a pro-German coalition consisting of Lord Lansdowne, Arthur Balfour, and Joseph Chamberlain. Salisbury had been forced to retire because of ill health, over the issues of constitutional reform, and the rather sorry spectacle of the British Army in the Boer War. The new Prime Minister, Arthur Balfour, wanted an understanding with Germany, but as time passed he became aware of Germany's hostility.[3] German hegemony over Europe would place England in greater isolation; this Balfour could not permit.

In France, the colonialists tried to quiet the ill will caused by

Fashoda. Assuming the lead, and speaking for a majority of the colonial party, Etienne wrote in the influential British *National Review* that the long-standing colonial differences had to be resolved or both states would be isolated. He told the British that their effort for land reclamation on the Nile was worthy of French admiration and praise.[4] Paul Cambon told Delcassé that Etienne's move was well received in Great Britain. He also remarked that, '[Etienne] senses quite well that he can do nothing in the colonies if he remains a staunch enemy of the British.'[5] Etienne's basic colonial policy had not altered. He continued to believe in the basic value of France's African expansion; he himself wished to expand in the western Maghrib rather than toward the Nile and Red Sea. Britain was obviously too solidly entrenched in Egypt to be driven out, and to try to dislodge her would probably lead to serious European complications.[6] In 1900 the imperialists' changing colonial policy could be summed up in two simple words: consolidation and conciliation. They believed that France's pressing need was an immediate unification of the empire. The gigantic territory in the Maghrib and in Africa south of the Sahara had to be joined with Algeria. Most annexationists, by 1900, considered Morocco a part of French North Africa, and any moves to expand the French empire in Africa, they thought, eventually had to include Morocco. Etienne, for example, believed that it was time to reach an accord with Britain which would guarantee peace and security for French Africa. To prepare the way for a French take-over in Morocco, it was first necessary to win the total support of Great Britain.

As another part of the problem the colonialists were concerned with the attitude of the Ottoman Empire toward any Moroccan action. The spectre of a Muslim uprising, fostered by Constantinople, bothered the colonial group. If, on the eve of the move to the west, the Algerians and Tunisians revolted, the whole Moroccan venture could be damaged beyond repair. Jean Constans, the French ambassador in Constantinople, was one of the imperialists' staunchest allies. From his post near the Sultan's court, he kept Etienne and the colonialists informed of the strong currents of opposition to any French advance. Probably better informed than Delcassé, the deputy from Oran knew that France would have to be careful in Morocco. In February 1899, Constans informed Etienne that the young Turks were very antagonistic toward a French colonial take-over in any Muslim land, and that they would urge Muslim resistance to any French designs on nations which professed Islam.[7]

Many of the imperialists misunderstood Delcassé's deliberate policy in regard to Morocco. Delcassé was convinced of the need for a slow, methodical penetration of the western Maghrib, and his very deliberate policy of first obtaining a European concurrence irritated the colonial party. Constans was certain that Delcassé's stand over the collection of the Ottoman debt would cause trouble for France.[8] The chief of the Quai d'Orsay pushed for a European collection commission, because he saw the Ottoman debt question as a stepping stone for greater diplomatic intercourse between the continental powers.[9] The gulf which appeared between Delcassé and Etienne over the entire Moroccan question caused trouble for the Quai d'Orsay. Delcassé, frustrated by Etienne's growing hostility toward his Maghribi policies, informed him that '. . . there can not be two contradictory policies in Morocco', and urged him to bide his time.[10] Delcassé and Etienne shared the goal of Moroccan annexation, but they differed on the means to that end, and they slowly drifted apart over the question of timing because each man had to cope with colonial questions on different levels. Etienne could afford to be very vocal in his criticism of Delcassé's policy in Morocco or Constantinople. The full weight of ministerial responsibility was not placed on his shoulders. Delcassé had to concern himself with steering a careful course through stormy European waters. For example, the British responded slowly to the new colonialist stance after Fashoda. The Germans appeared to be hostile to both Britain and France, and the Spanish were undecided as to what course to follow. Etienne, on the other hand, did not have to live with the day-to-day complexities of European diplomacy while Delcassé could not afford to use excessive or unguarded words. The two men acted quite differently and rarely found areas of exact agreement.

One area of full agreement between Delcassé and the colonialists was the remote possibility of the annexation of Ethiopia. As a part of France's policy of finding a rapprochement with England, Delcassé and Etienne, as spokesman for the annexationists, considered diverting attention from the Nile to Ethiopia. In January

1902, Etienne told the Chamber that France had only one small colony in East Africa, but he thought that French Somaliland could serve as a base for action in Ethiopia. In this context Etienne advocated a railroad linking Jibouti in Somaliland to Addis Ababa.[11] The *Comité* hinted that Britain had designs on Ethiopia because, as the *Bulletin* stated, the British wanted to run a railroad from Khartoum to Uganda and the line to Urganda was '. . . only possible through Ethiopia'.[12] General Galliéni advised Etienne that a railway from Dakar in Senegal to Jibouti would have to run through Addis Ababa. This, the general believed, would bring about the final linking of all French Africa.[13] Etienne, no stranger to the map of Africa, had grave doubts about the trans-African project. Dakar to Jibouti was a colonialists' dream: it was simply not practical to think about laying track across the vast expanses of central Africa. Besides, both Delcassé and Etienne realised that it might simply be too costly in diplomatic and economic terms to turn France's attention to Ethiopia. France's relationship with London was, at that point, too fragile to risk a rupture over so doubtful an adventure. There remained an Ethiopian group within the *Comité de l'Afrique française* which demanded that France assume its 'historic role' in that country. But the founding of the *Comité du Maroc* in 1904 for the penetration of Morocco ended the siphoning of colonialist energy for the Ethiopian question. After 1904, the Moroccan question dominated the colonial party, and the *Comité du Maroc* pushed the Dakar-Jibouti via Addis Ababa project far into the background.

The Ethiopian group was officially silenced by Robert de Caix at the February meeting of the Moroccan Committee. He introduced a series of resolutions, backed by Eugène Etienne and other influential leaders, which called for international arbitration on the Ethiopian railway question. The *Comité* approved his programme, and for the time being the Moroccan issue became the sole concern of the imperialists.[14] In the March edition of the *Bulletin* de Caix wrote that there were other more pressing questions than Ethiopia. Morocco, de Caix stated, had to come first, and while France had to watch over her interests in the area, the best policy, he believed, was to seek at least an international 'neutralisation of Ethiopia'.[15]

The handling of the Ethiopian question by the colonialists was an important step in the cooling of relations between France and Britain. Determined not to permit French and English interests to clash over a railroad, the colonialists, led by Etienne, displayed their desire for good relations. The Khartoum-Uganda line and the Dakar-Jibouti project could have developed into another conflict, possibly as serious as Fashoda, but the French colonialists did not permit it to get out of hand. The recourse to caution and negotiations with England were what Delcassé had urged, and these he got.

On the other hand, the British had to adjust to the new diplomatic situation in Europe. Salisbury, ousted in 1900, had worked for a *detente* with France, but his successor, Lord Lansdowne, had been a part of that pro-German group which ousted him. However, fearing the Franco-Russian alliance, the British government dreaded the possibility of a war, and Lansdowne's failure to secure an understanding with Germany over the Far Eastern question caused great concern over Britain's isolation from the continental powers.[16] Kaiser Wilhelm II, appearing most aggressive, caused England a great deal of irritation when he announced the construction of new warships. Despite Joseph Chamberlain's initial enthusiasm over the possibility of an Anglo-German understanding, Lansdowne felt that Britain should look around and make a careful decision as to her course of action.

In 1902, in the state of growing fear over the isolation of England, the Committee for Imperial Defence (CID) met in London. Under Balfour's guiding hand, the CID began to analyse England's weaknesses vis-à-vis Russia and France. In the debate over the relative strengths of Russia and France, it was decided that in any war with the two, France would have to be struck first because she was the strongest, but also the most vulnerable to an attack directed against the colonies. The leaders of the CID felt that, 'The "colonial party" in France, though increasingly powerful, did not represent national opinion, and it is doubtful if the French lower classes would . . . continue a war, unless national soil was invaded.'[17] The main thrust of a British assault on France would come against Bizerte, Dakar, Martinique, Diego-Suarez, Saigon, and Jibouti. The main blow would be against Bizerte, and the British hoped to occupy it and to promote a Muslim revolution in all of Tunisia and Algeria. The

Committee for Imperial Defence also believed that a native rebellion in the Maghrib would force France to divert forces to protect the *colons*: this would have the effect of quickly ending the war.[18]

The CID considered that, of all the possibilities for war, one probability of a conflict with France was greatest. On the eve of the *entente cordiale*, the CID, under Balfour's administration, again stressed this idea to the British government.[19] In the face of such confusion in the British government, Delcassé and Etienne would have to play the role that Lord Salisbury played in 1898. It was the Quai d'Orsay's turn to be a moderating influence in European diplomacy when the pro-Germans in the British cabinet received a rude shock when Wilhelm II announced his pro-Boer attitude in South Africa.[20] Even Joseph Chamberlain knew that his policy of seeking a rapprochement with Imperial Germany was a fruitless search. After a stinging defeat on the free trade issue, and rather than accept the total failure of his policy, Chamberlain resigned from the Colonial Office in 1903.

The resignation of Chamberlain also heralded a basic change in the attitudes of the personnel in both the colonial and foreign offices. Sir Francis Bertie, appointed to succeed Edmond Monson in Paris, Sir Arthur Hardinge, and Sir Arthur Nicolson began to reshape British policy. These men were increasingly suspicious of German ambitions in Europe.[21] The initial pressure to consummate changing British opinion fell on Paris. Paul Cambon, Delcassé, and the Quai d'Orsay would have to decide what action to take. Delcassé wanted to be convinced that the time was ripe to begin overtures to England before reaching an understanding with Spain over Morocco.[22] Leon y Castillo, the Spanish ambassador to Paris, was such a noted Francophile that Delcassé could have dealt with England first without offending the Spanish. Senora Leon y Castillo had the reputation of being more French than the French. Her lifelong dream had been to be the wife of the Spanish ambassador to Paris, and she had expressed this desire while still a young girl in school at the College of the Sacred Heart in Madrid. Her pressure on Leon y Castillo to serve French interests would eventually give the Quai d'Orsay the needed latitude to deal with Britain over Morocco.[23]

While Delcassé grappled with the complexities of European

diplomacy, Etienne helped in searching out new areas of agreement with England. With the full force of the colonial party and the *Comité de l' Afrique française* behind the new policy of goodwill toward England, the Quai d'Orsay could act with some certainty. Auguste Terrier, secretary-general of the *Comité*, wrote in the *Bulletin* that it was high time that England and France settled their long-standing differences over the Chad and the Niger. Terrier urged that the line from the Chad to Say be fixed by negotiations in which neither side made excessive claims. The time had come, he told his readers, to end the friction between England and France and to get on with bettering relations between the two countries.[24] During the debates on the budget for the Quai d'Orsay in January 1902, the colonial party clearly championed the changing policy toward Britain. Most speakers pointed to the French New Hebrides Islands, where England and France had made simultaneous claims of ownership. While believing that the major portion of the New Hebrides belonged to the French Pacific Island complex including New Caledonia, Tahiti and French Oceania, Etienne told the Chamber that the proximity of the New Hebrides to Australia did make the claim for France somewhat doubtful. Etienne, speaking at length on the changing climate between the two states, urged fair talks between the two contesting nations to decide the fate of the New Hebrides Islands.[25]

During his speech to the Chamber, Etienne touched on another problem with Great Britain—Siam. Both the British and French wanted a predominance in that south-east Asian country. Because of the nearness to Indochina, Etienne added, Siam should be in the French orbit, but he believed that there should be a fair negotiation between Great Britain and France over the future of the area. He told the amazed Chamber that he was not an Anglophobe. On the contrary, Etienne stated that he wanted to live in perfect harmony with the English and that it would be a sad time indeed if the two nations should ever have to meet on the field of battle. The colonialist deputies were not especially surprised by Etienne's open wooing of the English since his change of heart had been apparent for some time. Several colonialists shouted disapproval at Etienne during his speech, but he was able to counter by stating the obvious: continual conflict was against the

H

best interests of France in the colonies and in Europe. Even President Emile Loubet sent his hearty approval via a letter for Etienne's speech on behalf of better Anglo-French relations.[26]

The call of Morocco was growing in the imperialists' ears. Never, since Etienne first entered the Chamber, had the time seemed so right for action in regard to Morocco. Delcassé had been unwilling to offer England more than a guarantee of neutrality for Tangier and freedom of trade in a French Morocco.[27] But Cambon, Etienne, and the colonialists pressured Delcassé, who had second thoughts—England could possibly be won over to a total commitment for French Morocco, they all seemed to argue. In 1903, the imperialists' political influence was reaching an all-time high in the Chamber, as they held the position of vice-president, which guided opposition or support for the government.[28] What the imperialists wrote would be studied by the British with great care, and, as many of their number had hoped, it was enticing enough to win an invitation from Lord Lansdowne to visit London and discuss Moroccan policy and Anglo-French colonial differences in general.

In Etienne's 1903 article in the *National Review* he dealt with four key areas. He was concerned with clearing the air between England and France. After he had lavished praise on Great Britain, for, of all things, her work in Egypt and the Nile, he suggested solutions for problems of the Niger, Chad, Siam, and the New Hebrides. Etienne stated that Britain's work of pacifying the Nile region merited the admiration of the civilised world. The reclamation of the farmlands near the Nile was astounding, Etienne said.[29] On the Niger and Chad, Etienne said what he had refused to admit since 1890—that Britain and France had equally important spheres of influence which both sides should recognise. The treaties arranged with native kings in western Africa, Etienne admitted, were worthless, because the African sovereigns signed the same treaties for identical rights with France and England.[30]

In regard to the New Hebrides question, Etienne proposed the same solution. Simply, the two powers should discuss the issues. A continuance of the conflict would bring about the possibility of war in the Pacific, which would endanger Australia as well as New Caledonia. After praising the pioneering spirit of the

Australians, Etienne wrote that he believed that France and England could find speedy conclusions to their colonial problems in the Pacific.[31] The Siamese question was to be handled similarly.

What was so surprising about Etienne's position was its conciliatory tone. He had decided, as had Paul Cambon, that the time had come to make public the French desire for an understanding with Britain.[32] Slowly Delcassé realised that Etienne could serve the best interests of French policy by going to London to talk with the British government. Through the good offices of the respected Paul Cambon, Etienne was invited to Whitehall to confer about colonial problems and Moroccan policy.[33]

Etienne's evolving Moroccan policy became quite clear when he wrote a lengthy article on France's Saharan policy in the summer edition of *Questions diplomatiques et coloniales*. Etienne stated that the Sahara had no real value, being simply a vast waste land, but that in the context of Algero-Moroccan policy it was vital. To pacify the region, he said, it was necessary to seize and hold the oases and to force recognition of French control by the Moroccan sultan.[34] The deputy from Oran stopped just short of declaring that the Saharan question was one of the keystones in the French plans to penetrate Morocco. Colonel Marie Laperrine, commandant of the Saharan Oases Area, wrote to Etienne that the pacification of the tribes in the Algerian section of the Sahara was going along slowly. Etienne also knew that resistance to the march of the French was opposed from the Moroccan side of the frontier.[35]

Later in the summer of 1903, Laperrine wrote Etienne about plans for a military railroad which were under way in the Sahara. The project which the general proposed for the Saharan railroad was important in the context of Morocco penetration. There were to be a set number of kilometres between watering stations. Each water location would be well guarded. The tracks would run as close to the frontier as possible to facilitate troop movements.[36] Laperrine, devoted to Moroccan annexation, also wrote that the famous hermit Charles de Foucauld, who knew this region, was contemplating a move deeper into the Sahara to proselytise the Touaregs. Laperrine, who knew of de Foucauld's difficulties in bringing many converts to Christianity, believed that the monk could serve as a source of information on the various tribes in the

Sahara. The renowned monk said he was not willing to become an intelligence agent for the military, but Laperrine felt that it was possible to interpret what the recluse might relate.[37]

Etienne had a valuable confederate in Colonel Laperrine, and he also had a strong ally in Charles Jonnart, the governor general of Algeria. During the summer of 1903, Jonnart, who partially owed his position in Algiers to Etienne's staunch support,[38] wrote that the whole force of his office was preoccupied with the growing tension in the Sahara and the *Sud Oranais*.[39] Etienne realised that Jonnart's energetic action had aided in the process of pacification in Algeria to the extent that the colonialists need not fear a revolt over the Moroccan penetration.[40]

With the situation becoming clearer for Etienne and his imperialist friend, he prepared for his trip to London to meet with Lansdowne. On 2 July Etienne and Lansdowne dined together, and the latter broached the subject of French Moroccan policy. In the English plan for Morocco, it had been decided that France should have a free hand to settle the situation, and Etienne was told as much.[41] The Frenchman was overjoyed at the prospect of the Anglo-French accord over Morocco. Etienne's visit with Lansdowne was intended to sound out British opinion. Cambon skilfully brought the traditional enemies together, and with equal skill he had convinced Delcassé that Etienne was paying homage to him by adopting his policy of conciliation with the English.[42] Delcassé, preparing to visit Lansdowne in July, felt the time was ripe to confront Lansdowne with French plans for Morocco. He wanted to gauge the Foreign Office's response, and he authorised Cambon to begin talks with Lansdowne over Morocco.[43] The year 1903 was the turning point in Anglo-French relations because it was the year that saw a serious effort by the French colonialists to reverse the two decades of antagonism over colonial problems. For Paul Cambon, 1903 meant the culmination of his policy of trying to find a common ground for a rapprochement. For Etienne the turn of events brought the possibility of Moroccan annexation closer. Delcassé could turn his energy toward cementing the new alliance.

The changes which occurred in 1903 were of great significance. With the British and French able to solve long-standing colonial disputes in a peaceful and calm manner, the way was clear for a more formal, military *entente*. Etienne emerged, much to the surprise of the colonialists, as a man who was one of the strongest champions of the Anglo-French *entente*. A decade before, Etienne would have exploded in rage at the thought of such settlements. As he once said, however, the imperialists were men of decisive action, and their action had to be practical. Etienne stood at the zenith of his power in the Chamber and in a year he would enter the government again, this time as Minister of the Interior. He remained permanently committed to the French settlement of the Moroccan crisis. The *entente* which was developing was at least partially his brain child and the events in Morocco that followed were the direct results of the shift which the colonial party made in 1903. Paul Cambon, Théophile Delcassé, and a host of supporters within the colonial movement enabled France to decide on a course of action. While tensions developed between Delcassé and Etienne, general co-operation in regard to Morocco prevailed, and this era of mutual goals greatly aided Delcassé's overall policy. However, the overwhelming problem of exactly how to annex Morocco, and when, troubled both Delcassé and the imperialists. This problem would eventually break up the alliance between the chief of the Quai d'Orsay and Etienne, the spokesman for the colonial lobby.

Notes to Chapter 8 will be found on pages 192–4.

Chapter 9 THE IMPERIALISTS AND THE TANGIER CRISIS 1904-5

THE DIPLOMATIC turning point in the process of Moroccan penetration came in 1904 and 1905. The Paris-based colonialists moved more toward an understanding with England in 1903, while in Morocco the French imperialists, Tallandier and Count de Saint-Aulaire, prepared the way for the eventual seizure of that state. Lyautey, who was becoming more independent and often insubordinate, waited for orders to begin the long march to Fez. At Ain Sefra the small army was ready for the command to invade the western Maghrib. While Lyautey and the colonial expeditionary force prepared for the day of action, Charles Jonnart kept Etienne informed of the rising tide of disorder in the Oranais, and often Etienne was better informed of activities in Algeria and Morocco than was Théophile Delcassé.

In early 1904 Jonnart wrote to Etienne that the preparations for action in Morocco were proceeding in South Algeria as well as the colonialists had expected. Jonnart had been allocated large sums of money to bribe certain influential members of the *Mahkzen* to keep them loyal to France. Algeria's energetic governor general urged that more money be allotted to keep corrupt Moroccan officials corrupt.[1] The alleged outbreaks of banditry near the oasis of Figuig convinced him that steps would have to be taken to speed up the pace of penetration. After ascertaining that much of the agitation along the undefined border originated at the Sultan's court,[2] he demanded that more mounted troops be sent for duty on the Oranais frontier. He told Etienne that it would be necessary to occupy a number of strategic villages there.[3]

From Tangier, Captain Léon Jouinot-Gambetta, a nephew of the illustrious Gambetta, wrote to his patron Etienne that as the French increased their activity along the Algero-Moroccan frontier, the authority of the Sultan as a defender of an Islamic land declined. Gambetta, knowing that bribery would serve the French ends, offered lucrative administrative positions to members of the *Mahkzen*.[4] The gold French franc became one of the keys to the penetration of Morocco. In an attempt to resist France the Moroccan Foreign Minister, Mohammed Torres, approached the American consul to inquire if the United States would negotiate a loan with the Moroccan government. The amount was not set because Torres realised that Abdel Aziz needed any sum he could get. The American government, however, was not inclined to lend anything to the Sultan.[5]

While Morocco was collapsing into financial chaos and civil anarchy, the *Comité de l'Afrique française* and the colonial party decided that the time had come to concentrate on a massive effort to add Morocco to the empire. In February 1904 a number of influential imperialists formed the *Comité du Maroc* to speed the annexation of Morocco. Etienne was elected as the committee's first president, Charles Roux assumed the vice-presidency, and Robert de Caix and Auguste Terrier became secretaries. As Etienne stated, 'The *Comité du Maroc* is a branch of the *Comité de l'Afrique française*; it will have the same organ—the *Bulletin*.'[6] Later the president announced that Robert de Caix, the editor of the *Bulletin*, promised that first priority would be given to the Moroccan question.[7] The entire thrust of the colonialists aimed at preparing official and public opinion for the annexation of Morocco.

At the first public meeting of the new committee in June 1904, Etienne made the keynote speech. After praising Jonnart and Lyautey, the deputy from Oran told his enthusiastic audience that the time had come for France to act with dispatch and decision in the western Maghrib.[8] French pre-eminence in Morocco would be established by a massive influx of civil administrators from France, and these men would mould the Moroccan executive apparatus to fit into the French imperial scheme. This in turn would keep Morocco welded to France.[9] Emerging as the prime advocate of French action in Morocco, Etienne set the tone for the ultimate addition of Morocco to France's Maghribi empire.[10] He revealed that the main goal of the imperialists was to make Morocco a colony of France, and the claim that France only wanted to supplement the Sultan's authority and restore order was a smoke screen to hide the actual aims of Etienne and the colonialists. During his speech Etienne praised Delcassé and England for the growing understanding between the two countries. Soon, Etienne said, all Europe would recognise France's predominance in the western Maghrib. Through the energetic work of Paul Cambon, the French ambassador to Britain, and Lord Lansdowne, an agreement between the two states was near.[11]

Robert de Caix lauded the growing accords and stated, 'For the first time France and England have regulated the problems that have menaced [Europe]. . . .'[12] The accords, signed by Cambon and Lansdowne in April 1904, were praised by Etienne who added his 'heartfelt gratitude' for the first step in ending the dangerous colonial rivalry in Africa. Perhaps, he told the *Comité du Maroc*, it would be possible to extend the colonial accords into a working military alliance between the two states.[13] The colonial activists were several steps ahead of Delcassé and the Quai d'Orsay. While neither Delcassé nor Lansdowne felt, in April 1904, the need openly to speculate on the future possibilities for the *entente*, it was obvious that the relations between Great Britain and France were better than at any time in the nineteenth century. In England, Edward Grey, the future Prime Minister, felt that the course of European diplomacy had changed and reached an irreversible stage of friendship.[14]

Evidence of the change came when the British *National Review* asked Etienne to write a lengthy article explaining France's Moroccan policy. Etienne began his article by telling the English that the major problem in Morocco was one of basic legal and fiscal reform. Citing a speech by Delcassé on the western Maghrib, he said that France had definite plans for financial and police reform in Morocco. Etienne pointed out that the court officials did not receive regular salary; consequently they took a portion of the taxes which they collected. Like leeches, these royal officials raised taxes to increase their own incomes. This, Etienne claimed, had to be ended by France, and to foster reform, Franco-Arab schools would be introduced as well as a number of French-staffed medical centres. All this, the militant deputy told his readers, the French people were willing to undertake in the name of humanitarianism and civilisation.[15]

The British were somewhat impressed by the imperialist leader's arguments: the Germans, however, were not. Prince von Radolin, the German ambassador in Paris, misunderstood the colonialists' offers to the British for more understanding. Von Radolin incorrectly judged that there was a great difference of opinion between Delcassé and the colonial party over the ultimate fate of Morocco. The German correctly saw that a gulf of distrust and dislike was growing between the militants and Delcassé, but he failed to see that in the long run the final goals of annexation were the same. In a dispatch to Prince von Bulow in Berlin he stated that the chief of the Quai d'Orsay was at odds with the leadership of the colonial party, and that Delcassé intended only to enforce a peace along the Oranais frontier.[16] In 1904, von Radolin tried to place doubts in the minds of Delcassé and Tallandier over the resolve of the British to recognise France's interests in Morocco. He warned Tallandier that the British legation in Tangier would try to obstruct French progress in the western Maghrib. Not citing any source, von Radolin told Tallandier that the British regarded the *entente* as a vehicle for stopping the French in Morocco.[17] Obviously, Berlin did not relish the *entente* between France and Britain. Wilhelm II wrote to his cousin, Czar Nicholas II of Russia, 'Though Delcassé is an anglophile *enragé*, he will be wise enough to understand that the British fleet is utterly unable to save Paris.'[18] Angered and petulant over the emerging friendship between London and Paris, the Kaiser tried to find a way to split the alliance. The clumsy attempts of von Radolin to place doubts in Tallandier's mind, and Wilhelm's bellicose statements were calculated to shake France's resolve to rely on British goodwill.

In Morocco, however, Tallandier and Sir Arthur Nicolson worked together on the very difficult problems arising from the growing state of civil disorder. Nicolson indicated that he would support the French efforts to reform the police of Tangier by introducing police officers trained by France. An Algerian officer and three Muslim noncommissioned officers were chosen to begin the process of reconstructing the city's police force.[19] Nicolson told his French colleague that British bankers were lending money to Abdel Aziz at extraordinarily high interest rates which made repayment a virtual impossibility.[20] The

French and British consuls continually complained about the unsafe conditions on the major road from Rabat to Casablanca. Bandits had attacked European tradesmen on the highways, and Tallandier and Nicolson petitioned the Sultan and the *Mahkzen* to take steps to see that the roads be made as safe as possible for European travellers.[21] Both consuls were well aware their demands for more police protection on the roads were unrealistic. The Sultan's representatives could not even collect the traditional Islamic taxes in many of the smallest villages; consequently, it would be impossible to enforce security on the roads. The decline of the Sultan's authority had its repercussions on the Oranais border as well.

Lyautey explained to Etienne that the explosive situation along the Oranais frontier was rapidly deteriorating. In February 1904, Moroccan bandits attacked French *colon* settlements north of the oasis of Figuig. Convoys from the French Sudan destined for the Tuat oasis complex were looted by several hundred Moorish brigands. The irritated Lyautey asked Etienne to inform the Chamber that the situation had reached the crisis level and that money should be voted to increase the numbers of troops in the area.[22] The commander of Ain Sefra believed that his troubles along the border were a direct result of the civil disorder within Morocco. As Abdel Aziz lost prestige, the tribes on the Moroccan side of the frontier felt freed from the Sultan's authority and became bolder. The Sultan, refused loans from the French and the British, was unable to pay his soldiers. This in turn meant that Abdel Aziz could no longer count on their loyalty.[23]

However, Colonel Hubert Lyautey presented something of a problem for Delcassé and the Quai d'Orsay. Since his arrival at the Ain Sefra garrison in 1903, the aristocratic soldier had manifested an independence of mind which bordered on near insubordination. Algerian governor general Charles Jonnart promised that the office of the chief executive would devote all its time and energy to insure that the situation in the South Oranais was well publicised in Paris.[24] Lyautey was in full agreement with Jonnart's plan of action, but he decided to go beyond the governor's plans. In February 1904, the Ain Sefra commander told a group of visiting French officials that he and Jonnart were in full accord, and to preserve peace along the Algero-Moroccan border stern, military measures had to be taken against Moroccan bandits.[25] To preserve law and order, Lyautey warned, immediate steps had to be taken to suppress Bou Ammama.[26] In 1904 Bou Ammama was an aged and rather insignificant Moroccan leader. Lyautey took this old Muslim and made out of him a threat to French authority in western Algeria. Once the colonial soldier manufactured the idea of a widespread rebellion led by the old man, he continually bombarded Paris with dire warnings of a massive invasion of Algerian territory. No incident was too trivial for Lyautey to report to the colonialist leadership, and in turn they blasted Delcassé for acting too slowly in respect to Moroccan annexation. At a banquet for the *Comité du Maroc* Etienne went out of his way to laud the energetic actions of Jonnart and Lyautey in the Sud Oranais, and Tallandier's diplomatic work in Tangiers; on the other hand he had little praise for Delcassé and the Quai d'Orsay.[27] The colonialists, while hoping that the Foreign Minister would take action, preferred to concentrate on winning over minor colonial and diplomatic officials to the cause of Moroccan annexation. The implication for the Quai d'Orsay was clear: the colonialists had lost faith in Théophile Delcassé. Reliance would have to be placed in Jonnart, Lyautey, and Tallandier.

Tallandier also worked to weaken the Sultan's political authority; he wrote Etienne that he had established a number of Franco-Moroccan schools, located in Tangier, Fez, and Larache. These educational centres, he told Etienne, would be a giant step toward accomplishing France's propaganda goals of winning the Moroccans to the cause of annexation. Tallandier added that the schools were to be staffed by Frenchmen and Algerians of unquestioned loyalty to France.[28] While Tallandier worked to win the fidelity of Moroccans in the country, General Lyautey tried to subvert the Sultan's authority along the border.

Lyautey boasted to Etienne that he had scored a great success in secretly winning over to France the Sultan's representative at the oasis of Tafilalet.[29] The continual subversion of Abdel Aziz's position as well as the addition of allies and territory along the frontier suited the French plan of annexation. Supported by the British in Morocco, Tallandier, Saint-Aulaire, and Jouinot-Gambetta continually tried to undermine the court's influence.

The three men convinced important Moroccan merchants of the overwhelming value of French protection for their trade and commerce. The Quai d'Orsay and Etienne believed that this conversion was the primary mission of the Tangier legation.[30] While the Tangier legation prepared the way for the eventual French occupation, Paul Cambon worked to consolidate the Anglo-French understanding with Lord Lansdowne and the British Foreign Office. Lansdowne and Cambon conferred at length to find a lasting solution to the various colonial problems. In a letter to his son, Paul Cambon explained that France had won her freedom of action in the western Maghrib as far as Lansdowne was concerned. Believing that the African controversies were close to being officially ended between the two powers, the inner circle of the British government pledged their support of the French solution in Morocco.[31] Having promised their support, the London government felt that 'national honour' demanded total support for France.[32] Lord Grey, a supporter of the growing Anglo-French cordiality, recalled that, 'The real cause for satisfaction [in 1904] was that the exasperating friction with France was at an end, and that the menace of war with France had dissipated.'[33] Evidently, the Cambon-Lansdowne talks went far beyond the scope of the Egypt-Morocco barter. Both men meant the new cordiality to culminate finally in full military discussions of some sort. Military and naval co-operation must have been fully discussed between the two men, and indeed, Lord Grey recalled that when he became Prime Minister he discovered that Lansdowne had authorised joint military and naval conferences between France and England in early 1905.[34]

As Cambon predicted, the German government was far from pleased with the *entente*. Wilhelm II wrote to von Bulow, 'I think the French have used the advantage of their momentary political situation [in Morocco] with the utmost skill. They have succeeded in making England pay dearly for their friendship without losing their bond with Russia.'[35] The unpredictable Kaiser, realising the danger to Germany which was created by the Cambon-Lansdowne accords, smouldered with resentment at his cousin King Edward VII of England, at Delcassé, and at Lansdowne. Wilhelm decided that he had to try to divide the *entente* members, and in a series of letters to Nicholas II, he began to formulate plans to draw France into a general alliance with Germany and Russia. An agreement between the three powers to mediate and end the conflict between Russia and Japan, with whom Britain was allied, would embarrass England. This would, Wilhelm hoped, cause London to repudiate the *entente*.[36] As he told von Bulow, '[This *entente*] will have the result that English consideration for us will pass more and more into the background. . . .'[37] This the Kaiser could not permit.

While the Germans were evaluating the changing climate in Anglo-French relations, the French colonial party urged action in Morocco. Robert de Caix wrote that since the accords between France and England were a working reality, France had to take advantage of British support in the western Maghrib. Warning that an excessive display of force would only engender hatred and a bloody resistance, de Caix urged that the *Mahkzen* be retained and used during the time of penetration and pacification. He wrote, '. . . we must make sure to present our actions in a manner acceptable to all of France.'[38] Soon thereafter, Etienne told the readers of the *Bulletin*, '. . . nothing is more important to our national destiny than the future of Morocco. That country is very vital to our North African colonial domination. . . .'[39] The role of colonial committees, Etienne claimed, was to educate the French public about Morocco and to keep pressure on the Chamber of Deputies.

Lyautey informed the colonialists in Paris that he had visited Oran to arrange for the transfer of colonial troops from their posts in northern Algeria to the combat zone along the Oranais border. He claimed that Moroccan cavalry continued to harass French mounted patrols operating out of Tuat. Friction along the frontier was growing, and the colonel believed that France would have to act within the year to end it.[40] Lyautey believed, as did most imperialists, that Delcassé was simply not energetic enough in pushing the cause of Moroccan annexation. The commander of Ain Sefra continually complained to the leadership of the *Comité de l'Afrique française* about the policies of the Quai d'Orsay. Almost every imperialist journal assailed Delcassé also. Joseph Chailley-Bert, one of the most influential colonial leaders and a member of the inner circles of the colonial lobby and the *Comité*, accused Delcassé of being too prudent, reserved, 'and even timid',[41] and Robert de Caix, writing in the *Bulletin*, blasted French policy in Morocco and urged an end to all hesitation in the process of penetration.[42] De Caix, Chailley-Bert, and the imperialists of the *Comité de l'Afrique française* were united on the issue of annexation, and their efforts were felt by all representatives of the French government. Paul Cambon laboured in London as Lyautey prepared for action in Algeria. Informed that all of the European powers, except Germany, believed that France should be responsible for order and security in Morocco, Cambon felt that France should begin the process. He told his son, '. . . it might be necessary to penetrate Morocco by force, but that action should be well prepared in advance in order to avoid a general rebellion. . . .'[43]

At every opportunity, the leadership of the *Comité* encouraged their colonial colleagues in the Chamber to strive harder for the Moroccan cause. In an article in the *Bulletin*, Etienne pointed out that order had ceased to exist in the western Maghrib. Abdel Aziz and the *Mahkzen* found themselves unable to collect taxes. This state of affairs did not displease Etienne, because the crumbling executive structure of the Sultan's government meant that France was closer to occupying the country. 'Our ambition is, not as some pretend, to stop the confusion in Morocco,' Etienne told his readers, 'but to take advantage of the huge inventory of resources which Morocco can offer.'[44] This candid declaration of intent showed the true meaning in Etienne's western Maghribi policy. As a man of pragmatic action, which he so often claimed he was, Etienne believed that the acquisition of Morocco must be based on the anticipation of profit. The benefits from the annexation would be great only if the costs of penetration could be held to a minimum. Tallandier praised Etienne's declaration, stating that the Sultan's government had reached the end of its ability to borrow money from the European powers. French bankers consolidated the Moroccan debt at an extraordinarily high profit for themselves. As the sources of income dried up, financial chaos took hold of the country as unpaid officials and soldiers refused to work.[45]

Lyautey, still smouldering in Oran, sent Paris another fiery letter. Conditions, the colonel said, were going rapidly downhill and he was in Oran to confer with other army officers about the eventual actions which France would have to take in regard to the Moroccan penetration.[46] Unknown to Lyautey or to Etienne, however, the French military drew up a secret plan for the rapid seizure of Morocco. Acting in secret with the Quai d'Orsay, the War Ministry proposed a comprehensive schedule for the occupation of Tetouan, Tangier, Larache, Rabat, Mazagan, Mogador, and Agadir. Colonial troops would board their ships at Toulon, and the regular infantry would embark at Algiers and Oran.[47] The entire action, which was a basic amphibious operation, could be completed within four days with Algerian frontier troops acting in concert with the seaborne invasion. Lyautey, having been informed of the operation, told Etienne that with such a plan in the War Office, he could rest assured of eventual action. In fact, Lyautey, raising the exaggerated spectre of Bou Ammama again, occupied and fortified the oasis of Ras el Ain near the Moroccan frontier on his own initiative. The colonialists felt that steps were being taken to complete the Moroccan preparations.[48] Lyautey's independent action evoked an anguished response from Théophile Delcassé. In a letter to Etienne, Delcassé bitterly complained of Lyautey's unauthorised occupation which seemed intent on circumventing the diplomatic policies of the Quai d'Orsay.[49] Etienne, convinced of the correctness of Lyautey's actions, coldly informed the minister that he would not interfere with the commandant of Ain Sefra who 'has done his duty and no more than his duty'.[50] Even at official social functions, Delcassé and Etienne greeted each other in an extremely cold manner, and the break between the two men had become obvious.[51]

The Ras el Ain occupation irritated the Moroccan government. Marquis de Segonzac, the famous French explorer, on a visit to Tangier, wrote that he doubted if the *Mahkzen*, in the face of the recent occupation, could permit the French to make any more advances at the expense of the Sultan.[52] The danger of a religious rebellion within Morocco was, in fact, so strong that the War Ministry was prompted to order Lyautey to evacuate Ras el Ain. The colonel, in a rage, claimed the value of the oasis was in its fine water supply which could be of benefit to the invasion forces. Why surrender it to the Moors, he argued, when the French would have to expend lives to retake it? Lyautey protested the retreat to the commander of the XIXth Corps in Oran—but to no avail.[53]

Etienne received a bitter letter from the aristocratic officer who, in a petulant mood after the Ras el Ain evacuation order, objected to such a backward step just so that Abdel Aziz could save face. What counter-measure, he asked Etienne, would 'save our face' when the recall became known in Morocco? In fact, claimed Lyautey, 'it is the eternal starting again, Siam, Egypt, positions which we have given up without firing a shot . . . I will never be a party to these crimes of treason.'[54] Tallandier did not agree, however, with the strong position that Lyautey had taken. As he told Etienne, France had to present a united front to the Sultan and the *Mahkzen*. Weakness and division would certainly impede the progress of the penetration, and the *Mahkzen* had to be used by the French even if this meant handing out large bribes.[55] Tallandier believed that Lyautey was too rash. The general was frustrated with Delcassé's policy of slow preparation for Morocco's annexation, and Tallandier also thought that the ultra-secretive chief of the Quai d'Orsay was overly cautious. Tallandier wanted Lyautey, Jonnart, and Etienne to present a unified programme to Delcassé for the annexation of the western Maghrib, and once in possession of a single plan, Delcassé would have to push for the culmination of the Moroccan penetration.[56]

The idea of a joint meeting appealed to the colonialists, and in October Jonnart, Lyautey, and Tallandier visited Paris to confer with the imperialist leadership on the Moroccan situation. The Paris conference was observed by Sir Edmond Monson, who believed that some new, fairly militant policy would come out of the assembly. He thought that France followed two policies concerning Morocco. On the frontier there was an aggressive military policy of building up large concentrations of soldiers. The Tangier legation worked to subvert the authority of Abdel Aziz and the *Mahkzen*.[57] These two approaches were obvious to anyone observing the events in the western Maghrib. However, in August 1904 Delcassé had written to Etienne that, '. . . there are not two contradictory policies for Morocco'.[58] Symptomatic of the gulf which was slowly dividing the colonialists and Delcassé was the colonial activists' opposition in regard to Delcassé's policy toward Morocco, which the militants believed was rent with indecision and hesitation. Those advocates of rapid Moroccan annexation centred around Etienne did not realise, as did Delcassé, that the Germans would probably react to a French move in Morocco. For Delcassé, there were two quite different policies for necessary reasons. Haste could bring on a violent reaction from the Moors, and the Quai d'Orsay was not certain of the European and American reactions. Already inflamed Moroccan mobs had sacked several French homes in Tangier, and even Saint-Aulaire, an imperialist militant himself, wrote Etienne that Tangier's Muslim population was seething; the only realistic policy seemed to be prudence.[59]

Paul Cambon, an advocate of deliberate progress and a supporter of Delcassé's administration at the Quai d'Orsay, wrote to his son that the Spanish recognition of the Franco-British accords had given France a preponderant position in Morocco. Spain had considered asking Germany for diplomatic aid in pressing her claims to the northern tier of the Cheriffian Empire, but decided to reconsider.[60] From Paris, Leon y Castillo urged his government in Madrid to accept the 1904 accords as a *fait accompli*. Through the Spanish ambassador Delcassé received the welcome news that Madrid was willing to assume her diminished role in the western Maghrib. The Spanish government's mistrust was balanced by the actions of the Francophile Leon y Castillo who was determined to please the Quai d'Orsay.[61]

Delcassé, feeling somewhat stronger now that Spain seemed agreeable, decided to call a conference at the Quai d'Orsay to discuss fully the differing opinions in respect to the penetration of the western Maghrib. Spurred on by the news of Madrid's recognition of France's special relationship vis-à-vis Morocco, the Paris conference was joined by Paul Cambon. Delcassé invited Cambon, Jonnart, Lyautey, Tallandier and Etienne to his private offices in the Quai d'Orsay. Lyautey was the staunchest advocate of immediate action, and Cambon suspected that the commander of Ain Sefra wanted to carve out for himself a small personal empire in the South Oranais or in Morocco. Jonnart supported Lyautey's position but Delcassé sided with the cautious diplomat Cambon.[62] The British watched the entire proceedings with great interest and noted that in November Etienne made a definitive speech in the Chamber on the Moroccan situation. Monson informed Lansdowne that when Etienne, then president of the Chamber's Foreign Affairs Committee, rose to speak the galleries filled with foreign diplomats and journalists. Etienne, Monson reported, praised the *entente cordiale* and England's recognition of France's preponderance in the western Maghrib. At the end of his speech he called for the joining of England, France, and Russia into a general military alliance.[63]

Etienne's address to the Chamber marked the high point of the Paris talks on Morocco. The conflict over the approach to penetration was not resolved, but as Saint-Aulaire later wrote, all of the men involved, regardless of their position, were very optimistic. The members of the conference, except Cambon and Delcassé, whose absence was marked, made Maxim's restaurant their headquarters while in Paris. Etienne, nicknamed 'The Great Marabout' and 'Our Lady of the Colonies', charged Saint-René Tallandier and Jouinot-Gambetta with the duty of preparing the way in Morocco by bribery and subversion.[64] While Etienne and his circle of colonialists enjoyed Paris' finest cuisine and plotted, the situation in the South Oranais collapsed.

The Moroccan troops at Figuig mutinied against their officers and ravaged the countryside. By January 1905, nomadic tribes in the area crossed the border and raided Algerian *colon* settlements. Local French officials claimed that the tribes were inflamed by Islamic Marabouts from Morocco; the tribes were in a hostile state.[65] Mohammed Torres, in reaction to the forced reorganisation of the Tangier police, dismissed all British and French employees from the Moroccan customs house in Tangier.[66] The situation became so unsettled that the entire Algerian Oranais was declared under military rule. Some caravans bound for Algiers and Oran were looted by Moroccan bandits, but other caravans reached their destination intact.[67]

Many French officials firmly believed that the German government encouraged the Moroccans to raid into Algeria. Richard von Kuhlmann, the German chargé in Tangier, was a forceful proponent of Germany's anti-French policy in Morocco, and many officials in the French legation at Tangier speculated that von Kuhlmann had a great hand in the formulation of German Moroccan intervention.[68] In January 1905, von Kuhlmann suggested to von Bulow that since French leftists and some stalwart *revanchards* opposed any colonial action in Morocco, it could be an excellent coup to inform Abdel Aziz that Germany took more than a passing interest in the future of the independence of the western Maghrib. Von Bulow replied to the chargé, 'The suggestion [that you] put forward . . . that it should be made clear in the appropriate quarters in Morocco that Germany takes a political interest is worthy of consideration. . . . [but] we cannot go so far as to say that we will give open support to the Moroccans. . . .'[69]

In late January 1905, von Bulow informed von Kuhlmann of certain aspects of Germany's Moroccan policy which should be stressed to the Sultan. Abdel Aziz, von Bulow said, must be made to believe that German and French Moroccan policies were almost identical. The German government would not acknowledge any formal notification of an impending change in the independent status of the kingdom. The entire tone of von Bulow's instructions was menacing, possibly denoting that some sort of German action in Morocco was near.[70] Unsettling to the Germans was the change that occurred in the French government when in early February 1905, Maurice Rouvier, an old politician with definite connections with Etienne and the imperial activists, formed a cabinet. While retaining Delcassé at the Quai d'Orsay, he asked Etienne to take the portfolio of the Ministry of Interior. This, however, had the effect of weakening Delcassé's position since the elevation of Etienne to cabinet rank had the earmarks of approval for colonial militancy. Since Etienne could directly affect Algeria and the Oranais, Delcassé could be bypassed even more. The Ministry of the Interior controlled Algeria, and as such Etienne could work in concert with Jonnart and Lyautey. The immediate change was apparent to Hoffman Philips, the American vice-consul in Tangiers, who told Washington that there was feeling in Morocco that with the cabinet in Paris a move to take over a large portion of the administration of Morocco was close at hand.[71]

Robert de Caix noted this change when he wrote in the *Bulletin*, 'The danger which we see in uncertainty is at least that of [having to] abandon our entire Moroccan enterprise.'[72] The *Comité* expressed its satisfaction at Etienne's official position by stating, 'He enters the government at a very opportune time, since the Moroccan problem has arrived at an important phase. . . .'[73] In Morocco, the British consul informed the English residents of Tangier that Lord Lansdowne decided that the question of security for Europeans resided with the French. In the aftermath of the 1904 accords Lansdowne felt that England had to wait for the French to take action.[74] Auguste Terrier, secretary of the *Comité du Maroc*, told a meeting of the committee that the Moroccan advocates were pushing for a quick solution to the problem of disorder within the Cheriffian Empire.[75]

Suddenly the plans of the colonialists were rudely interrupted. In March 1905, Kaiser Wilhelm II landed at Tangier and made a speech proclaiming Abdel Aziz as the ruling sovereign of an independent state. The French plans for Morocco were thrown out of gear, and Abdel Aziz, assured by von Kuhlmann of some German support, called for an international conference on the future status of his country. Etienne reacted to the new situation by recalling Saint-Aulaire and Jouinot-Gambetta back to Paris for consultations. With Jouinot-Gambetta, he discussed the quick reorganisation of the Algerian-based colonial troops, and both men agreed to several methods of operation.[76] Etienne was forced to be brief with the two men because the government faced heavy anti-colonial opposition in the Chamber because of Delcassé's handling of Wilhelm II's visit to Tangier.

Paul Cambon watched the fall of Delcassé from the Chamber's gallery. Etienne and Maurice Rouvier remained silent while the chief of the Quai d'Orsay was forced to defend himself alone. Disgusted, Paul Cambon wrote to his son that, 'Delcassé did not parry the attacks; he responded badly. It was vital to come to grips with Jaurès. . . . It was a duel to the death. Delcassé . . . stunned, could not find the decisive words; he was lost. . . .'[77] Emile Combes and General André, the Minister of War, attacked the chief of the Foreign Ministry in a personal vendetta since Delcassé had opposed André's anti-Catholic, anti-clerical policies.[78] Only at that point did Etienne and Rouvier, who were also opposed to André's vehement policies, try to defend Delcassé.[79] The British did not like the events in Paris and Lord Grey felt that the French were showing a grave weakness by giving in to the Kaiser's demands that Delcassé be removed from the Quai d'Orsay. London wondered if the *entente* would survive the German onslaught.[80]

In Madrid, Sir Arthur Nicolson, the British ambassador to Spain, talked with Spanish officials concerning the forthcoming conference to be held in Algeciras. To reassure the French they were not alone, Nicolson stressed to Marquis Villa-Urrutia that Spain had to act in agreement with England and France. Nicolson informed Lansdowne that he stressed several times to the Madrid government that Britain stood firmly with her ally.[81] However, Germany misinterpreted the resolve of London to stand by France and keep the *entente* intact. In a memorandum to Wilhelm II, von Bulow stated that Germany would strengthen the opposition to Delcassé and his Moroccan policy by stressing before the Algeciras conference began Germany's high price for her agreement to a French preponderance in the western Maghrib. European territorial rights had to be given up and equal economic rights for all states had to be established. Von Bulow told Wilhelm that this meant the 'open door' in the widest sense of the term.[82]

German policy toward France was based on poor intelligence. One of von Bulow's statements makes this quite clear. 'If it should happen that a conference is called together,' he said, 'we are already assured of the diplomatic support of America as regards the "open door". England will above all else wish to avoid the risk of opposing America.'[83] This odd declaration simply did not meet with the reality of Great Britain's open statements of support for France. Von Bulow may have misread dispatches from the United States, and if this were the case, it was a tragic mistake. In any case, von Bulow told Wilhelm II, 'I hold it unthinkable that a conference could have the result of enclosing Morocco in the exclusive sphere of French influence and interests.'[84] Not only was the Kaiser misinformed of American support, he was told that Theodore Roosevelt might even come to Algeciras. 'England', von Bulow stated, 'will find it very difficult to give France any more support in the face of the entry of President Roosevelt on the scene. . . .'[85] Where von Bulow got his information on the United States is not clear, but the British and French ambassadors found Washington unconcerned with Morocco. In Tangier, Samuel Gummere stressed that the United States had little interest in the future status of Morocco.

Von Bulow told von Kuhlmann the same thing that he told Wilhelm II except that he informed the German chargé d'affaires, 'Today, however, we have established confidential relations with

America, and know that she will give diplomatic support to the policy of the open door. Through this attitude of America, England will be obliged to change her tone.'[86] To add to the confusion in Berlin, von Radolin warned that France would cling to the 1904 accords to reach her goal in Morocco. The German ambassador believed that Rouvier was under the total influence of 'the colonial fanatics, of whom Etienne, the Minister of the Interior, is certainly one'.[87] Rouvier, von Radolin believed, was under the spell of the anti-German wing of the Quai d'Orsay and the colonialists. Baron von Holstein, unsure that England was going to change her tune at Algeciras, looked with horror at the direction of German foreign policy ordered by the Kaiser and von Bulow. The Kaiser, still trying to draw France into an alliance with Germany and Russia, believed that France would trade Morocco for the *entente* and von Bulow, acting on this idea, informed an amazed Holstein that, 'We must keep for ourselves the possibility of securing for France a free hand in Morocco at the moment when she decides as to her joining in the German-Russian understanding.'[88] Germany, Holstein believed, was about to receive a very unpleasant surprise at the Algeciras conference. American support, on which von Bulow and Wilhelm counted, simply did not materialise, and Britain stood beside France. The whole affair went badly for Berlin, and France won her preponderance in the western Maghrib—but the French timetable for annexation was delayed by several years. After the smoke of Algeciras cleared the French colonialists found themselves frustrated in their wishes for an immediate takeover.

Most French officials knew exactly what the Germans were trying to do by the Kaiser's forceful interjection in Moroccan affairs. Robert de Caix wrote, 'Germany will attempt to profit by her efforts to get us to end our excellent relations with England . . . to force us into a form of diplomatic slavery [by taking] part in a modern Germanic revival of a continental blockade against the British empire.'[89]

The possibility of military action in respect to Morocco was not ruled out in Paris. Etienne, as Minister of the Interior, had some control over events, especially in the Algerian Oranais. Colonel Marie Laperrine, commanding the Saharan oases posts, informed Etienne that he believed that the desert caravan routes would never be secure until France ruled all of the watering spots in southern Algeria. He urged a rapid seizure of the key oases on the Algero-Tripolitanian border as a means to protect the rich caravan routes.[90] The plan appealed to Etienne, and in July 1905 he suggested to Maurice Berteaux, the Minister of War, that the Saharan Corps should be reorganised into more compact mobile units. Etienne asked Berteaux to sign the necessary decrees to place the reorganisation in motion.[91] The Oranais became critical for France's new plans. The Saharan Corps had to protect mail riders because several of the dispatch riders had been murdered by Saharan bandits, and Telegraphic lines had to be repaired every day.[92] At the same time, Etienne began to look to the eastern Saharan oases as a potential source of difficulty. It would be necessary to guard the eastern flank against Muslim incursions to protect the lucrative Saharan caravan trade. Charles Jonnart was informed by Etienne that the French ambassador to Constantinople was sounding out Ottoman opinion on a French expedition to the oases complexes of Bilma and Djanet.[93]

While Etienne plotted the securing of Algeria's eastern flank, Morocco continued to dissolve into chaos. The *Bulletin* informed its readers that there was unrest in Marrakesh and Rabat where Europeans had been attacked by mobs. Tallandier took all Europeans and Americans under the protection of the French legation.[94] He informed Rouvier that the Muslim agitation was growing to a crisis level, and that Tangier was in a state of anarchy. Europeans found it impossible to walk the streets in safety.[95] In the midst of the growing anarchy in Morocco Etienne became the Minister of War late in 1905. Because of the growing confusion in Morocco, he felt that it would be necessary to first seize Bilma and Djanet to protect the eastern Sahara before considering further action in respect to the penetration of the Cheriffian Empire. Simply, Etienne did not want to lose one element of the empire while securing another part.

For the militants of the colonial party and *Comité*, the years of penetration were over. Morocco was considered to be almost in the French orbit. The Moroccan advocates, Tallandier, Saint-Aulaire, Jonnart, Lyautey, and Jouinot-Gambetta, were ready for the last final push. As Minister of War, Etienne could give the order to occupy the oases of Bilma and Djanet and once that was accomplished he could prepare for the action in Morocco. The Anglo-French alliance was strong and had survived the attacks of the Kaiser and von Bulow.

However, overlooked in the general euphoria which followed the preparation for the Anglo-French accords of 1904 and the ousting of Delcassé in 1905, was the fact that a great change had occurred in the make-up of the French government. With the fall of Delcassé the colonial activists had gained greater power, especially within the cabinet, and the voices of moderation for a time at least were silenced. The seizure of Bilma and Djanet in 1906 and the Oujda and Casablanca occupation in 1907 were symptoms of a change in approach. While the colonial party and the *Comité de l'Afrique française* were enjoying their greatest period of power they did not realise that with every crisis, albeit major or minor, there was a tendency for the Paris government to interpret it in terms of European tension rather than in the light of imperialist expansion. European tensions, particularly with Germany, would win out over African expansion, and this from 1906 to 1910, the French imperialists failed to comprehend.

Notes to Chapter 9 will be found on pages 194–8.

Chapter 10 THE PENETRATION OF THE SAHARA: CONTINUED PREPARATION FOR THE MOROCCAN CAMPAIGN 1905-7

THE THREE years from 1905 to 1907 were a time of continual preparation for the Moroccan campaign, as the imperialists took advantage of every opportunity to weaken independent Morocco. Etienne, as Minister of War, foresaw the possibility of a Muslim reaction to the operations in Morocco, and to prevent an interruption in the rich caravan trade by Muslim activities in the eastern Sahara, he planned the takeover of the Tripolitanian oases of Bilma and Djanet. By first securing all of the eastern Sahara, Etienne could then concentrate on the larger, different Moroccan question. In 1906 Etienne became Minister of War: he was therefore directly responsible for the military commands in the Sahara, including the southern part of Oran Province. With the European powers meeting in Algeciras to decide the ultimate fate of the western Maghrib, the imperialists had time to consider their own role in the eventual addition of Morocco to the empire. They firmly believed that France had to have a definite, concrete plan for the Sahara. By 1904 the colonial leadership complained that the French colonialists and the French government did not actually consider the great Sahara as part of the empire. This, they believed, was unfortunate because the desert formed a vital link between North Africa and the great hinterlands of central Africa. For example, any programme pertaining to the future of the desert, Etienne stated, had to contain three basic points: to create there a political entity with its own military and administrative structures, to pacify it, and to administer it.[1] It was necessary to keep violence at a minimum in order for the Sahara to show a profit and continue to interest French political and colonial groups.

Germany was quite surprised to find that the United States did not support her at the conference as she had hoped because the Americans were mainly concerned with preserving their commercial interests in Morocco.[2] The French War Ministry, realising that they would benefit from the international discussions in south-eastern Spain, could prepare for the eventual takeover in Morocco. As the south Oranais became plunged in anarchy, the colonial forces believed that France could use the situation for leverage at the Algeciras conference. The question of security in the Oranais forced France to take serious measures to protect French settlers and the lucrative caravan trade.[3] The War Ministry granted additional funds for the expansion of the military forces. To supplement the number of the Foreign Legionnaires and the regular army units of the XIXth Corps, the War Ministry ordered the transfer of troops into southern Algeria.[4] The colonialists also requested Saint-Aulaire and Jouinot-Gambetta to return to Paris for consultations to help clarify French intentions in the western Maghrib and at the resulting meeting Etienne, acting for the imperial leadership, briefed the two men on the developments at Algeciras. Informing them that he was strengthening the forts and enlarging the military formations along the Algero-Moroccan border, the war minister charged Jouinot-Gambetta to prepare a plan to co-ordinate the efforts of the troops under Lyautey and of the French legation in Morocco.[5]

While Paris considered different military plans for Morocco, von Bulow tried to adjust German policy to its rude shock at Algeciras. He wrote Count Wolf von Metternich, the German ambassador to London, that, 'Our Moroccan policy throughout is no attempt to break up the Anglo-French *entente*. The whole Moroccan question is not of such importance that we should make it especially a question of our prestige.'[6] Thus, von Bulow had drastically changed his attitude toward the Moroccan situation less than a year after his misinterpretation of the American position concerning Morocco. Sir Edward Grey received an official visit from Count von Metternich and told the German ambassador that he, 'wanted to avoid trouble between Germany and France because I really thought that if there was trouble, [Great Britain] . . . should [have to] be involved in it.'[7] Metternich responded by rejecting France's contention that she had a natural preponderance in Morocco. Germany, the ambassador said, could not permit her economic interests to be guarded by a hostile France. Not even a guaranteed 'open door' would satisfy the German Foreign Office. Morocco, as Berlin saw it, simply could not pass uncontested into the French orbit.[8]

Edward Grey, concerned about the possibility of a diplomatic rupture over Morocco, met with Paul Cambon in late January 1906. Cambon, distressed over the possibility of German interjecting herself so openly into the Moroccan situation, believed the Germans might declare that an invasion of Morocco would be interpreted as an attack on German honour. He asked Grey to give an assurance that if a European war broke out, London would stand by her commitments to France.[9] Grey gave his word: England would honour her pledge to go to the aid of France in the event of continental hostilities. The French, naturally nervous over the possibility of facing Germany alone, were dissatisfied with anything less than repeated declarations of support, which London gave throughout 1906. In Tangier, the French colony announced that it was going to publish a daily French language newspaper, *La Dépêche morocaine*, which claimed to be militant in regard to immediate Moroccan annexation. The *Comité du Maroc* and the *Comité de l'Afrique Française* gave their full approval to the formation of the imperialist journal, another weapon in the assault on Moroccan independence.[10] The end was in sight for Abdel Aziz as a plethora of rumours about tribal rebellions spread throughout Morocco and the imperialist press delighted in finding any incident, no matter how trivial, to report.[11] Few tribal leaders were willing openly to support the Sultan, and many chieftains refused to pay taxes. Tax collectors from the *Mahkzen* were attacked and driven out of numerous villages and rebellious tribesmen also attacked *Mahkzen* cavalry units, while European consuls complained that bandits controlled the roads.[12] The disorders became so widespread that the French ordered caravans on the Oranais to travel in convoys of at least several hundred camels, while raids from the Moroccan side of the border struck several *colon* settlements in Algeria.[13] 'It is the first time in two and a half years,' Lyautey told Etienne, 'that I sense a cracking . . . [the Minister of Foreign Affairs] told me to shun the shadow of a frontier incident. I certainly will not look for one, [but the Moroccan bandits] only respect force and its appearance. . . .'[14]

Jonnart, as anxious to penetrate Morocco as Lyautey, complained in a long dispatch to Etienne that the Moroccans continually invaded Algerian territory and ravaged the countryside. He devoted, he claimed, most of his time as governor general of Algeria to reviewing the serious depredations in the South Oranais. On his own authority, Jonnart had dispatched to southern Algeria the penal sections of the Second Regiment of the Foreign Legion to construct new forts along the frontier. Before being certain of Etienne's support for such a venture, Jonnart had already given his consent for the building of the needed posts.[15] Etienne praised Jonnart for his energetic, individual action, and to protect his imperialist ally, Etienne issued a War Ministry minute acknowledging the creation of these posts as an integral part of French army policy in the Oranais. Etienne added to the minute that the posts should be as close as possible to the Moroccan frontier. The creation of the forts would, '. . . aid the police and intelligence [officers] in that region so close to the Moroccan frontier'.[16] Meanwhile, the War Ministry also turned its attention to a longstanding military problem. On 1 May 1906, Etienne wrote Léon Bourgeois, the chief of the Quai d'Orsay, that he was promoting a number of Muslim sergeants to officer grades in the Saharan troops who were attached to the First Regiment of Zouaves on the Moroccan frontier. The War Ministry, totally assured of their loyalty to France, wanted to keep these new officers with their regiment. When Tallandier asked for Muslim officers of undoubted fidelity to France to serve in Morocco, Etienne continued in his letter to Bourgeois, he sent a few Muslim commissioned officers to staff the French military mission at Rabat.[17]

As minister of war, Etienne also planned a quick seizure of the oases complex of Bilma-Djanet to guard France's eastern flank in the Sahara. Concerned about German friendship with the Young Turks in Constantinople, France wanted to know if England would stand with them if the Germans and Ottomans contested their eastern operations. Diplomat Philippe Crozier was ordered to question the British resolve to sustain the *entente*. Grey, frustrated by this continual French sign of insecurity, informed Sir Francis Bertie that, 'We have given such assurances at Algeciras and will continue so long as the French wish it and trust us. Cordial co-operation remains a cardinal point of British policy. You speak in this sense if necessary to Bourgeois. Etienne should know it too.'[18]

Bertie either did not receive Grey's dispatch on time, or else he did not grasp the seriousness of the French fear at once. In any case, Etienne approached Bertie at a party given by the German ambassador to Paris, to request assurances of Britain's intent to stand by the *entente*. After giving this pledge verbally, Bertie realised that he needed to state England's position in a formal diplomatic interview with Bourgeois, Etienne, and Clemenceau. On 16 March 1906, Bertie called on each man and explained that Grey had authorised him to state categorically that Great Britain stood firmly by her French allies.[19]

With the British assurance in mind, Etienne began to plan for the eastern Saharan action. Léon Bourgeois, a partner to the plan, kept the War Ministry fully aware of the diplomatic correspondence on the French action. He told the colonial leaders that Marabouts were crossing the French Sahara exhorting Muslims to resist the French. To complicate matters, these holy men brought into the Sahara modern rifles which the representatives of the Moroccan sultan issued from the royal armoury at Fez. Despite the obvious fact that Bourgeois cited no specific examples of such an activity, and certainly despite the fact that such an act by the Moroccan government was tantamount to political suicide, Etienne accepted the report. In the margin of the report, Etienne scrawled, '. . . this information will be useful'.[20] The claims of modern rifles made the eastern action indeed more easy. Fighting would not probably occur when the French made their final move, but the activists in that ministry had the power to commit France's full Saharan military capabilities to the oasis seizure if such a doubtful event occurred.

George Myer, director of African affairs at the Quai d'Orsay, worked closely with Etienne on the Bilma-Djanet campaign. Myer, the professional diplomat, believed that Germany and the Ottoman Empire were urging the Tripolitanian tribes forcefully to oppose the French. He told Etienne that in the long run France would need to take these areas to protect her forts on Lake Chad as well as in eastern Algeria. Finally, Myer also informed the governors of Algeria and French West Africa that orders from the War Ministry and the Quai d'Orsay would be sent to spell out the details of their part of this occupation.[21] Lyautey was even asked to suggest plans for the military aspect of the seizure, and in a note to the general, the Minister of War restated an obvious fact that all messages should be in code because, 'Success depends on secrecy. I await intelligence [reports] from you in order to make definitive judgements and to give the final orders for the expedition.'[22] The Paris colonialists were thinking about the most expeditious manner of taking and holding Bilma and Djanet.

In a dispatch to Jonnart, Etienne stated that while the Quai d'Orsay was in the process of collecting information from the ambassadors in Constantinople, Cairo, and Berlin on the expected reaction to the Bilma and Djanet expeditions, Jonnart could aid the occupation by working in close co-operation with the governor of French West Africa. Eastern Algerian posts must co-ordinate their efforts with those in West Africa and on the Chad, and Etienne charged Jonnart to '. . . send the most numerous, most frequent, and most pertinent intelligence you can'.[23] The French consul in Tripoli informed Bourgeois that he had learned through spies well placed in the Tripolitanian administration that the Sultan, under pressure from the Young Turks with the Ottoman administration, authorised the preparation of an expedition to oppose the French in the oases. The Ottoman officers, he learned, also received orders to occupy and entrench Bilma and Djanet as separate forts. Over 400 soldiers and six pieces of heavy artillery were assigned to the command. The consul, who had paid his agents well, stated that he received the same information from several reliable sources.[24]

On 23 May 1906, Etienne telegraphed Jonnart that he had given the command of the French expedition to Colonel Marie Laperrine, and that this officer was ordered to take and hold the oases by force if necessary. France was going to use as a pretext for the occupation the necessity to restore order on the Tunisian-Tripolitanian frontier and to protect French caravan commerce. Informing Jonnart of the expedition being formed in Tripoli, Etienne indicated that the Ottomans hoped to be in the oases by the last day of May. Jonnart was to begin to execute the Algerian part of the plan as soon as possible to facilitate the movement of the French.[25] On 26 May Etienne wired Jonnart that the occupation plan was to be set in motion in order to get French troops into the region before the Ottoman troops arrived.[26] The French arrived and took command of much of the oases complex while the Ottoman command took smaller oases near the French. However, the main object of the occupation had been accomplished: the French were secure on their eastern Saharan flank.

In a telegram to Lyautey, Etienne asked about the problem of military transport in the Oranais. With the key oases of the eastern Sahara under French control, the Moroccan advocates concentrated on the preparation for the penetration of Morocco. Lyautey and Etienne, concerned with the transportation of arms and reinforcements to the posts in the Oranais, felt that the rail line from Colomb-Bechar south into the Sahara would need to be strengthened in order to carry an increased quantity of supplies.[27] When the final push into Morocco came, the Army and the War Ministry had to feel secure in their preparations, and to do so they co-operated with the other departments of the government in order to speed along the pace of the plans for Morocco. In late May the Quai d'Orsay requested that the intelligence branch of that ministry supply all possible geographic information on Morocco. The Foreign Ministry especially wanted detailed maps of Tangier and Casablanca. Etienne informed Bourgeois that he was sending all available maps of the two cities and also a detailed map of the western coast line.[28]

The need for maps and detailed information of the coast came in response to the growing violence and bloodshed. French agents in Morocco reported that several ships had unloaded over eighty cases of modern German rifles for the Sultan's armoury. The exporter was based in Belgium, but French secret agents in Tangier reported that they discovered the weapons were ordered and shipped from an arms manufacturer in Germany. The agents were certain that the rifles were sold to the Moroccan government with the blessings of Berlin.[29] To make matters worse, Muslim holy men, infuriated by France's imperialist efforts, continued to preach a *jihad* against the French and, in July, Albert Charbonnier, a young French resident of Tangier, was murdered by a Muslim fanatic. The French government reacted swiftly by sending three gunboats to Tangier. In a typical act of gunboat diplomacy, the *Kléber*, *Jeanne d'Arc*, and *Galilée* trained their guns on the Arab quarters while Tallandier placed six demands on the desk of Mohammed Torres. The French hoped to embarrass the *Mahkzen* completely before its subjects by demanding punishment for the guilty persons (even though everyone knew the murder was the act of one Muslim), a heavy indemnity, and public apologies.[30] Meanwhile, Moroccan mobs also attacked a number of French citizens in Casablanca. The assaults nearly killed a number of the victims. Much of the hostility toward the French originated at the court in Fez. The *Bulletin* reported that much of the religious consternation in southern Morocco came because of official court policy.[31] The colonialist organ claimed that couriers, carrying letters from Abdel Aziz to Muslim tribal leaders urging open warfare against the French in the oasis regions, were captured by French cavalry near Figuig. A few days after the letters were intercepted, the imperialists claimed, the War Ministry placed the troops of Figuig, Tifalelet, Tuat, and Ain Sefra on a war footing. Troops were dispatched from northern Oran to bolster the forces along the frontier.[32] To assure the security of southern Algeria in case of an attack in Morocco, Etienne and the governor of French West Africa reorganised the local colonial troop units into smaller, more mobile forces.[33]

However, Etienne expected that most of the Moroccan penetration would be carried on by the Foreign Legion. The War Minister was therefore concerned about the conduct of the Legion, which was always a superb fighting force, but which also had a reputation for being rather hard to handle in garrison or on occupation duty. In a brief note to the Army Chief of Staff, Etienne suggested that within each regiment a new disciplinary company be created to handle offenders. Usually, the War Minister noted, the regiments had at least one company for penal labour, but since the occupation of Morocco would require highly disciplined troops, Etienne believed another such company was needed. Perhaps the institution of the penal company would act to curb any illegal act.[34] Phrasing his suggestion so as to denote a direct order, Etienne urged the Chief of Staff to act quickly. In November, after Etienne left the War Office in the wake of the fall of the Sarrien ministry, the Chief of Staff recorded that

Etienne's order in regard to the Legion's penal units had been carried out. General Picquart, who replaced Etienne at the War Office, approved the action and it remained in force.[35]

Etienne left his ministerial post in October 1906 and, returning to the Chamber, he continued to urge a conclusion to the Moroccan question. Because of his leadership of the colonial party, Etienne continued to have an active role in the final stages for the penetration of Morocco. He had, as War Minister, for example, increased the number of troops in the South Oranais and had ordered the occupation of Bilma and Djanet. As leader of the colonial party he could keep the pressure on the government to take further action. The French government, Etienne was convinced, was almost ready to annex Morocco. The imperialists, from 1905 to 1907, had shown a willingness to gamble over the future of Morocco and the Sahara. However, they also revealed the basic weakness in their policy. Simply put, the Moroccan crisis of 1905 had not totally focused attention on imperialism, as the activists had hoped. Instead, the strain in European diplomacy had shown France's basic antagonism to Germany and also her basic strength in the alliance with England, who supported her at the Algeciras conference. The moves toward Morocco and the Sahara were made easier by the agreement and benevolent action of England. But, the overriding fact that the *entente cordiale* was not mainly a colonial alignment was not lost on the non-militants in Paris. By using this alliance for colonial issues such as Morocco, the leaders of the colonial party and the *Comité* weakened their own position.

Notes to Chapter 10 will be found on pages 198–200.

Chapter 11 THE FINAL PREPARATION FOR THE MOROCCAN CAMPAIGN 1907-10

FROM 1907 to 1910 the French imperialists were busy with the final preparations for the annexation of Morocco. With the fall of the cabinet of Jean Sarrien in October 1906, a new ministry under Clemenceau came to power and surprisingly maintained a basic continuity in colonial affairs because the leader of the new government saw the imperial issues in the light of the *entente cordiale* with England. Clemenceau, still the old tiger of the *revanche*, correctly believed that the 1904 alliance gave strength to France's anti-German position. Clemenceau thought that if France withdrew from the proposed annexation of Morocco, the newly forged *entente* might split, and this would only serve Germany's interests. Therefore Clemenceau fought successfully to keep the Moroccan finances in the hands of the French throughout his entire three-year administration.

In the Clemenceau cabinet, Stephen Pichon took charge of the Ministry of Foreign Affairs and General Picquart succeeded Etienne at the War Ministry. The first indication of the continuity came when Picquart upheld Etienne's order transferring emergency troops from Oran to south Algeria. Two companies of infantry and a battery of artillery were sent to Beni Ounif and Ain Sefra to bolster Lyautey's forces,[1] and Picquart supported Etienne's order despite the provocative nature of an act which placed such heavy siege guns in the region. The mountain guns were certain to be used as a support for any French invasion of Morocco, but the Clemenceau cabinet allowed the movement to stand. Stephen Pichon had served as resident minister in Tunis before being called to the Quai d'Orsay, and while in Tunisia he had supported the Bilma-Djanet operation openly. His duty during the eastern operation had been to keep military pressure on the Tunisian-Tripolitanian frontier, and, without hesitation, he had sent troops to engage Ottoman cavalry on the border.[2] Like Picquart, Pichon became a dedicated colonial expansionist even before he became Minister of Foreign Affairs. He maintained the foreign policies of Bourgeois, while Picquart kept the basic aggressive colonial and imperial policies of Etienne.

Lyautey did not immediately fully appreciate the change, and he told the colonialists that he opened his newspaper every morning with fear, because he doubted if the new administration in Paris would continue to pursue an activist Moroccan policy. He told the former War Minister that France would do well to occupy all the oases in the Sahara because of their obvious strategic value in the event of the expected French invasion of Morocco. To permit the Moroccan tribes to cross the Algerian Sahara was a stupid policy because, Lyautey warned, the army could never be sure when those tribes might attack posts inside the Oranais. Exaggerating the dangers from the Moroccan tribes, he told Etienne that he had urged immediate action, yet the Chamber hesitated. 'I knew my place', he wrote while in a petulant mood. He then suggested that if the pseudo-academic colonialists 'of the Chamber know better than I [do about Morocco] they have only to come to take the handle of the frying pan.'[3]

As the year ended, talk of rebellion against Abdel Aziz and his European entourage at court circulated throughout the western Maghrib. The *Bulletin* dredged up every possible horror which occurred in Morocco. In Marrakesh, the governor was openly anti-European, and he agitated his people against the non-Muslim population. However, in Marrakesh there were also pro-French Moroccan Muslims who openly supported a French occupation of Morocco. One such citizen of Marrakesh was Moulay Hafid, a close relative of the Sultan. The *Comité du Maroc* cited Moulay Hafid as a possible ally of France and named him as a possible successor to Abdel Aziz. When addressing himself to the Muslims of that city, however, he claimed that he was more faithful to the word of the Prophet than the discredited Sultan Abdel Aziz.[4] Meanwhile, Abdel Ben Sliman replaced Mohammed Torres, and the new Moroccan Foreign Minister enjoyed a reputation in the French diplomatic mission as something of a progressive reformist. However, Muslims attacked Sliman's conciliatory policies and the marabouts and the very powerful *Ulama* condemned his attempts to institute European diplomatic and fiscal reforms contrary to basic Islamic policy. In the mosques of Fez, the *Ulama* preached very violent sermons in reaction to Sliman's reform programmes.[5]

In the spring of 1907 it became obvious that the whole governmental structure of Morocco was rapidly decaying. Unless something drastic was done, civil war might break out and endanger European lives and commerce there. Everywhere in Morocco talk of a revolt against Abdel Aziz continued to spread. Some Muslims now compared him to Abul Hamid, the Ottoman sultan who was overthrown by the Young Turks.[6] The French decided to throw their support behind a coup d'état led by the intelligent and energetic Moulay Hafid of Marrakesh. However, before France could actively support Hafid or intervene on his behalf, German neutrality had to be secured. The possibility of such a benevolent German attitute toward French action in Morocco was raised by Philippe Crozier, the French ambassador to Vienna. On 5 May 1904, he reported that Vienna indicated Wilhelm II might be willing to talk about the Moroccan situation with a French representative.[7]

Jules Cambon, the French ambassador to Berlin, wrote Pichon that he believed the Kaiser might be willing to meet with a French representative. 'I am inclined to think that the Kaiser is filled with goodwill . . .', he sarcastically told the Quai d'Orsay as he advised his superiors to explore the chance of resolving an aggravated situation.[8] However, the Paris government knew that any talks with Wilhelm II had to be predicated on a German recognition that France would not break up the alliance with Great Britain. In March the Kaiser had violently attacked the Anglo-French *entente* during an official interview with Jules Cambon, and he seemed determined to smash it if possible. The knowledge that the German government still clung to the hope of breaking up the Western alliance made the choice of a French representative much more difficult. The Quai d'Orsay felt that the Minister of Foreign Affairs could not journey to Berlin to hear Wilhelm II propose a dissolution of the Anglo-French alliance. The man who went to speak with the German emperor had to be influential, but not an actual governmental official.

As already stated, the Emperor's main purpose behind these clumsy overtures to France was to break up the *entente*. 'Your Majesty hit the nail on the head', von Bulow wrote to his master, 'when you pointed out that an alliance with France is the only price for which our position in Morocco could be saleable.' Germany, von Bulow continued, '. . . ought to remove entirely the impression that we could sell Morocco for small benefits, as though for a tip [*trinkgeld*].'[9] The price von Bulow and Wilhelm II asked for Morocco was the recognition of German hegemony over Europe. The breaking of the *entente* would leave the German-dominated Triple Alliance as the greatest military power on the continent. The Morocco trade, if France accepted it, would mean the double isolation of England and France.

Pichon, in June 1907, was interested in hearing exactly what the Kaiser would offer, and he asked Eugène Etienne to go to Germany as a semi-official representative of the Quai d'Orsay. Pichon's plan was not well received by everyone, however. Paul Cambon, the French architect of the 1904 accords, opposed the mission, as did Delcassé. Von Bulow, hoping that the meeting would lead to the breaking of the alliance, told the Kaiser, '. . . thinking Frenchmen will not continue to close their eyes to the fact [of German might] and to the necessity for them . . . to turn to us. It is to be hoped that Your Majesty's conversation with such men of note as Etienne . . . will help to spread cognizance of this.'[10] Again, von Bulow misinterpreted the basic facts of European diplomacy. Pichon did not rush to Berlin to sit at the feet of the German Kaiser; he sent Etienne, a semi-official representative. During a preliminary talk with Etienne, von Bulow stated that Wilhelm thought there might be some hostile feeling against Germany in France. After this classic bit of under-statement, the German chancellor informed Etienne that France's future in Morocco depended on German goodwill and on a diminution of the tensions between the two countries.[11] However, Etienne refrained from making any comment to von Bulow's rather clumsy overture.

On 25 June 1907, Etienne journeyed to Kiel to meet with Wilhelm II. The Kaiser was impressed with Etienne as a man of obvious energy, and he questioned the former Minister of War about France's intent in Morocco. Etienne carefully informed the German ruler that France had, through her established interests in the Maghrib, the natural preponderant influence in Morocco. Secondly, the disturbances in the western Maghrib had to be ended by France because Paris feared that the Moroccan trouble could spill over into Algeria.[12] The Kaiser had already outlined to von Bulow the German 'Policy against France',[13] and he proceeded to tell Etienne what Germany expected in return for support in Morocco. 'The great questions of the future which are cropping up in the world require a united Europe, and Germany and France ought to go into them hand in hand.'[14] But, Wilhelm II warned his semi-official visitor:

> France had concluded the Morocco understanding with England in the spring of 1904 behind our backs, and therefore against us. Our interests have been seriously imperilled, as have the interests of all European powers in Morocco. I knew this personally from the heads of other states. I had allowed France a whole year in which to communicate with me on the subject, but no communication had come to me. . . .[15]

The Kaiser became irritated with Etienne because the latter continued to urge the Germans to acknowledge what the other European powers had to recognise at Algeciras. After the meeting with Wilhelm II, the former War Minister returned to Berlin as a guest of von Bulow; there, Etienne told his host quite frankly that as long as the Germans refused to recognise the realities of Algeciras, France could never consider any agreement with Germany. France's *entente* with Great Britain, while not aggressive, would not be subordinated to Berlin's wishes. Von Bulow replied that the German government knew that there were always reckless politicians in France who called for a war of revenge against Germany. There were still unresolved colonial conflicts in Africa between England and France, but the *revanchists* would subordinate them to the combined effort against Germany.[16]

The semi-official diplomatic waves caused by the meeting in Germany were felt in London, Vienna, and Tangier. Saint-Aulaire reported to Pichon that the German legation in Tangier had been given a full report of the Kiel encounter. From an unnamed source within the German legation, Saint-Aulaire learned that the German Foreign Ministry was highly irritated with Wilhelm II and von Bulow's fruitless talks with the French representative. The British government, reported Paul Cambon, had some serious misgivings over the Etienne mission; however, *The Times* (London) stated that if France really expected a fair deal from Germany over Morocco, they would have to wait a very long time.[17] In London the Foreign office was concerned over the offers of Wilhelm II and over France's resolve to continue the working alliance.[18]

Philip Crozier wrote Pichon from Vienna that the Austrian Foreign Ministry was distressed by the French denial of the official status of the Etienne mission. The Austrian government hinted that if France would take advantage of Wilhelm II's new interest in an accord with France, there could be a lessening of international tension. Crozier felt, however, that the Austrian Foreign Office was simply repeating the official German position.[19] Paul Cambon was totally disgusted with his own government because of the semi-official Etienne trip to Kiel, and he wrote to his son that the French representative rambled over many colonial subjects with the Kaiser, but it was the Kaiser who suggested an immediate alliance between the two states. The colonial leader, according to the ambassador, was amazed, but countered, 'To contract such an alliance it would be necessary to remake France first.' At the Quai d'Orsay, Jean Constans, Stephen Pichon, Jules Cambon, and Etienne discussed the trip to Kiel. Jean Constans summed up a widely shared feeling when he told the chief of the Quai d'Orsay, '. . . that was a mission which it will not be necessary to undertake again.'[20]

Jules Cambon reported that the Wilhelmstrasse and Baron von Holstein were also upset over the Kaiser's meeting with Etienne. Von Holstein demanded an exact transcript of the talks from the French Embassy, and Cambon learned that the only thing von Holstein felt could come from the Kiel talks would be a slight counterbalance to Britain's naval superiority.[21] Pichon warned Cambon that Paris was well aware of Berlin's attempts to break up the Anglo-French *entente*, and advised him to be very careful of the Germans and to promise the erratic Wilhelm II nothing.[22] Paul Cambon, obviously distrusting the colonialist's diplomatic ability, then asked Paris if Etienne had promised anything concerning France's participation in the proposed Berlin-Baghdad Railroad. He hoped that Etienne had not even discussed such a matter with the Kaiser.[23]

Von Bulow felt that the Wilhelm II-Etienne meeting might eventually produce some tangible results. He hinted to Sir Charles Hardinge, the British ambassador, that, in spite of everything, there was a possibility of a *rapprochement* between France and Germany. Hardinge reported that the German chancellor indicated that 'there was already a visible *dentente* in the relations of France and Germany', but the Englishman doubted the accuracy of von Bulow's source of information.[24] The German chancellor either intentionally overstated the importance of the Etienne visit to frighten the British, or he misconstrued French willingness to listen to the Kaiser. There was a wide gulf between Gallic curiosity and an inclination in Paris to destroy the hard-won *entente*. Could any German really believe that France would prefer to surrender the continent to German hegemony? If von Bulow was spinning beautiful dreams, von Holstein was not, since the master of the Wilhelmstrasse saw the Etienne mission with brutal clarity. As he told von Bulow, 'It is childish diplomacy when von Radolin or Etienne dangles before us the possibility of drawing France away from England to our side. What can England offer the French, and what have we to offer?'[25] One of the concrete results of the mission was the irritation of Sir Francis Bertie, the British ambassador to Paris. Bertie told Grey that there was a small pro-German group in the French government who claimed that France's slow progress in Morocco was due to some alleged British weakness in supporting France in the year after Algeciras.[26] This Grey did not like. Being a member of the pro-*entente* element in London, Lord Grey wanted to assure France of unending support. He told Sir Frank Lascelles, the British ambassador in Berlin, 'The present moment is a critical one in our relations with France: her present position in Morocco is just now not enviable, and the enemies of our *entente* . . . are only too ready to point out her difficulties.' Grey therefore told Lascelles that British efforts should be directed toward assuring the French that the *entente* was real and workable for both states.[27]

These problems for France in Morocco were indeed serious. The champion of Marrakesh, Moulay Hafid, revolted against Abdel Aziz in 1907, and Charles René-Leclerc, the representative of the *Comité du Maroc* in Morocco, reported that the tribes around Marrakesh had proclaimed Moulay Hafid as the true sultan. Hafid, supposedly a friend of France, tried to placate the French officials in Tangier as well as the Muslims of Marrakesh. At the same time, Rabat's military garrison also rebelled against Abdel Aziz.[28] Tribal chieftains proclaimed Hafid as Sultan in the Great Mosque of Marrakesh in September 1907, and since that time there was a virtual civil war in the western Maghrib.[29] Charles Jonnart had been warned by Clemenceau that the violence in the western Maghrib was bound to influence the border situation for the better. The rebellion, the old tiger believed, would aid the French designs on Morocco. Jonnart was assured that France would take the action necessary to serve France's colonial policy in the western Maghrib.[30]

Jonnart wrote Stephen Pichon that the troubles in Morocco were causing serious repercussions in western Algeria, and that France should take swift measures to ensure Algerian security. The inaction of France, in Jonnart's opinion, only encouraged the enemies of French Moroccan policy who wanted to force Abdel Aziz to show some backbone by attempting to resist the inevitable annexation. Jonnart, demanding military intervention, called on Pichon to take conclusive action.[31] As Jonnart feared, the rebellion against Abdel Aziz spilled over into southern Algeria. The military command reported to Paris that several Moroccan Turkish officers had been captured in the Sahara with a large number of rifles.[32] The *Bulletin* reported that the citizens of Fez had risen in rebellion against Abdel Aziz, proclaimed Moulay Hafid as their sultan, and that civil war raged in almost every city, even Rabat, where Abdel Aziz resided.[33]

While civil war ravaged Morocco, a serious problem developed in the colony of Mauritania, south of the Algero-Moroccan border. In early 1908 over twenty French officials and civilians had been killed as a result of Islamic, anti-colonial agitation in the region. The *Bulletin* reported the rumour that many of the tribesmen had new Mauser rifles which had been issued by the royal armoury at Fez.[34] Auguste Terrier claimed in September

1908 that that whole area of Africa was in a state of siege as
Mauritanians, led by Moroccan officers, raided throughout the
area almost at will. The governor general of French West Africa
dispatched 250 combat-hardened Senegalese infantrymen to
Mauritania to aid what was described as the hard-pressed French
outposts there.[35] However, as was the case with many imperialist
claims, Terrier failed to cite specific evidence, nor did he comment
on why the Moroccan government would chance a strong
French counteraction by such hostile activity.

Colonel Marie Laperrine, commander of the southern oases,
informed the colonial leadership that the religious discontent in
Mauritania was due, he believed, to the Turks in the eastern
Sahara as well as the Moroccans in the western Sahara. Much of
the confusion originated with the militantly nationalistic Young
Turk officers stationed in the Tripolitanian capital. Laperrine
stated that he would use all the force at his command to keep the
Turks and the Moroccans from subverting French authority in
the area.[36]

Laperrine also thought that much of the subversion in the area
originated not only in Constantinople but in Berlin. Because of
reports originating with agents in Tripoli the colonel decided that
the Germans had to have a hand in the situation. The Germans,
Laperrine speculated, wielded a great influence over the Young
Turks, and this moral authority was felt in the eastern oases.[37]
Stephen Pichon wrote to Etienne that the eastern situation was of
great concern to the Quai d'Orsay. Like Laperrine, Pichon
believed the Germans and the Young Turks were upsetting the
situation near the French-held oases of Bilma and Djanet. Any
aggressive Turkish attitude, Pichon stated, would not be tolerated
by the French government.[38]

The French imperialists fully believed that the situation in
the eastern Sahara and in Mauritania was somehow related to the
Moroccan question. A conflict on two fronts in the Maghrib
worried the colonialists, and a Turkish threat or a Mauritanian
rebellion on the eve of the invasion of Morocco could destroy all
of France's plans for the western Maghrib as easily as an internal
Algerian uprising, against which the French had already prepared.
The leaders of the colonial party and the *Comité* felt that Morocco
was the most important project for France. Any hostilities, either

by the Turks or Mauritanians, could be handled by the French military authorities, but Morocco was not as simple. Most colonial militants wanted France to act in the western Maghrib as quickly as possible, and in February 1908 Etienne spoke for the activists on the crumbling authority in Morocco. Obviously hoping to force the government to act, Etienne told the Chamber, 'Since 1904 the Moroccan question has been resolved. Yes, it has been resolved in favour of France.' At Algeciras, all nations, except Germany and Austria, recognised the French preponderance in the western Maghrib and the time had come for France to intervene in Morocco, to stop the war, and to restore order.[39] Pointing to the left, and to Jean Jaurès in particular, Etienne claimed that the leftists forgot the mutilated victims of the civil war in the Cheriffian Empire. One of Jaurès' deputies shouted at Etienne, 'To avenge a few men you must kill hundreds?' Jaurès jumped to his feet and said, 'Yes M. Etienne, how many victims do you need?' Etienne asked the Socialist leader if he meant that France should remain idle and allow massacres and outrages, when with a little effort order could be restored in the western Maghrib.[40] For Etienne, the question of Morocco could be boiled down to three main points: because of her preponderance in the Maghrib France had the right to annex Morocco; the Algeciras conference recognised France's right in the area; and France had a duty to protect Algeria and Tunisia.

The problems in Morocco increased with anti-European riots at Casablanca, and at the oasis of Figuig on the undefined Algero-Moroccan border Moroccan guards had even opened fire on French troops. With the breakdown of discipline the Moroccan frontier army ceased to be an effective military force. To make matters worse, the French could not fully trust Moulay Hafid to recognise French sovereignty in Morocco. Meanwhile, to add to the confusion, Abdel Aziz made a last-ditch effort to save his crumbling authority by asking the French legation to intervene on his side. After declaring a *jihad* from the mosque at Rabat to please the *Ulama* of that city, Abdel Aziz promised the Europeans he would institute reforms within Morocco on a massive scale.[41] Short of military intervention, however, little could be done to restore calm to the western Maghrib.

Throughout the summer of 1909, the situation in Morocco

crumbled. Battles were fought between the armies of the two contenders for the Sultan's throne. In Paris, the colonialists reported with satisfaction that Abdel Aziz suffered defeat after defeat, and by the end of the year his armies would be decimated and unable to continue resistance against the rebels of Moulay Hafid. Etienne and the imperialists chafed under the restraints of waiting. They knew that within a few years the French tricolour would fly over Morocco, but the expectation of 1904-5 had given way to the tedium of hesitation. The time was drawing near when Lyautey would begin his long march across the Algerian border, but the years of preparation made the time of waiting bitter.

Finally, Abdel Aziz's forces deserted him, and in late 1909 he was forced to abdicate in favour of Sultan Moulay Hafid. The French, quick to take advantage of the new shift of power, urged Moulay Hafid to be merciful to the vanquished Abdel Aziz. The deposed Sultan, allowed to live in silent exile in a small villa near Tangier, was given an allowance from the Moroccan treasury which permitted a small staff of servants. By early 1910, the march of French penetration was showing excellent progress. The *Alliance française* announced that it would subsidise the building of new Franco-Arab schools at Fez and Safi.[42] The building of such a school, financed and controlled by French interests, but in the heart of the holy city of Fez, marked the vast changes which were taking place throughout Morocco. Fifteen years before the cornerstone was laid, in 1910, for the Alliance school in Fez, the French had demanded and received the permission to install a European Christian consul there. By 1910, the Moors, already confused by their own bloody fratricidal conflict, were in no position to resist the French 'infidels'. Moroccan independence was only an illusion maintained because of the tortured course of European diplomacy. In late December 1910, Eugène Etienne returned to the presidency of the *Comité du Maroc* in order to preside over the demise of an independent Cheriffian Empire.[43] The culmination of the French empire was clearly in sight. But the power of the colonial party and their allies had peaked simply because of the increased international tensions. Ironically, the annexation of Morocco would be the last gasp of the old imperialist order because the gathering clouds of war would subordinate annexationist interests to national goals and defence. Perhaps this was the fatal flaw in the imperialist movement. Once the issue of war with Germany was raised, all other items became secondary and almost unimportant.

Notes to Chapter 11 will be found on pages 200–2.

Chapter 12 THE TWILIGHT OF
IMPERIALISM 1910-19

THE FOUR years prior to the outbreak of World War I marked a decline in the interest in colonial expansion. Morocco was finally added to the French North African empire in March 1912. Overshadowing all other events, however, was the outbreak of the war in the summer of 1914. The imperialist militants who had played such a vital role in expansion had built up a vast base of power in the Chamber and in the government, but after 1910 they were forced to turn their attention to matters of national defence rather than to colonial acquisition. As international tensions increased, the imperial sphere of interests necessarily decreased. Those colonial activists who held positions in the government and in the Chamber reluctantly subordinated their expansionist desires. Only a few imperialists who were totally involved with imperial administration in the field could devote their full attention to colonial matters.

After 1910 imperialists held many positions within various governments. Delcassé, for example, served as Minister of Marine in 1912. Despite the fact that the former Minister of Foreign Affairs had been a prime advocate of colonialism based on maritime power, he simply had to devote all his energy to the preparations of the French fleets for eventual war. Etienne, now ageing, his hair turning grey, was named as War Minister in 1913. In the same cabinet was Charles Jonnart, who held the portfolio of the Ministry of Foreign Affairs.

The colonial block tended to decline as its members sided more and more with their parties' official positions on matters of national necessity. That was perhaps the overall weakness of the *Parti Colonial*: not a party in the strict sense of the word, it was unable to impose any special discipline. Fortunate for the colonialists was the fact that most of the colonial leadership, including Etienne, were associated with the Group of the Democratic Left. This party was composed of Joseph Chailley-Bert, Etienne, Gaston Thompson, Joseph Reinach, and others.[1] But the old leadership, out of patriotic motives, refused to allow expansionist questions to overwhelm the preparations for war.

In the Chamber the colonialists controlled the appointments to many key committees such as the Army Commission, and on 12 July 1910, Etienne, an ex-Minister of War, was named to that key post as its president. During one session of that body in 1911 the military committee considered and recommended to the deputies over fifty separate pieces of legislation. Believing that European rivalry and tensions could bring on a general conflict Etienne fought hard for a complete examination of recruiting policies. What Etienne wanted was primarily a substantial increase in the number of troops in the French army in case of a clash with Germany.[2] Opposed by the formidable Jaurès, who was also a member of the Army Commission, Etienne led the fight for modifications of the Army Law, and he won. During the general budget debates of 1911 the imperialist leader was a key figure in the fight for appropriations for the military establishment.[3] As he fought harder for France's military establishment, he participated less in the debates over the monetary requests for the colonies, as was the case with most other imperialists. The colonialists controlled the Chamber's Commission for Protectorates and Colonies. Lead by Paul Deschanel, this official committee could boast of a membership which was strikingly similar to the leadership of the colonial party and the *Comité de l'Afrique française*. Serving with men like Lucien Hubert, Joseph Chailley-Bert, Denys Cochin, Alexandre Millerand and Hippolyte Laroche, Etienne continued to guide carefully the doctrines of the French empire,[4] and interestingly, most of the proposed laws which the commission considered were directly concerned with the governmental administration of Algeria.

In 1910 the colonial party, distressed at their declining political fortunes, chided the Chamber for a lack of interest. Most believed that their greatest achievements had been the founding of the colonial party and the guiding of French efforts in western Africa and throughout all the African continent. Reflecting with some bitterness on France's hesitation to accept the concepts of colonialism, Etienne said, 'But how many [young] Frenchmen will recall or know the great efforts or long time which it has taken to obtain [French Africa]. How many do not know anything of the sacrifices, the valour, energy, money, and also the tears. . . .'[5] The noble visions of Ferry and Gambetta, he complained, were almost forgotten, and only by the faith of the colonial party could France continue to be strong in her empire, and because of her empire, in Europe.[6]

The colonialists could point with pride to that vast area in Africa which they helped to add to the empire. In late 1910 the area known as French West Africa extended over 3,913,000 square kilometres, and only through continual pressure was it unified and pacified. The 'union of all of French Africa', one imperialist claimed, 'is not an adventurous concept. . . . it is a living reality.'[7] The Chamber was told on 24 December 1910, that France should judge imperialism by its results. What has the empire done for France the imperialists asked? Answering their own question, Etienne, acting as their spokesman, stated that it had added prestige and strengthened the economy of France. 'Have you any doubts for [the empire's] future?' he continued.[8] In the same speech before the Chamber, the annexationist lavishly praised the work of Lyautey and Laperrine in the southern Oranais. These men were representative of the many dedicated officers who prepared the way for the addition of Morocco to the empire. Their actions pacified the south Oranais and the Algero-Tripolitanian frontier, and the threats to France's eventual occupation of the western Maghrib had been ended.[9]

However, the final solution to the Moroccan problem bothered a number of the French colonialists. Robert de Caix wrote early in 1911 that the conditions in Morocco were so serious that military occupation was only a matter of time. Moulay Hafid was unable to keep order in Morocco. While de Caix claimed that the Oran Division, an element of the XIXth Army Corps, was concentrated on the frontier in order to give battle to dissident Moroccan tribes, these French troops could be ordered to march to Fez and seize the capital.[10]

While de Caix urged a seizure in the western Maghrib, imperialists within the government were busy laying the political groundwork for just such an action. As vice-president of the Chamber, Etienne had great latitude in his dealings with governmental officials, and he had many important personal contacts. In the spring of 1911 he asked his old friend, the Marquis de Segonzac, to go to Morocco to talk with Moulay Hafid regarding the situation in Fez. In May de Segonzac wrote a long letter to report his clear and accurate impressions. De Segonzac found a distinct undercurrent of subversion and competition among the cliques at the court, and Moulay Hafid was obviously torn between the advice of differing groups on how to react to the French demands for reforms.[11]

While in Morocco, de Segonzac lived at the home of General Henri Gaillard, the French consul at Fez. During talks with Gaillard, de Segonzac came to believe that the proposed occupation would lead to the need for a reorganisation of the French military command there.[12] French soldiers supported the rule of Moulay Hafid and de Segonzac reasoned that the Sultan needed this support for his own weak throne. Moulay Hafid confirmed this opinion when he told de Segonzac, 'If you leave, I shall leave with you.'[13]

The annexationists knew that the time was nearing when the French would have to invade Morocco, and they had demanded that the government consider the appointment of Lyautey as the chief of Morocco whenever the occupation began.[14] There could be little doubt that the French had to guide the Sultan and most military men already in the western Maghrib had little faith in Moulay Hafid's ability to govern his own state. General Dalbiez, attached to the legation in Tangier, wrote to Paris that the Sultan was 'a fat buffoon, mediocre in all things'.[15] Dalbiez related that in Fez there was a shortage of meat and grain but in Tangier there were large flocks of sheep, and the public storehouses were filled to overflowing with grain. Political conditions were so unsettled that the necessary meats and grains could not be transported from Tangier to Fez. It would probably serve French interests, the general advised, to depose Moulay Hafid and replace him with a strong yet loyal member of the *Mahkzen*.[16]

However, most of the imperialists wanted to maintain the sultanic government as a convenient vehicle for colonial control since the French hoped to govern Morocco through a dependent sultan. Robert de Caix wrote that the French government and army would have to undergird the sultan's position. It is necessary, he said, to continue a process of building up the number of French advisers and military attachés in Morocco for the sake of securing all of North Africa.[17] The French colonialists had reason to be concerned about Morocco because the Germans, irritated over the continual French advances in Morocco without proper compensations to them, dispatched on 1 July 1911 the gunboat *Panther* to Agadir. But in the Franco-German talks that followed, German Foreign Minister Kiderlen Wachter and Joseph Caillaux, the French premier, reached a compromise on the situation. France got her free hand in Morocco and Germany obtained territory in western Africa.[18] The imperialists were furious at the deal. Joined by Clemenceau, the colonialists atatcked the Caillaux government. The onetime anti-imperial *revanchard* Clemenceau and the arch-colonialist Etienne fought side by side for the territorial integrity of the French African empire.

While France was in the midst of the Agadir crisis, the Italians moved to take Libya into their very modest empire.[19] The French colonialists did not oppose Italy's occupation because they felt that their eastern Algerian border would be secured by a European power. Had the French felt any great desire to take Libya they would have enlarged the military occupation which began with the Bilma and Djanet campaign of 1906. But as Robert de Caix stated, French colonial opinion was sympathetic to Italian efforts in North Africa.[20] Because of the Italo-French 1900 agreements over Libya and Morocco, France could afford to be generous in her support for this Italian imperial effort.

In 1911/12 the French government realised that the probability of war with Germany was probably very real, and it would be indeed politic to show some attention to the least committed member of the Triple Alliance. There was a governmental crisis in France which tended to lessen French interest in Italy's Tripolitanian operation. Raymond Poincaré replaced Joseph Caillaux on 14 January 1912,[21] and the Poincaré ministry was interested in pushing the Moroccan military occupation. The men around Poincaré—Louis Barthou, Charles Jonnart, Maurice Rouvier, and Eugène Etienne—despite their official party allegiances, supported a government which would be dedicated to colonial expansion in the western Maghrib.[22] Most of the colonialists had attacked the Caillaux government for dragging out the start of a serious occupation of the western Maghrib. Robert de Caix, speaking for the colonialists, stated that this government had procrastinated for two months over Morocco, and had left office with nothing done to consolidate France's gains. Morocco could not wait, and with the new government possibly the western Maghrib would fall into the hands of the French.[23]

A delegation of colonialist deputies and members of the *Comité de l'Afrique française* went to see Poincaré, the chief of the new ministry, to urge the nomination of Lyautey as the commander of the full Moroccan occupation. Because of their great influence on the Chamber, they were able to convince Poincaré to agree to this appointment.[24] All of the annexationists were openly concerned about the Moroccan resistance to French penetration because in January 1912 Colonel Henry Brulard of the French Foreign Legion wrote to Paris that the French troops, even the Algerian regiments, were having difficulties in pacifying the region. Brulard, a tough veteran of the Second Legion Regiment, advised that a corps of Moroccans be formed to aid in the penetration.[25] The problem of a violent Moroccan reaction was on Etienne's mind when he began a tour of the South Oranais in April 1912. At the post at Colomb-Bechar, he said that the time had come to penetrate Morocco regardless of armed opposition. France's pre-eminence in the Maghrib demanded that she act. Lyautey was especially praised as a soldier of great leadership. The gallant soldiers of the XIXth Corps, Etienne said, should applaud a great military leader.[26]

Because of the strong colonial party and the position of Etienne as vice-president of the Chamber, the imperialists were in an excellent spot to praise and urge the promotion of Lyautey. Because of their longstanding influence in the Chamber they could also be privy to much diplomatic information. One of their valuable contacts was René Normand, a legation official in Fez, and Etienne often requested that Normand give him reports of the situation in Morocco which would be passed on to other colonial leaders. On 30 March 1912 Moulay Hafid signed the Treaty of Fez which recognised a French protectorate over Morocco. This marked the official start of the French annexation of the Maghribi state. French troops were ordered into the country to guard against a rebellion. It was this situation which prompted the imperialist leadership to request detailed reports from Normand.

In April 1912, Normand wrote that the Moroccans were putting up a stiff armed resistance to the French penetration. However, the Moorish merchant element seemed to welcome the presence of the French military. Normand believed that the takeover was going better than anyone had expected. In fact, he reported that there was a 'Society of the Friends of France' established in Fez, and that, 'Fez is slowly losing its appearance of a totally Muslim city.'[27]

How the conservative Muslim elements of the western Maghrib would react to European penetration always troubled the imperialists. In the Atlas Mountains, despite the presence of the el Glaoua family, tribes armed with modern rapid-firing rifles fought against the French. The el Glaoua family controlled the Atlas region and also the city of Marrakesh. Opportunists of the first degree, the el Glaoua political machine attached themselves to the French invaders. Throughout the decades which followed the signing of the Treaty of Fez, the family became the most powerful in all of Morocco.[28] In Marrakesh, the capital of the el Glaoua empire, a Muslim was struck by an automobile containing three French diplomats. The Moor was only slightly injured, but a riot followed and Frenchmen, Germans, and a Swiss national were beaten and struck with rocks. However, Moroccan soldiers under the command of a member of the el Glaoua family finally restored order.[29]

Order was rare in Morocco during the first spring of the occupation in 1912. Moroccans, seething with rage over the French operations, voiced their protests with violence and rioting. Moors, filled with resentment, tried to fight back. René Normand told his supporters in Paris that there had been great bloodshed in Fez. Normand, who was trained in the crucible of the South Oranais, advised the imperialists to urge that the Foreign Legion and colonial army begin to train Moroccans. Only Moroccans, collaborating with France, could restore order.[30]

However, the colonialists were not overly concerned with the Moroccan protests, and as long as the Legion and Army kept the resistance at a minimum, the process of occupation could continue at a satisfactory pace. The bulk of the fighting fell to the Legion, who served France well in the early days of the penetration. The demand that the Legion create military units of collaborationist Moors was well taken and later acted on. The fighting in Morocco by the colonial forces and the Legion marked the end of the long struggle to add the western Maghrib to France's North African empire. For the imperialists also, the military pacification of the kingdom meant the culmination of a struggle for Morocco which began in earnest in 1898. By the end of 1912, as far as they were concerned, the ambition of giving France a mighty imperial edifice was fulfilled. But most French colonial leaders, including Eugène Etienne, were caught up now in the preparation for European war.

The decline of interest in colonial activities was accelerated in 1913 when the Chamber considered the Three Year Law which would increase the two-year term of service in the French army by one year. Involved with the legislation were most of the leadership of the Colonial Party in the Chamber. Charles Jonnart and Eugène Etienne served in the Briand government, which was constituted on 30 January 1913.[31] Despite their imperial concerns, especially with the newly acquired area of Morocco, these annexationists had to devote all their time to the fight over the new military service Bill. Etienne, as Minister of War, was forced by necessity constantly to defend his legislation before a hostile Chamber, and as he did so the colonial block became leaderless.

Etienne believed, as did most of the French politicians, that an eventual clash with Germany was almost inevitable. The generation who faced the growing tensions in Europe, like the deputy from Oran, had been greatly affected by the defeat and humiliation of 1870. However, few Frenchmen really desired a general European war, and because of the alliance system any clash between France and Germany automatically meant a general confrontation. Perhaps wrongly, it was felt in Paris that the Three Year Law would ease European tensions once France became the military equal of Germany.[32] Most imperialists preferred peace to armed conflict simply because they were not certain the empire could survive the shock of war. Morocco, for example, had been a part of the French empire for only two years, and the colonialists knew that it was only partially pacified. From their contacts within the colonial administration in Morocco—Lyautey, de Segonzac, Dalbiez, and Brulard—the imperialists learned that it would take a large number of troops and a great amount of time to complete the process of pacification. Military columns moving from south-western Algeria into south-eastern Morocco had to be halted because of more pressing needs elsewhere in the protectorate. Consequently, few colonialists were anxious to confront Germany for the sake of the *revanche* at that critical time. However, a distaste for the memory of 1870 plus a patriotic love for France motivated them during the months that preceded the lengthy, heated debates over the proposed Three Year Law.

In early June 1913, the debates began on the Three Year Law, and the colonialists were one of the major forces defending the new laws. Jaurès and Etienne continually clashed over the increase in military service during the discussions. Basically they wanted all Frenchmen between the ages of 18 and 35 to see some service and for the term of enlistment to be raised to three years.[33] Support came from every political group within the Chamber. The opposition of Jaurès to the proposal had alienated the Right within the Chamber, and the government was assured of the vocal support of Albert de Mun,[34] who was a leader of the Catholic co-operationists. De Mun's active support would mean a great deal in the debates. Being a vice-president of the Chamber's Commission on Work and a member of the Commission on Protectorates and Colonies meant that de Mun would be able to influence a number of uncommitted deputies. After several weeks of debate the Three Year Law was passed by the Chamber. Dozens of resolutions and counter resolutions had been discussed by the deputies, and the final vote came on 19 July 1913. Most of the deputies realised the great part played by the colonial party in the passage of that important piece of legislation.

While the annexationists were involved with the passage of the Three Year Law, they had little time for colonial matters. They did maintain contact with General Lyautey in Morocco, and in late April 1913 Lyautey wrote to Paris to suggest that the War Ministry establish training schools for officers in Morocco. Military schools, Lyautey hoped, would be established in Fez, Algiers, and Tunis. These educational centres would promote

the study of the Muslim and his language. The general believed
that this would help France maintain peace and security in all of
the Maghrib.[35]

The pacification of Morocco was not totally forgotten during
the hectic summer of 1913. The War Ministry created a Moroccan
Bureau to oversee the process of pacification. Interestingly, it
secretly began to transfer large tracts of Moroccan territory to
Algerian administration; Algeria was being enlarged at the ex-
pense of Morocco. The ministry informed the commander at Ain
Sefra that in a directive he had ordered the limits of the fort at
Colomb-Bechar to be moved far to the west, deep into Moroccan
territory. Paris apparently wanted to add as much territory to the
Oran Province as possible.[36]

On 9 December 1913 the Barthou cabinet came to an end.
Gaston Domergue replaced Barthou, and Joseph Noulens assumed the portfolio of the War Ministry.[37] Etienne's year at the War
Office was a busy one considering his advanced age and physical
condition, but he was able to concentrate some of his efforts on
Algerian affairs. The pushing of the Algerian border to the west,
enlarging Algeria, was typical of Etienne's concern for his native
land. This act, and others like it, would cause great difficulties at a
later date when both Morocco and Algeria were independent states.

The consolidation of France's gains in Morocco continued to
occupy a good deal of time for the imperialists. In June 1914, on
the eve of the outbreak of the Great War, a long letter from
General Henri Gaillard, who had been promoted to the position
of secretary general of the protectorate of Morocco, indicated that
the Spanish agitated the Moors in the French zone.[38] Lyautey,
Gaillard's superior, took immediate steps to stop the subversion.
Several Muslim religious leaders were arrested in Tangier and
sent into exile. Slowly the country was returned to a state of
relative peace and order.

Morocco was affected by the outbreak of the war in August
1914. Moroccans, like the rest of the Maghribi Muslims, served
on the western front and in French industry. During the early
months of the war imperialism became a lost issue, as most
deputies were deeply concerned about the confused conduct of
the early military campaign. Galliéni, an old colonialist soldier,
commanded the troops in the Paris area, and the deputy from

Oran, as president of the Chamber, constantly wrote to the ailing general to find out if the capital was truly safe from the Germans. Galliéni, disheartened by the enemy advance, was determined to rescue the city. Under his direct command were Moroccan and Algerian Muslims who were ready, Galliéni boasted, to throw themselves on the enemy. The only problem for the Paris commandant was how to get his small command out to the Marne River to confront the opponents.[39] Galliéni's daring and famous taxicab army contributed to the halting of the Germans on the Marne River, and, flushed with initial success, he wrote Etienne to praise his North African troops. While not approving of the overall Allied strategy, Galliéni said that the defence of Paris was due in part to the great courage of the Maghribi natives.[40] But how much of an impression did Galliéni's praise have on the colonial leadership's basic beliefs about the colonial subjects?

Obviously, while willing to use Muslims to fight for France, many imperialists still did not fully trust them. In letters to Charles Lutaud, the new governor general of Algeria, Etienne continually asked about the internal security of Algeria. Lutaud, appointed governor in 1911, responded to his 'dear master's' inquiry that the Muslims remained peaceful. The Maghribi natives remained quiet even though most of France's XIXth Corps was fighting on the western front. The natives, according to the staunchly imperialist governor general, 'did not cause us any concern'.[41] A firm believer in *colon* superiority, Lutaud related that even in the face of rising grain prices, the Algerians were as docile as usual. The grain problem, especially acute for the Muslims since it constituted the base of their diet, had to be dealt with by strict regulation. Speculators, warned the governor, could cause difficulties because the Algerian Muslims simply did not have enough money to purchase such high-priced items, even if they were very necessary.[42]

Never realising that Muslim docility was related to hunger, Lutaud wrote that the colonialists in Paris did not have to worry about a rebellion of any sort. The Italians in Tripolitania had effectively sealed the border with Tunisia and Algeria, and consequently Islamic agitators could not cross over into French territory.[43] In early March 1915, Lutaud had to face some disturbances caused by the lack of food. In a typical colonialist reaction, he warned that any outbreak of violence would be handled with great dispatch. Warning that order would be preserved, Lutaud stated that a well-aimed fusillade was the proper solution. If trouble came to Algeria, the governor would be quite willing to fall back on the mass of *colons* and crush any resistance.[44]

Again in 1916 rioting broke out in the Aures area of Algeria, and Lutaud responded with as much force as was possible. Believing himself to be the champion of the *colons*, the governor general in his zeal alienated many within the French government who were truly grateful for the Muslim participation in the war effort. Even Etienne had to admit that the natives had done a great deal to strengthen French industry and to bolster the sagging French military. When the Clemenceau ministry took power in 1917, the 'Old Tiger' decided to take a long look at Algerian affairs, and one of his first acts was to remove Lutaud and replace him with the more moderate Charles Jonnart. Jonnart's appointment was not hailed as a great step forward toward Muslim equality, but, as many knew, the governor general did favour some limited reforms.

Most of the old line colonialists found that they could do little to head off some basic alterations in Algeria, and even Etienne, now weak with a serious heart condition, had to give his grudging approval to a series of laws proposed by Jonnart in 1918. The Jonnart Laws became a reality on 4 February 1919, and some *colons* hailed it as the first sign of the decay of *Algérie française*. However, the new laws, as moderate as they were, failed to enfranchise a large number of the Muslims of that North African colony. But in the context of the imperial movement they were meaningful since this step revealed two things about the annexationists. They emerged from World War I as a less potent political force, and most of the old activist leadership had passed from the scene by 1920. This heralded a drastic change in France's imperial policy, and in the long run it meant simply a downgrading of the colonial question. What had been started in 1870 as a result of a humiliating defeat, ended in 1920 as a result of a resounding, but draining victory. Energy which hitherto had been expended on annexation was gone. The victory over Germany in 1918 spelled the death knell of New French Imperialism

in 1920. For forty years the drive to expand France overseas had
been an almost overriding issue, but in the post-World War I
world the reason for it disappeared. The era of New French
Imperialism had come to an end.

Notes to Chapter 12 will be found on pages 202–4.

Conclusion

It is a difficult task to evaluate the lasting legacy of the French empire as it existed from 1880 to 1910. Since World War II the process of decolonisation has reversed the efforts of the annexationists. Damned by such writers as Frantz Fanon and Germaine Tillion, the expansionists appeared to be heartless and ruthless, and many were exactly that. But others, probably the vast majority, urged France to seek new areas of overseas expansion out of the best of patriotic motives. Men like Lyautey, Etienne, Galliéni, and Delcassé lived during a particular period in history, and what is a valid moral judgement for the historian and the critic of the mid-twentieth century is not applicable, in all cases, to the French imperialist of the late nineteenth century. However, two questions must come to mind about the French empire: were the empires built in Africa and Asia solid in their political and economic foundations, and did the French leave behind a lasting legacy in those colonial areas?

Eugène Etienne, the figurehead of New French Imperialism, died of a heart attack in May 1921, but even at the time of his death there were forces at work, especially within North Africa's majority Muslim population, which would eventually bring about the end of imperial rule. With the Jonnart Laws of 1919 the imperial edifice showed a slight crack, but even the mighty Etienne had grudgingly accepted those minor alterations in the political structure in North Africa. But more significant than the laws of 1919 was the list of Muslim candidates in the Algerian municipal elections of 1921. The list, headed by Emir Khaled, a descendant of the famed resistance leader Abdel Khadir, won a number of seats, causing a near panic in Algiers. Despite the fact that the election was quickly invalidated and Khaled exiled a year later, the symbolic act was committed as far as Algeria was concerned.

In 1912 the Young Tunisian movement had boycotted tram lines in Tunis and caused great distress among the *colons* and the French administrators in the capital city. Certainly, this was clear indication that the natives of North Africa were not as docile, nor as slow-witted, as the anti-assimilationists had claimed. There were faint stirrings of nationalist thought not only in North Africa, but in the rest of the French empire.

The founding of the *Etoile Nord Africain* in Paris in 1926 by Abdel Kader Hadjali, a member of the Algerian Communist Party, added a new dimension to the stirrings in the empire. The ENA, under its new leader Messali Hadj, called for 'the total struggle for independence of . . . Algeria, Morocco, and Tunisia'. Such a thought would have been inconceivable to Etienne and the stalwarts of the *Comité de l'Afrique française* a decade earlier. What the staunch associationists failed to realise was that the empire could not be effectively sealed off from the rest of the outside world. Wilsonian idealism as well as France's plight after the bloody conflict of 1914–18 made an impact on the colonial subjects. The struggle by Kemalist Turkey against Greece and her western supporters stirred the subject peoples of the empire, especially in the Maghrib.

The flaw in the colonialists' philosophy was simply an under-estimation of the intellectuals and the post-war youth in the empire. They were so certain of their social darwinist ideology and their associationist principles that they failed to judge correctly the tenor of their subjects' minds. Probably so used were they to the *Beni oui-oui*, or natives who sided with the imperial administration, that the colonialists did not listen to other voices within the overseas territories.

It would be too simple to criticise the stalwarts of the colonial party and the *Comité de l'Afrique française* for being short-sighted and unresponsive to the aspirations of the people which France governed. However, it is wise to consider that these men saw annexation as the means to a national end. After 1870 colonialism existed not only for the acquisition of colonies, but also for the revitalisation of France, and after the defeat by Prussia, France needed all the resources she could muster in re-establishing her place in the European community of nations. Most expansionists were single-minded men who had that one goal in mind, and this was, as they saw it, a patriotic endeavour. Men like Etienne, for example, believed that imperialism was the means to reforge France's prestige and a certain route to the eventual *revanche*.

To restructure France and to enhance her position vis-à-vis the European community of nations, the imperialist pushed industrialisation in the overseas territories at the expense of all other internal development. This was especially true in Africa south of the Sahara, where the huge commercial concessions were granted. While the concept of the concession was continually questioned by men such as Joseph Chailley-Bert, the idea was firmly implanted in the minds of many new colonialists. After World War I the necessity for such rapid exploitation changed, and the metropole did increase the scope of African development, but in the long run the anti-concessionists were proved correct. Actual progress, owing to post-war economic and political conditions in France, was retarded.

But again, it is well to remember what overwhelming forces motivated the imperialists. Certainly, the imperial militants can be criticised for their attitudes concerning colonial exploitation and industrialisation, and in the associationist context, the native and his welfare was secondary to expansion. This was an accepted part of that ideology, but the concessionists, especially Delcassé and Etienne, believed firmly that immediate exploitation was a national necessity. In their patriotic zeal all else became secondary and lost importance. Assimilation and all that attended that ideal, as the colonialist saw it, was simply not practical for France when she had to cope with the internal and international situation after 1870.

What few imperialist activists failed to perceive was the basic fact that wherever the French flag flew there was also French history. During the scramble for Africa France was still the France of 1789. This was a vital part of the French existence, and it was a part which the native, be he Algerian, Dahomean, or Indochinese, would not help but notice. If the revolutionary ideals of 1789 were valid for the Frenchmen of 1890, why was it not also valid for the native. They lived under the same flag, and eventually spoke the same language. It was simply unrealistic to expect the Maghribi, African, or Asian to ignore the great history of French revolutionary ideology. Did not Liberty, Brotherhood, and Equality mean the same thing for the African as it meant for the metropolitan Frenchman? As more education filtered down to the native the contradiction of French rule and the ideals of the revolution became apparent. While teaching French grammar and history, the seeds of revolt were planted. When young colonial subjects were asked to sacrifice and die for France during World War II, the questioning of French honesty and dedication to their own revolutionary, equalitarian heritage was open to serious question.

Certainly, few of the New Imperialists could have envisioned the collapse of the French empire after 1945. Dien Bien Phu and Evian sur Bains would have been beyond their comprehension since they believed they were building an eternal empire. Etienne, a staunch republican patriot, had warned in the early 1880s against giving any political concessions to the natives, for in his mind, it would mean, '. . . the official end to the colonial era'. Frantz Fanon, almost seventy years later, wrote, 'I am a French man. . . . I am personally interested in the future of France, in French values, in the French nation.' To Fanon, like so many other young subjects in the empire, French values, in which they believed they shared, were simply ignored outside of the mother country.

It was a strange and contradictory legacy which the imperialist activists left to the empire and the French state. Perhaps, most importantly, they did push the concepts of acquisitions, and through their energies France planted her flag on a huge portion of the earth's surface. Without their efforts the French empire might not have been created. Rightly or not, they believed that they were serving the short-term and long-term interests of the nation which they saw in 1870 humiliated by Germany. They can be criticised for their attitudes and actions, but not their patriotic dedication. Without Delcassé, Etienne, Mizon, de Maistre, and other colonial militants, the history of France after 1870 would have been quite different indeed. They set in motion forces which would affect Europe and Africa long after they had passed from the French political scene.

References

Chapter 1 PRELUDE TO NEW IMPERIALISM 1880–7
(pages 13–24)

1 Gabriel Hanotaux once described Etienne as 'ardent, alert, practical, receptive, . . . who was to be our colonial [policies' greatest exponent] . . ., psychologically certain, familiar with the man and affairs [of state].' Gabriel Hanotaux, 'Exposé général', in *L'empire colonial français* (Paris: 1929), xiii.

2 Vincent Confer, *France and Algeria: The Problem of Civil and Political Reform, 1870–1920* (Syracuse: 1966), 14–15.

3 Raymond F. Betts, *Assimilation and Association in French Colonial Theory 1870–1914* (New York: 1961), 137.

4 Eugène Etienne, 'Report to the Colonial Congress, 1904' as quoted in ibid, 201.

5 Gabriel Hanotaux, 'Discours: les principes généraux de notre organisation coloniale', a chapter in Henry Brenier et al, *La politique coloniale de la France* (Paris: 1924), 174.

6 Confer, *France and Algeria*, 74–5

7 Betts, *Assimilation and Association*, 137.

8 Eugène Etienne, *Son oeuvre—Algérienne et politique 1881–1906* (Paris: 1907), I, 417.

9 Henri Brunschwig, *Mythes et réalités de l'imperialisme colonial français 1871–1914* (Paris: 1960), 80.

10 Stephen H. Roberts, *The History of French Colonial Policy*, 2nd edn (London: 1963), 15.

11 Military Decree of 1 July 1882, as quoted in France, Service des affaires indigènes, Residence générale de France à Tunis, *Historique de service des affaires indigènes de Tunisie* (Bourg: 1931), 13.

12 Military Decree of 10 June 1882, as quoted in ibid, 18–19.

13 Etienne, *Son oeuvre*, I, 415–16.

14 Jacques Chastenet, *La république des républicains 1879–1893* (Paris: 1954), 142.

15 Etienne to Faure, Paris, 16 August 1882, as found in Marcel Blanchard, ed, 'Correspondance de Félix Faure touchant les affaires coloniales 1882–1889', *Revue d'histoire des coloniales*, 44 (1955), 138–9.

16 Etienne to Faure, Paris, 17 August 1882, ibid, 139.

17 Ibid.

18 Brunschwig, *Mythes et réalités*, 111–12.

175

19 Jean Jaurès, *Textes choisis I, contre la guerre et la politique coloniale* (Paris: 1959), 75.
20 Ibid.
21 Etienne, *Son oeuvre*, I, 418. Etienne was not an alarmist over the situation of the Spanish workers in Oran. The problems with them were noted by the American consul in Algiers. Alexander Joudan to John Davis, Algiers, 12 September 1882, United States Department of State. *Consular Dispatches from Algiers*, roll 103.
22 Etienne, *Son oeuvre*, I, 417.
23 Ibid, 427–8.
24 Betts, *Assimilation and Association*, 59.
25 Etienne, *Son oeuvre*, I, 456.
26 Ibid.
27 'Colonies françaises: Algérie', *Bulletin*, 5 no 1 (January 1895), 15.
28 Military Decree of 1 July 1882, as quoted in Service des affaires indigènes, *Historique de service*, 14.
29 Etienne, *Son oeuvre*, I, 443–4.
30 Ibid, 451.
31 Letter from Paul Dislere to Félix Faure, Lille, 9 April 1885, as quoted in Blanchard, 'Correspondance de Félix Faure', 154–5.
32 Blanchard, in his collection of Faure letters, included many letters from Jules Ferry to Faure concerning Indochinese affairs. This is also apparent in Eric Schmieder's 'La Chambre de 1885–1889 et les affaires du Tonkin', *Revue française d'histoire d'outre-mer*, LIII (1966), 153–214.
33 See note by Blanchard, 'Correspondance de Félix Faure', 156–7.
34 Schmieder, 'La Chambre de 1885–1889', 177–80.
35 Ibid.

Chapter 2 ANNEXATION AND EXPANSION 1887–90
(pages 25–36)

 1 For an important article on Faure and his tenure as undersecretary see: Marcel Blanchard, 'Correspondance de Félix Faure'. Of special importance are his many letters to and from Ferry, the Minister of the Navy, and colonial officials in Indochina.
 2 Joseph Galliéni to Etienne, Niagossola, Sudan, 16 January 1888, found in the *Eugène Etienne Correspondance*, vol 24, 327, Nouvelle acquisition française, Bibliothèque nationale, Paris, letter number 5.
 3 Edouard Petit, *Organisation des colonies françaises et des pays de protectorat*, I (Paris: 1894), 204–5.
 4 Ibid, 205.
 5 Ibid.
 6 Colonial Agents to Faure, Paris, 7 January 1888. Blanchard, 'Correspondance de Félix Faure', 162.
 7 Gordon Wright, *France in Modern Times* (Chicago: 1966), 312–13.

8   Wythe Williams, *The Tiger of France: Conversations with Clemenceau* (New York: 1949), 84–7.

9   Dispatch from McLane to Bayard, Paris, 19 November 1887, as found in United States, *Dispatches, France*, roll 103. United States, Department of State, *Dispatches from the US Ministers to France 1789–1906* (Washington: National Archives, Microfilm, 1959).

10 Dispatch from McLane to Bayard, Paris, 1 December 1887, as found in ibid.

11 Galliéni to Etienne, Niagossola, Sudan, 16 January 1888, *Etienne Correspondance*, letter number 5. Evidently Galliéni was somewhat mistaken in his evaluation of Faure's position on the colonies. Many colonial representatives in south-east Asia, Indochina in particular, felt that Faure was a better undersecretary than Etienne. See letter from Colonial Agents to Faure, Paris, 7 January 1888, Blanchard, 'Correspondance de Félix Faure', 162.

12 Galliéni to Etienne, *Etienne Correspondence*, letter number 5.

13 Petit, *Organisation des colonies*, I, 242–3.

14 Ibid, 243–4.

15 Ibid, 244.

16 Ferry to Etienne, Paris, 13 October 1887, *Etienne Correspondence*, letter number 2.

17 Eric Schmieder, 'La Chambre de 1885–1889 et les affaires du Tonkin', *Revue française d'histoire d'outre-mer*, LIII (1966), 188.

18 Ibid, 208–9.

19 Etienne, *Son oeuvre*, I, 41.

20 Ibid.

21 Ibid, 56.

22 Ibid, 58–9.

23 Ibid, 62.

24 Galliéni to Etienne, np, 10 February 1888, as found in *Etienne Correspondence*, letter number 9.

25 Dispatch from McLane to Bayard, Paris, 29 March 1888, United States, *Dispatches, France*, roll 104.

26 Jacques Mangolte, 'Le chemin de fer de Konakry au Niger (1890–1914)', *Revue française d'histoire d'outre-mer*, LV (1968), 38–9.

27 Etienne, *Son oeuvre*, I, 73–5.

28 Ibid, 75.

29 Petit, *Organisation des colonies*, I, 195. The course of study at the school was pragmatic in approach. Finalised in a decree of 30 April 1906, signed by Georges Leygues, Minister of Colonies, the course of study included lessons on the colonial policy of France, foreign languages, and administrative procedures. Decree 105, 30 April 1906, as found in France, Ministère des colonies, *Bulletin officiel du Ministère des colonies*, 20 (Paris: imprimerie nationale, 1907), 398–9; Villot, *Etienne*, 151–2.

30 Petit, *Organisation des colonies*, 195.

M

31 Ibid, 196.
32 Ronald Robinson and John Gallagher, *Africa and the Victorians* (London: 1961), 389.
33 George Taubman Goldie to Lord Frederick Lugard, London, 24 July 1894, as found in Margery Perham and Mary Bull, eds, *The Diaries of Lord Lugard*, vol 4, *Nigeria* (Evanston, Illinois: Northwestern University Press, 1963), 58.
34 Ibid.
35 Brunschwig, *Mythes et réalités*, 116–17.
36 Betts, *Assimilation and Association*, 6. Percher, or Harry Alis, has not been the subject of a detailed study. Alis, perhaps one of the most important colonialists, was a master propagandist. His positions on colonial matters reflected the views of the militant annexationists. His successor was Robert de Caix who was as articulate as Alis, and who became famous for his articles in the *Bulletin* on French designs in Morocco. For more information on Alis and the *Comité* see George N. Sanderson, *England, Europe, and the Upper Nile 1882–1899* (Edinburgh: 1965), 118–19.
37 Jan Stengers, 'Correspondance de Leopold II avec van Eetvelde', *Academic Royale des Sciences d'outre-mer*, XXIV (1953), 477–80, 483–5.
38 Ibid, 481, 486.

Chapter 3   THE OPENING OF AFRICA 1890–2
(pages 37–51)

 1 Villot, *Etienne*, 69; Etienne served through several ministries while at Rue Saint-Florentin. He was appointed by Pierre Tirard in February 1889 and served during the de Freycinet ministry which came to power in March 1890. The de Freycinet ministry fell in February 1892. Jean Jolly, ed, *Dictionnaire des parlementaires français*, I (Paris: 1960), 37–9.
 2 Henri Brunschwig, *L'avènement de l'Afrique noire du XIXᵉ siècle à nos jours* (Paris: 1963), 135.
 3 Brunschwig, *Mythes et réalités*, 118–19.
 4 Eugène-Melchior de Vogüé, 'Les Indes Noires: L'Europe et la France en Afrique', *Revue des Deux Mondes*, LX (November 1890), 74, 76.
 5 The irritation of the French colonialists over the 1890 agreements was long-lasting. As late as 1899, in the wake of the Fashoda crisis, Etienne was still complaining about the Zanzibar protectorate. Etienne, *Son oeuvre*, I, 312.
 6 'La convention franco-anglais du Août 5, 1890', *Bulletin* 8 no 1 (January 1898), 10–11; Petit, *Organisation des colonies*, I, 16–17, 19.
 7 Speech by Paul Crampel before the Comité as quoted in Fernand Rouget, *L'expansion coloniale au Congo français* (Paris: 1906), 138–9.
 8 Ibid, 139.
 9 Letter from de Brazza to Etienne, Libreville, 18 April 1891, as

quoted in M. A. Menier, 'La Marche au Tchad', *Bulletin de l'Institut des Etudes Centrafricaines* (NS 5, 1953), 10–11.

10 Charles de Maistre, 'La mission Congo-Niger', *Academie des Sciences coloniales*, 21 June 1933, 136.

11 Letter from Alis to de Maistre, Paris, 20 August 1891, as quoted in Ibid, 138.

12 Letter from de Brazza to Etienne, Libreville, 30 July 1891, as quoted in Ibid, 9.

13 Letter from d'Arenberg to Dybowski, Paris, 30 December 1891, as quoted in ibid, 140–1.

14 Instructions from Etienne to Dybowski as quoted in ibid, 143–4.

15 Ibid, 144.

16 Etienne, *Son oeuvre*, I, 81–2.

17 Ibid, 85.

18 Ibid, 92.

19 Ibid.

20 Petit, *Organisation des colonies*, I, 228–9.

21 Ibid.

22 Ibid.

23 Ibid.

24 Entry in Lord Lugard's Diary for 19 September 1894, as quoted in Perham, *Diaries of Lord Lugard*, IV, 107.

25 Brunschwig, *L'avènement de l'Afrique*, 176–7.

26 Sir George Goldie to Lord Lugard, London, 2 July 1894, as quoted in Perham, *Diaries of Lord Lugard*, IV, 52.

27 On 3 May 1890, Etienne issued a decree uniting the French Congo and Gabon into an area named the French Congo. The commissioner headed the executive department which had its capital in Brazzaville on the Congo River. The commissioner was appointed by the undersecretary in Paris. Petit, *Organisation des colonies*, II, 38–9.

28 Ibid, 567.

29 Ibid. Lord Lugard related that by the Act of Brussels, signed in 1890, the states of Europe who were participating in the opening of Africa were prohibited from arming the natives with rapid-firing rifles. A local official in Nigeria 'promised 10 guns. After all they are the very worse and most rotten class of flint locks . . . less dangerous than poisoned bows and arrows. The Brussels Act does not prohibit flintlocks.' Entry for 21 September 1894, as quoted in Perham, *Diaries of Lord Lugard*, IV, 109.

30 Etienne, *Son oeuvre*, I, 104–5.

31 Petit, *Organisation des colonies*, I, 457.

32 Ibid, 476.

33 Etienne, *Son oeuvre*, I, 174–5.

34 R. Jeaugeon, 'Les sociétés d'exploitation au Congo et l'opinion française de 1890–1906', *Revue française d'histoire d'outre-mer*, XLVIII (1961), 353–5.

35   Ibid, 354–6.
36   Etienne, *Son oeuvre*, I, 111–12.
37   Ibid. The formation of the *Tirailleurs annamites* and of the *Tirailleurs tonkinois* was done by decrees before Etienne's term at the Rue Saint-Florentin. However, Etienne reinforced these units by the decrees of 2 February and 26 June 1890. These forces were never able to cope with the rising tide of anarchy, and troops as well as Legionnaires had to be sent into Indochina in ever-increasing numbers. Petit, *Organisation des colonies*, II, 461–2.
38   André Maurois, *Lyautey* (New York: 1931), 73–4.
39   Commandant de Porter, *La question du Touat Sahara algérien* (Alger: 1891), 59.
40   Ibid, 60.
41   'Le conseil supérieur des colonies', *L'Illustration*, 31 January 1891, 118.
42   Petit, *Organisation des colonies*, I, 176–7.
43   'Le conseil', *L'Illustration*, 118.
44   Ibid.
45   Rouget, *L'expansion coloniale au Congo*, 39–40.
46   Ibid, 40.
47   Etienne, *Son oeuvre*, I, 176.
48   Ibid.
49   Ibid, 190.
50   Raymond Ronze, *La question d'Afrique* (Paris: 1918), 228.
51   Harry Alis, *Nos africains* (Paris: 1894), 552, as quoted in Rouget, *L'expansion coloniale au Congo*, 143.
52   Etienne, *Son oeuvre*, I, 156.
53   Ibid, 180–1.
54   Ibid, 181.

Chapter 4   THE EMERGENCE OF THE COLONIALISTS 1892–6
(pages 52–68)

1   Villot, *Etienne*, 70.
2   Hanotaux to Etienne, Paris, 12 March 1892, *Etienne Correspondence*, letter number 20.
3   Betts, *Assimilation and Association*, 7
4   Villot, *Etienne*, 70–1.
5   Jacques Chastenet, *La troisième république* (Paris: 1955), 266.
6   Etienne, *Son oeuvre*, I, 200.
7   Ibid, 201.
8   Sir Arthur Hardinge, *A Diplomatist in the East* (London: nd), 107.
9   Dispatch from Lucien Labosse to Gabriel Hanotaux, Zanzibar, 26 November 1894, #57, France. Ministère des Affaires étrangères, Archives diplomatique, *Correspondance Politique*, Paris, Tome Zanzibar, 19.

10 Lord Kimberley to Lord Dufferin, London, 13 January 1895, #26, Foreign Office Archives 403/201, PRO, Africa, Public Record Office, London.

11 Dufferin to Kimberley, Paris, 15 January 1895, #30, FO 403/222, PRO, Africa.

12 Hardinge, *Diplomatist*, 123.

13 Dispatch from Baron de Courcel to Baron d'Esteurnelles de Constant, London, 21 November 1894, #426 MdA, Tome 899.

14 James J. Cooke, 'Madagascar and Zanzibar: A Case Study in African Colonial Friction, 1894–1897', *African Studies Review*, XIII, 3 (December 1970), 435–44.

15 Pilkington to his father, Cambridge, 3 November 1889 as quoted in Charles Harford-Battersby, *Pilkington of Uganda* (New York: 1899), 53.

16 F. D. Lugard, *The Rise of Our East African Empire: Early Efforts in Nyasaland and Uganda*, II (London: reprinted 1968), 64–6.

17 Hardinge, *Diplomatist*, 123

18 Dispatch from Lord Dufferin to Lord Kimberley, Paris, 27 November 1894, #11b, FO 403/222 PRO, Africa.

19 Dispatch from Sauzier, Representative in Madagascar, to Lord Kimberley, Tamatave, 6 November 1894, #14, FO 403/222 PRO Africa.

20 Dispatch from Blanchon, French Consul in Zanzibar to Hanotaux, Zanzibar, 20 August 1894, #36, MdA, Tome Zanzibar, 19.

21 Dispatch from Hanotaux to Gues, French Consul in Aden, 6 February 1895, MdA, Tome Angleterre, Aden 1885–95, 113.

22 Hanotaux to de Courcel, Paris, 5 May 1895, #124, MdA, Tome Angleterre, 904; Hanotaux to de Courcel, Paris, 30 May 1895, ibid.

23 Hardinge, *Diplomatist*, 108.

24 Ibid.

25 Etienne, *Son oeuvre*, I, 473–4.

26 Ibid, 478–9.

27 Ibid, 226.

28 Ibid, II, 88–9.

29 Eugène Etienne, 'Préface' to Marquis de Segonzac, *Voyages au Maroc 1899–1901* (Paris: 1903), iv; Villot, *Etienne*, 226, 267.

30 De Porter, *La question du Touat*, 59–60.

31 The question of a French Consul and the recognition of Abdel Aziz in connection with Etienne and the colonialists will be discussed fully in Chapters 7–9.

32 Maximilien de la Martinière, *Souvenirs du Maroc: Voyages et missions 1882–1918* (Paris: 1920), 49–50; 'La frontière Marocaine du sud Oranais', *Nouvelle Revue*, 77 (July–August 1892), 831–3.

33 'Pays indepedants: Maroc', *Bulletin* 5, no 9 (September 1895), 283. Louis Sevin-Desplaces, 'La mission Monteil et al politique de la

France en Afrique du Nord', *Nouvelle Revue*, 81 (March 1893), 138–41.

34 'Colonies françaises: Algérie', *Bulletin* 5, no 10 (October 1895), 299.

35 For more on Delcassé and the administration of the colonies see: Marcel Blanchard, 'Théophile Delcassé au Pavillon de Flore 1893–1894', *Le Monde française* XII (1949), 3–34.

36 Rouget, *L'expansion coloniale au Congo*, 610.

37 Etienne, *Son oeuvre*, I, 228–9.

38 Joseph Chailley-Bert, *Dix années de politique coloniale* (Paris: 1902), 126.

39 Joseph Chailley-Bert, 'Le ministère des colonies', *Revue des deux mondes*, 122 (April 1894), 916.

40 Betts, *Assimilation and Association*, 48–9.

41 Chailley-Bert, *Dix années*, 126.

42 Jeaugeon, 'Les sociétés d'exploitation au Congo', 355–8.

43 Ibid.

44 Chailley-Bert, 'Le ministère', 908–12.

45 Betts, *Assimilation and Association*, 51.

46 Chailley-Bert, *Dix années*, 130–1.

47 Rouget, *L'expansion coloniale au Congo*, 426–7.

48 Blanchard, 'Delcassé', 9–14.

49 Marcel Blanchard, 'Français et Belges sur l'Oubanghi, 1890–1896', *Revue français d'histoire d'outre-mer*, XXXIV (1950), 13.

50 Ibid.

51 Letter from Mizon to Lebon, Paris, 6 July 1895, Carton Afrique III, 17 a et b; Arch FdOM.

52 Letter from Mizon to Flint, Sudan, 14 March 1893, Correspondance de vaisseau Mizon, vol 10726, Nouvelle acquisitions française, Bibliothèque nationale, letter 8.

53 Letter from Mizon to Delcassé, Sudan, 14 March 1893, ibid, letter 9.

54 Letter from Mizon to Flint, Sudan, nd, ibid, letter 17.

55 Letter from Mizon to Flint, Sudan, 6 May 1893, ibid, letter 19.

56 Blanchard, 'Delcassé', 12–15.

57 Mizon to Delcassé, Sudan, 24 May 1893, *Mizon Correspondence*, letter 25.

58 Dispatch from Mizon to Chabredier, Sudan, 12 August 1893, ibid, letter 71.

59 Robinson and Gallagher, *Africa and the Victorians*, 392.

60 Letter from Mizon to Wallace, Sudan, 13 August 1893, *Mizon Correspondence*, letter 76.

61 Blanchard, 'Français et Belges', 13.

62 'Côte d'Ivoire', *Bulletin* 5, no 3 (March 1895), 83.

63 'Dahomey: le budget de la colonie', ibid.

64 Ibid.

65 Chailley-Bert, *Dix années*, 126.

66 Etienne, *Son oeuvre*, I, 489.

67 'Colonies françaises: Dahomey', *Bulletin* 5, no 12 (December 1895), 364.
68 Louis Sevin-Desplaces, 'La politique Franco-Africaine', *Nouvelle Revue*, 84 (October 1893), 638–9.
69 Chailley-Bert, *Dix années*, 8–9.
70 Louis Liotard, 'Préface' to F. Foureau, *Mission saharienne Foureau-Lamy: D'Alger au Congo par le Tchard* (Paris: 1902), 7.
71 Sevin-Desplaces, 'La mission Monteil', 138. Sevin-Desplaces, 'La politique Franco-Africaine', 632.
72 Captain Monteil to André Lebon, Paris, 7 March 1894, as found in Carton Afrique III 19a, Archives de l'ex Ministère de la France d'Outre-Mer; Rue Oudinot, Paris, France.
73 Thomas M. Iiams, Jr, *Dreyfus, Diplomatists and the Dual Alliance: Gabriel Hanotaux at the Quai d'Orsay (1894–1898)* (Paris: 1962), 150.
74 Entry for 10 March 1895, as found in Gabriel Hanotaux, 'Carnets', *La Revue des deux mondes*, April 1948, 402.
75 Sevin-Desplaces, 'La politique Franco-Africaine', 632.

Chapter 5 COLONIAL PROBLEMS IN MOROCCO AND WEST AFRICA 1894–8 (pages 69–80)

1 Petit, *Organisation des colonies*, II, 567.
2 For an early survey of border affairs see 'La frontière morocaine du Sud Oranais', *Nouvelle Revue*, 77 (July-August 1892), 830–7; for a more recent article on the border problem see Anthony S. Reyner, 'Morocco's International Boundaries: A Factual Background', *The Journal of Modern African Studies*, 1 (September 1962), 313–26.
3 Hanotaux came to the Quai d'Orsay on 30 May 1894, in the second cabinet of Charles Dupuy. Jean Jolly, ed, *Dictionnaire des parlementaires français*, 44.
4 Dispatch from Hanotaux to d'Aubigny, Paris, 12 June 1894, number 41, MdA, Tome Maroc 70, 41.
5 Dispatch from Hanotaux to d'Aubigny, Paris, 12 June 1894, number 40, MdA, ibid, 39–40.
6 Etienne, *Son oeuvre*, I, 242–3.
7 Ibid, 482–4.
8 Dispatch from Hanotaux to d'Aubigny, Paris, 12 June 1894, MdA, Tome Espange 924, 201–3; it took several months for France, England, and Spain to extend de jure recognition to Abdel Aziz. The length of time weakened the young sultan.
9 Sevin-Desplaces, 'La politique Franco-Africaine', 629.
10 Etienne, *Son oeuvre*, I, 242–3.
11 Dispatch from Hanotaux to M. Franc of the Tangier legation, Paris, 18 June 1894, MdA, Tome Maroc 70, 74.
12 Dispatch from Hanotaux to d'Aubigny, Paris, 18 June 1894, MdA, ibid, 85.

13 Dispatch from Hanotaux to d'Aubigny, Paris, 18 June 1894, MdA, ibid, 54.

14 Dispatch from Roustan, Ambassador to Madrid, to Hanotaux, Madrid, 4 July 1894, MdA, ibid, 309–10.

15 Telegram from d'Aubigny to Hanotaux, Tangier, 6 July 1894, MdA, ibid, 175–7.

16 Betts, *Assimilation and Association*, 6.

17 Brunschwig, *Mythes et réalités*, 124–9.

18 The *Mahkzen* was the governmental establishment of Morocco. Growing out of the tribal leadership, this institution became the most powerful organisation in the western Maghrib prior to the French occupation in 1912.

19 Dispatch from Phipps to Kimberley, Paris, 12 September 1894, #157, FO 413/222, PRO, Africa.

20 Dispatch from de Monbel to Hanotaux, Tangier, 16 September 1894, MdA, Tome Maroc 70, 71.

21 Etienne, *Son oeuvre*, I, 483.

22 Dispatch from Phipps to Kimberley, Paris, 18 September 1894, FO 413/222, PRO, Africa.

23 Dispatch from Hanotaux to de Mombel, Paris, 9 November 1894, MdA, Tome Maroc 70, 253–5.

24 De Courcel to de Reverseaux, London, 27 November 1894, MdA, Tome Angleterre 899, 161–2.

25 Dispatch from de Reverseaux to Hanotaux, Madrid, 2 February 1895, Tome Espange 926, 59.

26 Dispatch from de Reverseaux to Hanotaux, Madrid, 18 February 1895, ibid, 80–1.

27 Hanotaux wanted Paul Cambon to accept the portfolio of the Quai d'Orsay. He urged Dupuy to offer it to Cambon rather than to himself. Entry for 13 February 1895, Hanotaux, 'Carnets', 390.

28 Dispatch from Paul Cambon to Hanotaux, London, 6 March 1895, MdA, Tome 905, 182–4.

29 Dufferin to Hanotaux, Paris, 22 June 1895, MdA, ibid, 182–4.

30 Jules Cambon to Louis Barthou, Algiers, 30 November 1895, as found in France, Archive nationale, *Series F80*, *Algérie*, Paris, Carton 1698. Both Paul and Jules Cambon began their brilliant diplomatic careers in the colonial service. The Cambon brothers were part of that colonialist group which included Gabriel Hanotaux, Théophile Delcassé, Eugène Etienne, and Charles Jonnart, who became governor general of Algeria. Paul Cambon was the resident in Tunis before Jules Cambon accepted the governor generalship of Algeria. Confer, *France and Algeria*, 40–1.

31 Etienne, *Son oeuvre*, I, 485–91.

32 The colonialists had great faith in Jules Cambon, the governor general of Algeria. In fact, Cambon did not hesitate to send troops into the Oranais without the agreement of Louis Barthou, the Minister

of the Interior. In 1896–7 Barthou was won over to the cause of militant action and joined with Etienne many times to defend Algeria's interests before the Chamber.

33 Minute from Hanotaux to Baron d'Estournelles de Constant, Paris, 28 October 1894, MdA, Tome 898, 291.

34 Minute from d'Estournelles de Constant to Hanotaux, Paris, 31 October 1894, MdA, ibid, 331.

35 Dispatch from Delcassé to the Governor General of the Sudan, Paris, nd, Carton Soudan VI, 1; Arch FdOM.

36 Lord Dufferin to Hanotaux, Paris, 20 January 1895, MdA, Tome 900, 138–9.

37 Etienne's long speech came during an interpellation on foreign affairs. See Etienne, Son oeuvre, I, 227–43. In 1888 Galliéni, who influenced Etienne's colonial policy a great deal, felt that the British were 'adversaries' in western Africa. Galliéni worried about the possible subversion of France's colonies by Britain. Galliéni to Etienne, Niagassola, 16 January 1888, Etienne Correspondence, letter number 5. For a good survey of Etienne's militant African policy see Sevin-Desplaces, 'La politique Franco-Africaine', 627–32.

38 Hanotaux's policies have been well discussed in several works. For his African policy as it concerns Great Britain and western Africa see Alf Heggoy, 'The Colonial Policies of Gabriel Hanotaux in Africa, 1894–1898' (PhD diss, Duke University, 1963), 120–57; Iiams, Dreyfus, Diplomatists, 36–49.

39 Minute from Félix Chautempts to Hanotaux, Paris, 23 March 1895, Carton Afrique IV, 125a; Arch FdOM.

40 Dispatch from de Courcel to Hanotaux, London, 11 July 1895, MdA, Tome 905, 304–5.

41 André Lebon to Louis Barthou, Paris, 29 September 1896, Series F80, Carton 1969.

42 Note from Jules Méline on a report by Jules Cambon, Paris, 21 July 1896, ibid, Carton 1684. Jules Méline organised his cabinet on 29 April 1896. It fell on 15 June 1898 in the aftermath of the Fashoda affair. Jolly, Dictionnaire des parlementaires, 48–9.

43 Dispatch from Jules Cambon to Hanotaux, Algiers, 21 July 1896, ibid, Carton 1684.

44 Note from General Billot to Barthou, Paris, 20 August 1896, ibid, Carton 1684.

45 Jules Cambon to General Billot, Algiers, 8 September 1896, ibid, Carton 1695.

46 In fact, Hanotaux lost the respect of Jules and Paul Cambon by 1898. See Christopher Andrew, Théophile Delcassé and the Making of the Entente Cordiale: A Reappraisal of French Foreign Policy 1898–1905 (New York: 1968), 75–6.

47 Louis Barthou was one of Hanotaux's closest friends. Barthou was one of the few men with whom he used the familiar tu.

48 Hanotaux to Barthou, Paris, 16 November 1896, *Series F80*, Carton 1695.

49 Barthou to Méline, Paris, 14 January 1897, ibid, Carton 1684.

50 Dispatch from Cambon to Méline, Algiers, 24 May 1897, ibid, Carton 1684.

51 Dispatch from Cambon to Méline, Algiers, 28 May 1897, ibid, Carton 1684.

52 Undated minute by Méline, Paris, ibid, Carton 1684.

53 Hanotaux to Barthou, Paris, 10 December 1897, ibid, Carton 1698.

54 Etienne's remarks on the In Salah and Oranais action came in the Chamber in July 1900. See Etienne, *Son oeuvre*, I, 509–16.

55 Ba Ahmed remained a force until his death in 1901. After his Vizier's death, Abdel Aziz decided to rule alone. He came to lean heavily on European, non-Muslim advisers, and his authority declined. See Barbour, *North West Africa*, 88–9; Miège, *Le Maroc*, 40.

56 'Pays independants: Maroc', *Bulletin* 8, no 1 (January 1898), 30.

57 Paul Bourde to Etienne, Paris, 27 October 1898. *Etienne Correspondence*, letter number 36.

58 Etienne, *Son oeuvre*, II, 87–8.

59 Dispatch from Edouard Laferriere, Governor General of Algeria, to Louis Barthou, Minister of the Interior, Algiers, 26 April 1899, *Series F80*, Carton 1696.

60 Note from de Brazza to Barthou, Paris, 29 May 1899, ibid, Carton 1733.

61 'Pays indépendants: Maroc', *Bulletin* 9, no 2 (December 1899), 429.

Chapter 6 THE FRENCH COLONIALISTS AND FASHODA
1894–8   (pages 81–97)

1 Entry for 13 February 1895, Hanotaux, 'Carnets', 389–95; Iiams, *Dreyfus, Diplomatists*, 24–5; for the membership of the cabinet of Charles Dupuy see Jolly, *Dictionnaire des parlementaires*, 44.

2 Dispatch from Sir Francis Plunkett to Kimberley, Brussels, 2 June 1894, FO 403/201, PRO, Africa.

3 In July 1898 Monson, commenting on Delcassé's acceptance of the portfolio of the Ministry of Foreign Affairs, stated, 'For the moment the only important personage . . . is Delcassé, and I cannot say that his antecedents at the Ministry of Colonies inspire me with any other expectation than that HM Government will find him a very combative Minister.' Dispatch from Monson to Salisbury, Paris, 1 July 1898, as found in G. P. Gooch and Harold Temperley, *British Documents on the Origins of the War 1898–1914*, I (London: 1927), 158.

4 Entry for 10 March 1895, Hanotaux, 'Carnets', 402; Andrew, *Delcassé*, 36.

5 William I. Langer, *European Alliances and Alignments 1871–1890* (New York: 1957), 251–85.

6 Letter from Mizon to André Lebon, Paris, 6 July 1895, Carton Afrique III, 17 a et b, FdOM.

7 Sevin-Desplaces, 'La politique Franco-Africaine', 627.

8 See Pierre Renouvin, 'Les orgins d l'expedition de Fachoda', *Revue historique*, 200 (1948), 180–97.

9 Blanchard, 'Delcassé', 16.

10 Blanchard, 'Français et Belges', 16.

11 Ibid, 19. Also see letter from Monteil to Delcassé, Ubangui Posts, 7 March 1894, as found in Carton Afrique III 19a, FdOM.

12 Hanotaux, in 1894, devoted a great deal of time to preparing for the mission even though he had some personal reservations. See note from Hanotaux to the British Government, Paris, 6 August 1894, France, Ministère des Affaires Etrangères, *Documents Diplomatiques Françaises 1871–1914*, 1 sér, XI (Paris: 1947), 333–5.

13 Etienne, *Son oeuvre*, I, 242–3.

14 Rouget, *L'expansion coloniale au Congo*, 75: Louis Seven-Desplaces, 'La mission Monteil et la politique de la France en Afrique du Nord', *Nouvelle Revue*, 81 (March, 1893), 138–41.

15 Andrew, *Delcassé*, 43.

16 Blanchard, 'Français et Belges', 15.

17 Ibid, 16.

18 Blanchard, 'Delcassé', 31.

19 Ibid.

20 Dispatch from Lord Dufferin to Kimberley, Paris, 30 June 1894, #18, FO 403/202, PRO, Africa. For a recent study of Britain's policies in Egypt and the Sudan see Denis Judd, *Balfour and the British Empire: A Study in Imperial Evolution 1874–1932* (New York: 1968).

21 Iiams, *Dreyfus, Diplomatists*, 26.

22 Dispatch from Kimberley to Dufferin, London, 17 July 1894, #36, FO 403/202, PRO, Africa.

23 Andrew, *Delcassé*, 30–1.

24 J. A. S. Grenville, *Lord Salisbury and Foreign Policy: The Close of the Nineteenth Century* (London: 1964), 19.

25 Joseph Chamberlain to Salisbury, Highbury, England, 6 June 1897, Joseph Chamberlain Papers, University of Birmingham, Birmingham, England, JC 11/6, 204.

26 Dispatch from Lord Cromer to Salisbury, Cairo, 26 February 1898, #298, FO 633/6, PRO, Africa.

27 Confidential dispatch from Salisbury to Chamberlain, London, 17 September 1897, Chamberlain Papers, JC 5/7.

28 Dispatch from Plunkett to Kimberley, Brussels, 10 June 1894, #148, FO 403/201, PRO, Africa. For Etienne's speech on the Ubangui project see Etienne, *Son oeuvre*, I, 227–43.

29 André Lebon, 'La mission Marchand et le cabinet Méline', *Revue des deux mondes*, 70 (March–April 1900), 275.

30 Salisbury to Cromer, London, 1 April 1896, #173, FO 403/201. PRO, Africa.

31 In August 1894, in a secret dispatch, Plunkett informed Kimberley that he had access to secret information from the Belgian Foreign Office. Dispatch from Plunkett to Kimberley, Brussels, 4 August 1894, #61, FO 403/202, PRO, Africa.

32 Dispatch from Plunkett to Salisbury, Brussels, 6 September 1896, #56, FO 403/237, PRO, Africa.

33 Monteil to Delcassé, Ubangui Posts, 7 March 1894, Carton Afrique III 19a, FdOM; Iiams, *Dreyfus, Diplomatists*, 46.

34 From Monteil to André Lebon, Ubangui territory, 7 March 1894, as found in Carton Afrique III 190, FdOM.

35 From Monteil to Captain Decazes, Ubangui territory, 26 August 1894 as found in Carton Afrique III, 19c, ibid.

36 Lebon, 'Mission Marchand', 277.

37 Letter from Marchand to Liotard, Brazzaville, 17 November 1896, as found in Marc Michel (ed), 'Deux lettres de Marchand à Liotard', *Revue française d'histoire d'Outre-Mer*, LII (1965), 54.

38 Ibid, 50.

39 Letter from Marchand to Liotard, Zenga, [a post on the Ubangui] 5 April 1897, as found in ibid, 71, 80.

40 Charles Mangin to Madame Joseph Menard, Rafi, Sudan, as quoted in Charles Mangin, 'Lettres de la mission Marchand 1895–1898', *Revue des deux mondes* (15 September 1931), 246–7.

41 Memorandum from the Intelligence Division to Salisbury, Cairo, 27 October 1896, FO 403/237, PRO, Africa.

42 Etienne, *Son oeuvre*, II, 60.

43 Salisbury to Chamberlain, London, 18 November 1897, Chamberlain Papers, JC 5/7.

44 Sanderson, *England, Europe, and the Upper Nile*, 113.

45 On 1 November 1895, Léon Bourgeois formed a cabinet. Hanotaux was replaced by Bourgeois, and the portfolio of Colonies was given to Pierre Guieysse. Hanotaux was returned to the Quai d'Orsay on 29 April 1896, in the cabinet of Jules Méline. André Lebon became Minister of Colonies. Jolly, *Dictionnaire des parlementaires*, 47–8. The dispatching of the Marchand mission by Guieysse is recorded in Lebon, 'Mission Marchand', 275–8.

46 Pierre Renouvin, 'Les origines de l'expédition de Fachoda', *Revue histoique*, 200 (1948), 180–97.

47 Salisbury to Cromer, London, 24 December 1896, FO 633/7, PRO, Africa.

48 Private dispatch from Salisbury to Chamberlain, London, 13 December 1896, Chamberlain Papers, JC 5/7.

49 Dispatch from Geoffray, French chargé d'affaires in London, to Hanotaux, London, 17 May 1898, as found in France, *Documents diplomatiques*, 288–93.

50 Dispatch from Colonel Frederick Adam to Salisbury, Brussels, 2 January 1897, 2, FO #403/252, PRO, Africa.
51 Salisbury to Cromer, London, 12 February 1898, #186, FO 633/7, PRO, Africa.
52 Grenville, *Lord Salisbury*, 218.
53 The Etienne articles in *Le Temps* mainly dealt with the commercial companies, but from the tone it is easy to gather that he had changed his once hostile attitude toward England. Eugène Etienne, 'Les compagnies de colonisation', *Le Temps*, September 1897; Etienne, *Son oeuvre*, I, 17–54.
54 Chamberlain to Salisbury, London, 2 June 1898, Chamberlain Papers, JC 11/6, 218.
55 Salisbury wanted Marchand to withdraw without a great deal of fanfare or confusion. Dispatch from Salisbury to Cromer, London, 7 October 1898, Gooch and Temperley, *British Documents*, I, 176.
56 Lebon, 'Mission Marchand', 295–6.
57 Dispatch from Hanotaux to Cogordan, Paris, 21 June 1898, France, *Documents diplomatiques*, vol 16, 351.
58 Ministerial note from Georges Trouillot to Delcassé, Paris, 4 July 1898, ibid, 363–7; Paul Bourde to Etienne, Paris, 27 October 1898, *Etienne Correspondence*, letter number 36.
59 Dispatch from Geoffray to Delcassé, London, 9 August 1898, *Documents diplomatiques*, vol 16, 442–3.
60 Dispatch from Sir Edmund Monson to Salisbury, Paris, 4 August 1898, Gooch and Temperley, *British Documents*, I, 161–2.
61 Charles Mangin to Madame Henri Suquet, Fashoda, 9 October 1898, Mangin, 'Lettres de la mission', 266–8.
62 Dispatch from Geoffray to Delcassé, London, 25 August 1898, France, *Documents diplomatiques*, 480.
63 Etienne, *Son oeuvre*, II, 78.
64 Marchand to Etienne, Fashoda, 11 December 1898, *Etienne Correspondence*, letter number 40.
65 Ibid.
66 Robert de Caix, 'La question de Fachoda', *Bulletin* 8, no 10 (October 1898), 320.
67 Dispatch from Delcassé to Geoffray, Paris, 8 September 1898, France, *Documents diplomatiques*, 520–1.
68 Telegram from Salisbury to Delcassé, London, 9 September 1898, ibid, 529.
69 Dispatch from Geoffray to Delcassé, London, 12 September 1898, ibid, 543.
70 Andrew, *Delcassé*, 87–8. Delcassé's interest in naval problems continued. He served as Secretary of the Navy in three cabinets: the cabinet of Ernest Monis from 2 March 1911, to the Caillaux cabinet of 27 June 1911. Delcassé also maintained the portfolio of the Marine

in the cabinet of Raymond Poincaré which began on 14 January 1912. Jolly, *Dictionnaire des parlementaires*, 60–2.

71 Auguste Terrier, 'Les relations entre la France et l'Angleterre', *Bulletin* 9, no 2 (February 1899), 45.

72 Robert de Caix, *Fachoda, la France et l'Angleterre* (Paris: 1899), 320.

73 Etienne, *Son oeuvre*, I, 277–8.

74 Robert de Caix, 'Les relations franco-anglaises', *Bulletin* 9, no 3 (March 1899), 84.

75 Dispatch from de Courcel to Delcassé, London, 10 October 1898, France, *Documents diplomatiques*, 631–2.

76 Andrew, *Delcassé*, 112–13.

77 Dispatch from Paul Cambon to Delcassé, London, 10 December 1898, France, *Documents diplomatiques*, 864–6: Salisbury noted Cambon's conciliatory tone during these first official meetings. Dispatch from Salisbury to Monson, London, 11 January 1899, Gooch and Temperley, *British Documents*, I, 197–8.

78 Grenville, *Lord Salisbury*, 232.

79 Robert de Caix, 'L'accord franco-anglais', *Bulletin* 14, no 4 (April 1904), 107. Andrew, *Delcassé*, 103–4; Sanderson, *England, Europe, and the Upper Nile*, 376–7.

80 Sir Harry Johnston, *The Story of My Life* (Indianapolis: 1923), 332–3.

81 Ibid, 332–3. The arrival of the British prince in Paris was important because he was in favour of an alliance between England and France. Andrew, *Delcassé*, 194–5.

Chapter 7 THE OCCUPATION OF TUAT 1900–3
(pages 98–106)

1 Dispatch from de la Martinière to Delcassé, Tangier, 28 March 1900, *Series F80*, Carton 1698.

2 Delcassé to Waldeck-Rousseau, Paris, 23 June 1900, ibid, Carton 1696.

3 Georges Revoil to Delcassé, Tangier, 22 June 1900, ibid, Carton 1696.

4 Dispatch from General Grisot, CG of the XIXth Army Corps, to General André, Minister of War, Algiers, 1 September 1900, ibid, Carton 1696.

5 Delcassé to Waldeck-Rousseau, Paris, 7 December 1900, ibid, Carton 1696.

6 Etienne, *Son oeuvre*, II, 88.

7 'Pays indépendants: Maroc', *Bulletin* 10, no 1 (January 1900), 27.

8 Dispatch from Samuel R. Gummere to David Hill, Tangier, 9 March 1900, as found in United States, Department of State, *Dispatches from the US Consular Officials in Tangier* (Washington: 1962), roll 25.

9 Dispatch from Gummere to Hill, Tangier, 8 May 1900, ibid.

10 Mohammed Torres to Gummere, Tangier, 18 June 1900, ibid.

11 Etienne, *Son oeuvre*, I, 514–15.
12 Gummere to Hill, Tangier, 25 July 1900, United States, *Dispatches, Tangier*, roll 25.
13 Dispatch from de la Martinière to Delcassé, Tangier, 7 December 1900, as found in Carton Maroc 12, Dossier 95, Mission militaire au Maroc, année 1901, France, *Service Historique de l'Armée de terre, Section outre-mer*, Château de Vincennes (Val de Marne), Paris.
14 Burkhardt to General André, and to the Deuxième Bureau, Tangier, c 1900, ibid, Carton Maroc 12, Dossier 99.
15 Ibid.
16 Gummere to Hill, Tangier, 20 May 1901, United States, *Dispatches, Tangier*, roll 26.
17 Dispatch from Martinsen to Hill, Tangier, 9 August 1901, ibid.
18 Ibid.
19 Dispatch from Burkhardt to the War Ministry, Tangier, 30 August 1901, France, *Service Historique de l'Armée*, Carton Maroc 12, Dossier 99.
20 Burkhardt to the Deuxième Bureau, Marrakesh, 8 September 1901, ibid.
21 Etienne, *Son oeuvre*, I, 366–7.
22 Andrew, Delcassé, 198–9.
23 'Colonies françaises: Algérie', *Bulletin* 12, no 2 (Feburary 1902), 58.
24 'Pays indépendants: Maroc', ibid 12, no 4 (April 1902), 150.
25 The *Bled es Siba* was a section of Morocco in the hinterlands which was fairly free of *Mahkzen* control. It remained a centre of independence and dissidence for the Moroccan government. The area controlled by the government, usually near the larger cities and towns, was the *Bled es Mahkzen*.
26 Dispatch from Gummere to Hill, Tangier, 13 September 1902, United States, *Dispatches, Tangier*, roll 26.
27 Note from Delcassé to André, Paris, 3 December 1902, France, *Service Historique de l'Armée*, Carton Maroc 12, Dossier 95.
28 Etienne, 'Préface', de Segonzac, *Voyages au Maroc*, vi.
29 Hugo von Radolin to Baron von Holstein, Paris, 1 April 1903, as quoted in M. H. Fisher and Norman Rich, *The Holstein Papers, Correspondence 1897–1909*, IV (Cambridge: 1963), 274.
30 Etienne, *Son oeuvre*, I, 376–7.
31 Jonnart to Etienne, Algiers, c 1903, *Etienne Correspondence*, letter number 169.
32 Prince von Bulow to Wilhelm II, Berlin, c 1903, as quoted in Virginia Cowles, *The Kaiser* (New York: 1961), 208.
33 Jonnart to Etienne, Algiers, 20 May 1903, *Etienne Correspondence*, letter number 65.
34 Eugène Etienne, *Projet de loi ayant pour objet de l'éxploitation du Chemin du Fer à Beni Ounif* (Paris: Chambre des députés, Document 107, 8 June 1903), 1–3.

35 Jonnart to Etienne, Algiers, 18 June 1903, *Etienne Correspondence*, letter number 42.
36 Jonnart to Etienne, Algiers, 23 June 1903, ibid, letter number 43.
37 Tallandier to Etienne, Tangier, 31 July 1903, ibid, letter number 57.
38 Colonel Hubert Lyautey to Etienne, Ain Sefra, 28 October 1903, as quoted in Hubert Lyautey, *Vers le Maroc: Lettres du Sud Oranais 1903–1905* (Paris: 1937), 9.

Chapter 8 THE EUROPEAN IMPLICATIONS OF THE MOROC-CAN PROBLEM 1899–1904 (pages 107–17)

1 By the time of the constitution of the cabinet of Emile Combes on 7 June 1902, there were over two hundred deputies in the colonial party. Etienne was re-elected vice-president of the Chamber by a large vote. 'Colonies françaises: généralites', *Bulletin* 11, no 7 (July 1902), 266–7; Paul Bourde to Etienne, Paris, 27 October 1898, *Etienne Correspondence*, letter number 36.
2 Grenville, *Salisbury*, 427. Dispatch from Monson to Salisbury, Paris, 4 August 1898, Gooch and Temperley, *British Documents*, I, 161.
3 George W. Monger, *The End of Isolation: British Foreign Policy 1900–1907* (London: 1963), 19–20; Judd, *Balfour* 34–5. For an official picture see Memorandum by Sir Eyre Crowe, London, 1 January 1907, Gooch and Temperley, *British Documents*, I, 276–7.
4 Eugène Etienne, 'Colonial Litigation between France and England', *National Review*, July 1903, as quoted in Etienne, *Son oeuvre*, II, 204.
5 Paul Cambon to Delcassé, London, 2 July 1903, as found in Paul Cambon, *Correspondance 1870–1924*, ed Henri Cambon (Paris: 1924), II, 96–7.
6 Andrew, *Delcassé*, 107–10.
7 Jean Constans to Etienne, Constantinople, 13 February, 1899, *Etienne Correspondence*, letter number 22. For Delcassé's attitudes toward the Ottoman Empire see Andrew, *Delcassé*, 84–6, 233–7.
8 Jean Constans to Etienne, Constantinople, 19 December 1901, *Etienne Correspondence*, letter number 79.
9 Andrew, *Delcassé*, 84–5.
10 Delcassé to Etienne, Paris, 13 August 1904, *Etienne Correspondence*, letter number 46.
11 Etienne, *Son oeuvre*, I, 353–4; the Ethiopian railway from Adis Ababa to Jibouti, Somaliland was negotiated between England, France, and Ethiopia, The talks were completed by 1906.
12 'La France en Ethiopie', *Bulletin* 12, no 11 (November 1902), 378–9.
13 Joseph Galliéni to Etienne, Tananavaire, 31 January 1903, *Etienne Correspondence*, letter number 50.
14 Robert de Caix's resolutions, passed in February 1905, as quoted in the *Bulletin* 15, no 3 (March 1905), 104.
15 Robert de Caix's resolutions, passed in February 1905, as quoted in ibid 15, no 3 (March 1905), 105.

16 Grenville, *Salisbury*, 422–3.
17 E. A. Altham, Intelligence Division of the War Office, London, 'Military Needs of the Empire in a War with France and Russia', as found in Great Britain, Cabinet Documents, *Committee for Imperial Defence 1880–1914* (London: 1965), document 38/1, number 6, roll 1.
18 Ibid.
19 'The Strength of the Regular Army and Auxiliary Forces Having Regard to Peace and War Requirement', May 1904, Great Britain, *CID*, document 22a *Secret* number 40, roll 2.
20 A fuller discussion of this topic is found in note 3, supra [Chapter 8]. Also see Judd, *Balfour*, 19–20.
21 Monger, *End of Isolation*, 102–3.
22 Andrew, *Delcassé*, 180–1.
23 Marquis de Ramirez Villa-Urrutia, *Paleque diplomatico: Recuerdos de un Embajador*, I (Madrid: 1923), 80.
24 Auguste Terrier, 'Français et anglais autor du Tchad', *Bulletin* 12, no 3 (March 1902), 103.
25 Etienne, *Son oeuvre*, I, 367–8.
26 Emile Loubet to Etienne, Paris, 22 January 1902, *Etienne Correspondence*, letter number 61.
27 Andrew, *Delcassé*, 138.
28 Ibid, 198–9.
29 Etienne, 'Colonial Litigation', as quoted in Etienne, *Son oeuvre*, II, 204.
30 Ibid, 211–12.
31 Ibid, 217–19.
32 Andrew, *Delcassé*, 198–9.
33 Paul Cambon to Delcassé, London, 2 July 1903, Cambon, *Correspondance*, II, 96–7.
34 Eugène Etienne, 'Notre politique africaine (Algérie et Maroc)', *Questions diplomatiques et coloniales* (15 June 1903), as quoted in Etienne, *Son oeuvre*, II, 197–9.
35 Colonel Laperrine to Etienne, np, 8 July 1903, *Etienne Correspondence*, letter number 30.
36 Laperrine to Etienne, np, 11 August 1903, ibid, letter number 31.
37 Laperrine to Etienne, np, 30 December 1903, ibid, letter number 33. Laperrine gave the impression that de Foucauld was unwilling to aid the French. However, most of de Foucauld's biographers agree that he did in time assist the French military in the Sahara. See: Pierre Nord, *Charles de Foucauld: français d'Afrique* (Paris: 1957); Marion Mill Preminger, *Sands of Tamanrasset* (New York: 1963); Michel Carrouges, *Soldier of the Spirit: The Life of Charles de Foucauld* (New York: 1956); and also R. V. C. Bodley, *The Warrior Saint* (Boston: 1953).

38   Confer, *France and Algeria*, 59.

39   Charles Jonnart to Etienne, Algiers, c 1903, *Etienne Correspondence*, letter number 180.

40   Etienne, *Son oeuvre*, I, 386.

41   Lord Lansdowne to Sir Edmond Monson, London, 2 July 1903, Gooch and Temperley, *British Documents*, II, 292–3.

42   Paul Cambon to Delcassé, London, 2 July 1903, Cambon, *Correspondance*, II, 96–7.

43   Andrew, *Delcassé*, 199–201.

Chapter 9 THE IMPERIALISTS AND THE TANGIER CRISIS
        1904–5   (pages 118–36)

1   Jonnart to Etienne, Algiers, c 1904, *Etienne Correspondence*, letter number 172.

2   Jonnart to Etienne, Algiers, c 1904, ibid, letter number 181.

3   Jonnart to Etienne, Algiers, c 1904, ibid, letter number 184.

4   Captain Léon Jouinot-Gambetta to Etienne, Tangier, c 1904, ibid, letter number 54.

5   Mohammed Torres to Gummere, Tangier, 3 March 1904, United States, *Dispatches, Tangier*, roll 27.

6   Eugène Etienne, 'Notre Comité du Maroc', *Bulletin* 14, no 1 (January 1904), 3–4.

7   'Comité du Maroc', ibid, no 3 (March 1904), 76–7.

8   Etienne, *Son oeuvre*, II, 289–90.

9   Ibid, 293.

10   Jacques Caillé et François Charles Roux, *Missions diplomatiques françaises à Fes* (Paris: 1955), 151.

11   Paul Cambon talked a great deal with Lansdowne concerning Morocco. Cambon stressed that Delcassé wanted to take action in the western Maghrib only in accord with London. Lansdowne to Monson, London, 6 August 1902, Gooch and Temperley, *British Documents*, II, 264–5; Lansdowne to Monson, London, 15 October 1902, ibid, 269–70.

12   Robert de Caix, 'L'accord franco-anglais', *Bulletin* 14, no 4 (April 1904), 107.

13   Etienne, *Son oeuvre*, II, 290–1.

14   Lord Edward Grey, *Twenty-Five Years, 1892–1916*, I (New York: 1925), 50–1.

15   Eugène Etienne, 'La politique française au Maroc', *The National Review*, 1 August 1904, as quoted in Etienne, *Son oeuvre*, II, 314.

16   Prince von Radolin to Prince von Bulow, Paris, 20 October 1903, as quoted in Deutschland, Auswartiges Amt, *Die Grosse Politik der Europaischen Kabinette 1871–1914* (Berlin: 1924), 360.

17   Comte de Saint-Aulaire, *Confessions d'un vieux diplomate* (Paris: 1953), 124.

18   Kaiser Wilhelm II to Czar Nicholas II, Berlin, 27 October 1904, as

found in Herman Bernstein, ed, *The Willy-Nicky Correspondence* (New York: 1928), 69.

19 Saint-Aulaire, *Confessions*, 108.

20 'Pays indépendants: Maroc', *Bulletin* 14, no 1 (January 1904).

21 'Pays indépendants: Maroc', ibid, no 2 (February 1904), 58.

22 Lyautey to Etienne, Ain Sefra, 17 February 1904, Lyautey, *Vers le Maroc*, 37–8.

23 Gummere to Francis B. Loomis, Tangier, 14 March 1904, United States, *Dispatches, Tangier*, roll 27.

24 Letter from Jonnart to Etienne, Algiers, c 1903, *Etienne Correspondence*, letter number 180.

25 Speech by Lyautey, February 1904 as found in Hubert Lyautey, *Paroles d'Action—Madagascar, sud Oranais, Oran, Maroc 1900–1922* (Paris: 1927), 36–9.

26 Letter from Lyautey to Etienne, Ain Sefra, 17 February 1904 as found in Lyautey, *Vers le Maroc*, 37–8; Andrews, *Delcassé*, 261–3.

27 Etienne, *Son oeuvre*, II, 283–97.

28 Tallandier to Etienne, Tangier, 24 February 1904, *Etienne Correspondence*, letter number 59.

29 Lyautey to Etienne, Ain Sefra, 15 March 1904, Lyautey, *Vers le Maroc*, 42–3.

30 Jouinot-Gambetta to Etienne, Tangier, 16 April 1904, *Etienne Correspondence*, letter number 52.

31 Paul Cambon to Henri Cambon, London, 14 March 1904, Cambon, *Correspondence*, II, 128–9; Confidential dispatch from Lansdowne to Paul Cambon, London, 1 October 1903, Gooch and Temperley, *British Documents*, II, 311–14.

32 Sir Thomas Barclay, *Thirty Years: Anglo-French Reminiscences 1876–1906* (Boston: 1914), 280.

33 Grey, *Twenty-Five Years*, 50.

34 Ibid, 74–5; Monger, *End of Isolation*, 236.

35 Wilhelm II to von Bulow, Syracuse, Greece, 19 April 1904, as found in Bernhard von Bulow, *The Letters of Prince von Bulow 1903–1906*, trans Frederic Whyte (London: c 1930), 54.

36 Wilhelm II to Nicholas II, Berlin, 13 November 1904, Bernstein, *The Willy-Nicky Correspondence*, 85–8.

37 Wilhelm II to von Bulow, Syracuse, 19 April 1904, von Bulow, *Letters*, 54.

38 Robert de Caix, 'Après d'Accord', *Bulletin* 14, no 5 (May 1904), 144.

39 Eugène Etienne, 'Appel du Comité du Maroc', ibid, no 6 (June 1904), 175–6.

40 Lyautey to Etienne, Oran, 24 June 1904, Lyautey, *Vers le Maroc*, 76.

41 Joseph Chailley-Bert, 'La traité Franco-Anglais', *La Quinzaine Coloniale*, XV, 176 (April 1904), 249–51.

42 Robert de Caix, 'L'Accord Franco-anglais', *Bulletin* 12, no 4 (April 1904), 107–11.

43 Paul Cambon to Henri Cambon, London, 30 June 1904, Cambon, *Correspondence*, II, 144-5.

44 Eugène Etienne, 'L'oeuvre des comités coloniaux', *Bulletin* 14, no 7 (July 1904), 228.

45 Tallandier to Etienne, Tangier, 6 July 1904, *Etienne Correspondence*, letter number 60.

46 Lyautey to Etienne, Oran, 7 July 1904, Lyautey, *Vers le Maroc*, 77-9.

47 Secret dispatch, Etat-Major de l'Armée, Ière Bureau, 'Copie de la note secrété remise au département des affaires étrangères, le 23 Juillet, 1904', France, *Service Historique de l'Armée*, Carton Maroc D 1, Dossier 135.

48 Lyautey to Etienne, Oran, 31 July 1904, Lyautey, *Vers le Maroc*, 83.

49 Letter from Delcassé to Etienne, Paris, 13 August 1904, *Etienne Correspondence*, letter number 46.

50 Letter from Etienne to Delcassé, Paris, 16 August 1904, as cited in Andrew, *Delcassé*, 262.

51 Diary entry for 27 June 1904, as found in Maurice Paléologue, *The Turning Point: Three Critical Years 1904-1906* (London: 1935), 94.

52 Marquis de Segonzac to Etienne, Tangier, 6 August 1904, *Etienne Correspondence*, letter number 64.

53 Lyautey to Etienne, Ain Sefra, 6 August 1904, Lyautey, *Vers le Maroc*, 86-7.

54 Lyautey to Etienne, Ain Sefra, 8 August 1904, ibid, 93.

55 Tallandier to Etienne, Tangier, 12 September 1904, *Etienne Correspondence*, letter number 62.

56 Ibid.

57 Dispatch from Sir Edmond Monson to Lord Lansdowne, *British Documents*, III, 54-5.

58 Delcassé to Etienne, Paris, 13 August 1904, *Etienne Correspondence*, letter number 46.

59 Saint-Aulaire to Etienne, Tangier, 9 October 1904, ibid, letter number 46.

60 Paul Cambon to Henri Cambon, London, 8 October 1904, Cambon, *Correspondance*, II, 164-5.

61 Villa-Urrutia, *Palique Diplomatico*, I, 80-2.

62 Paul Cambon to Henri Cambon, London, 8 October 1904, Cambon, *Correspondance*, II, 164-5.

63 Dispatch from Monson to Lord Lansdowne, Paris, 9 November 1904, Gooch and Temperley, *British Documents*, III, 11.

64 Saint-Aulaire, *Confessions*, 167.

65 'Pays indépendants: Maroc', *Bulletin* 15, no 1 (January 1905), 36.

66 'Colonies française: Algérie', ibid, 26.

67 'Colonies française: Algérie', ibid, no 2 (February 1905), 75-6.

68 Saint-Aulaire, *Confessions*, 126.

69 Von Bulow to von Khulmann, Berlin, 2 January 1905, von Bulow,

Letters, 95. Von Bulow also warned von Khulmann that the opposition in France was growing toward Germany. That von Bulow knew Germany was courting serious difficulties there can be little doubt. Von Bulow to von Khulmann, Berlin, 2 January 1905, Deutschland, *Die Grosse Politik*, XX, 243.

70 Von Bulow to von Khulmann, Berlin, 30 January 1905, Von Bulow, *Letters*, 99.

71 Dispatch from Hoffman Philips to Francis B. Loomis, Tangier, 13 February 1905, United States, *Dispatches, Tangier*, roll 27.

72 Robert de Caix, 'Politique Morocaine', *Bulletin* 15, no 2 (February 1905), 61.

73 'Eugène Etienne: Ministre de l'Intérieur', ibid, 59.

74 'Pays indépendants: Maroc', ibid.

75 'Le programme du comité', ibid, no 3 (March 1905), 10–11.

76 Saint-Aulaire, *Confessions*, 167.

77 Paul Cambon to Henri Cambon, Paris, 24 April 1905, Cambon, *Correspondence*, II, 189.

78 Saint-Aulaire, *Confessions*, 85.

79 Paul Cambon to Henri Cambon, Paris, 24 April 1905, Cambon, *Correspondance*, II, 189.

80 Grey, *Twenty-Five Years*, 50–1.

81 Dispatch from Sir Arthur Nicolson to Lansdowne, Madrid, 4 April 1905, Gooch and Temperley, *British Documents*, III, 66.

82 Memorandum from von Bulow to Wilhelm II, Berlin, 4 April 1905, von Bulow, *Letters*, 122; memorandum from von Bulow to Wilhelm II, Berlin, 4 April 1905, Deutschland, *Die Grosse Politik*, XX, i, 301–3.

83 Ibid. Lansdowne was determined that the 1904 accords should develop into a working alliance. Very little could have swayed him from this support. Dispatch from Lansdowne to Monson, London, 29 April 1904, Gooch and Temperley, *British Documents*, II, 401.

84 Memorandum from von Bulow to Wilhelm II, Berlin, 4 April 1905, von Bulow, *Letters*, 122; memorandum from von Bulow to Wilhelm II, Berlin, 4 April 1905, Deutschland, *Die Grosse Politik*, XX, i, 301–1.

85 Ibid, 123. Most probably von Bulow got his information from Speck von Sternburg, the German ambassador in Washington. Von Sternburg indicated that President Roosevelt would support the German position in Morocco. Dispatch from von Sternburg to von Bulow, Washington, 9 March 1905, Deutschland, *Die Grosse Politik*, XXI, 259. Where von Sternburg received his information is unclear because in April 1905 the British ambassador Sir Mortimer Durand had a lengthy interview with William Howard Taft who stated officially, 'America does not care a cent for Morocco, and has no desire whatever to take sides between Germany and France.' Taft did state that President Roosevelt would help in mediation between Germany and France in Morocco. Dispatch from Durand to Lansdowne,

Washington, 26 April 1905, Gooch and Temperley, *British Documents*, III, 67–8.

86 Von Bulow to von Khulmann, Berlin, 6 April 1905, von Bulow, *Letters*, 123. The exact text reads, 'Heute aber stehen wir in vertrauensvollen Beziehunger zu Amerika und wissen dass dieses fur die "offene Tur" diplomatisch eintreten wird. Durch diese Stellungnahme Amerikas wird England sur Zuruckhaltung genotigt.' Von Bulow to von Khulmann, Berlin, 6 April 1905, Deutschland, *Die Grosse Politik*, XX, 319.

87 Von Radolin to von Holstein, Paris, 22 June 1905, Rich and Fisher, *Holstein Papers*, IV, 345.

88 Secret memorandum from von Bulow to von Holstein, Berlin, 31 July 1905, von Bulow, *Letters*, 163–4.

89 Robert de Caix, 'La crise Franco-Allemande', *Bulletin* 15, no 6 (June 1905), 237.

90 Colonel Marie Laperrine to Etienne, Southern Oases Command, Algeria, 19 February 1904, *Etienne Correspondence*, letter number 55.

91 Etienne to Berteaux, Paris, 29 July 1905, France, *Service historique de l'Armée*, Carton Algérie 30, Dossier sahariennes.

92 'Colonies françaises: Algérie', *Bulletin* 15, no 8 (August 1905), 308.

93 Dispatch from Etienne to Jonnart, Paris, 23 May 1906, France, *Service historique de l'Armée*, Carton Algérie 30, Dossier Bilma-Djanet 26–7.

94 'Pays indépendants: Maroc', *Bulletin* 15, no 9 (September 1905), 335.

95 Dispatch from Tallandier to Rouvier, Tangier, 12 November 1905, France, *Documents diplomatiques*, 174–5.

Chapter 10 THE PENETRATION OF THE SAHARA: CONTINUED PREPARATION FOR THE MOROCCAN CAMPAIGN 1905–7 (pages 137–45)

1 Etienne, *Son oeuvre*, II, 185–8.

2 Robert de Caix, 'Quinze jours de conférence', *Bulletin* 16, no 2 (February 1906), 36. Also, see Eugene N. Anderson, *The First Moroccan Crisis, 1904–1905* (Chicago: 1930).

3 'Colonies françaises: Algérie', ibid, no 1 (January 1906), 11.

4 'Pays independants: Maroc', ibid, 20.

5 Saint-Aulaire, *Confessions*, 167.

6 Von Bulow to Count Wolf von Metternich, Berlin, 9 January 1906, von Bulow, *Letters*, 195.

7 Sir Edward Grey to Sir Frank Lascelles, London, 9 January 1906, Grey, *Twenty-Five Years*, 80.

8 Ibid, 82.

9 Sir Edward Grey to Sir Francis Bertie, London, 31 January 1906, ibid, 77.

10 'Pays independants: Maroc', *Bulletin* 16, no 1 (January 1906), 19–20.

11 Ibid, 19.

12 'Colonies françaises: Algérie', ibid, no 2 (February 1906), 57.

13 'Colonies françaises: Algérie', ibid, 15, no 2 (February 1905), 75–6.

14 Lyautey to Etienne, Ain Sefra, 2 March 1906, Lyautey, *Vers le Maroc*, 255–6.

15 Dispatch from Jonnart to Etienne, Algiers, 2 April 1906, France, *Service historique de l'Armée*, Carton Maroc 18, Dossier 28–6 Frontière morocaine.

16 Eugène Etienne, Minute, 6 April 1906, 'Création du Postes à Sidi Auja sur la frontière morocaine', ibid.

17 Note from Etienne to Léon Bourgeois, Paris, 1 May 1906, ibid, Carton Maroc 15, 1904–8, Dossier 96.

18 Dispatch from Grey to Bertie, London, 15 March 1906, Gooch and Temperley, *British Documents*, II, 307.

19 Bertie to Grey, Paris, 16 March 1906, Grey, *Twenty-Five Years*, 105–6, Gooch and Temperley, *British Documents*, III, 306.

20 Note from Bourgeois to Etienne, Paris, 22 March 1906, France, *Service historique de l'Armée*, Carton Algérie 30, Dossier 1906 situation politique et militaire 26–7.

21 Note from George B. Myer to Etienne, Paris, 1 May 1906, ibid, Carton Algérie 30, Dossier Bilma-Djanet 2607. The Saharan problem is discussed in Bruno Verlet, *Le Sahara* (Paris: 1962), 53–61; also see Barbour, *North West Africa*, 258–9.

22 Telegram from Etienne to Lyautey, Paris, 3 May 1906, ibid.

23 Etienne to Jonnart, Paris, 8 May 1906, ibid.

24 Dispatch from Consul Rais to Bourgeois, Tripoli, 13 May 1906, ibid.

25 Telegram from Etienne to Jonnart, Paris, 23 May 1906, ibid.

26 Telegram from Etienne to Jonnart, Paris, 26 May 1906, ibid.

27 Telegram from Etienne to Lyautey, Paris, 30 May 1906, ibid, Carton Algérie 16, Dossier A I, 16.

28 Eugène Etienne, Minute, 20 June 1906, 'Documents géographiques relatifs au Maroc', ibid, Carton Maroc 20, études et projets 1899–1904, no special Dossier.

29 Confidential dispatch from the Deuxième Bureau, Tangier Branch, to the Chief of the Deuxième Bureau in the War Ministry, Tangier, 20 July 1906, ibid, Carton Maroc 15, Dossier 101.

30 'Pays indépendants: Maroc', *Bulletin* 16, no 7 (July 1906), 205–6; Gavin Maxwell, *Lords of the Atlas: The Rise and Fall of the House of Glaoua 1893–1956* (New York: 1966), 97.

31 'Pays indépendants: Maroc', *Bulletin* 16, no 9 (September 1906), 262.

32 'Colonies française: Algérie', ibid, no 10 (October 1906), 285

33 Eugène Etienne, 'Général ordre no 49, Afrique occidental française', 20 July 1906, France, *Service historique de l'Armée*, Carton AOF 2, Dossier Afrique 4, 1903–4.

34 Eugène Etienne, Minute, Paris, 18 October 1906, 'Disciplinaires des régiments étrangères' (pour L'Etat-Major de l'Armée), ibid, Carton

Legion Etrangère (Algérie 45), Dossier F création d'une compagnie étrangère de discipline.

35   Note from L'Etat-Major de l'Armée, Paris, 21 November 1906, ibid.

Chapter 11   THE FINAL PREPARATION FOR THE MOROCCAN CAMPAIGN 1907–10   (pages 146–57)

1   Telegram from Etienne to Jonnart, Paris, 24 October 1906, France, *Service historique de l'Armée*, Carton Algérie D 1, Dossier Ministère de la Guerre: Renforcements des postes au Sud Oranais.

2   Dispatch from Stephen Pichon to Bourgeouis, Tunis, 11 July 1906, ibid, Carton Algérie Sahara 1904–8, Dossier Bilma-Djanet.

3   Lyautey to Etienne, Oran, 21 October 1906, Lyautey, *Vers le Maroc*, 314.

4   'Pays indépendants: Maroc', *Bulletin* 17, no 1 (January 1907), 33–4. For a description of the intrigue around Moulay Hafid see Maxwell, *Lord of the Atlas*, 94–7.

5   'Pays indépendants: Maroc', ibid, no 3 (March 1907), 107. The *Ulama*, a body of learned Muslim doctors and theologians, had great influence, because of their exalted religious position, on the daily life of any Islamic state. See Wilfred C. Smith, *Islam in Modern History* (New York: 1957), 29, 307; Kenneth Cragg, *The Call of the Minaret* (New York: 1964), 162.

6   Charles René-Leclerc, 'A travers le Maroc', *Bulletin* 17, no 6 (June 1907), 231.

7   Dispatch from Phillipe Crozier to Stephen Pichon, Vienna, 5 May 1907, France, *Documents diplomatiques*, X, 794.

8   Dispatch from Jules Cambon to Pichon, Berlin, 24 June 1907, ibid, X, 85.

9   Von Bulow to Wilhelm II, Berlin, 27 June 1907, von Bulow, *Letters*, 218.

10   Ibid, 219.

11   Von Bulow to Wilhelm II, Berlin, 27 June 1907, ibid, 220.

12   Wilhelm II to von Bulow, Kiel, 26 June 1907, ibid, 216.

13   Secret dispatch from von Bulow to von Radolin, Berlin, 28 June 1907, Deutschland, *Die Grosse Politik*, XXI, ii, 577. The full text reads, 'His Majesty had, in the higher directives, telegraphed his first outline [of his Moroccan policy], in it, he himself fixed our Moroccan policy and made generally *our policy against France*. . . .' (The italics are mine.)

14   Wilhelm II to von Bulow, Kiel, 26 June 1907, von Bulow, *Letters*, 216.

15   Ibid, 215.

16   Von Bulow to Wilhelm II, Berlin, 30 June 1907, Deutschland, *Die Grosse Politik*, XXI, ii, 580.

17   Dispatch from Saint-Aulaire to Pichon, Tangier, 1 July 1907, France, *Documents diplomatiques*, XI, 103–4.

18 Dispatch from Paul Cambon to Stephen Pichon, London, 5 July
    1907, ibid, 114.
19 Dispatch from Crozier to Pichon, Vienna, 7 July 1907, ibid, 115–
    16.
20 Paul Cambon used a rather uncomplimentary description of Etienne's
    part in the Kiel meeting. Cambon wrote, 'Etienne, qui divide son
    echeveau', which means 'Etienne, who unravels his long ball of
    yarn'. Paul Cambon to Henri Cambon, London, 9 July 1907,
    Cambon, Correspondance, II, 232–3.
21 Dispatch from Jules Cambon to Pichon, Berlin, 18 July 1907,
    France, Documents diplomatiques, XI, 137–9.
22 Dispatch from Pichon to Jules Cambon, Paris, 18 July 1907, ibid,
    140–1.
23 Dispatch from Paul Cambon to Pichon, London, 24 July 1907, ibid,
    162. The British were concerned over the possibility of French
    investment in the proposed railroad, but Etienne was seemingly not
    interested at all in it.
24 Memorandum from Sir Charles Hardinge to Lord Grey, Berlin, 19
    August 1907, Gooch and Temperley, British Documents, VI, 44.
25 Baron von Holstein to von Bulow, Berlin, 29 August 1907, Fisher
    and Rich, Holstein Papers, IV, 488.
26 Dispatch from Sir Francis Bertie to Grey, Paris, 12 September 1907,
    Gooch and Temperley, British Documents, VI, 56–7.
27 Grey to Sir Frank Lascelles, London, 18 September 1907, ibid, 81.
28 Charles René-Leclerc, 'Maroc, l'Occupation de Casablanca',
    Bulletin 17, no 9 (September 1907), 332.
29 Charles René-Leclerc, 'Maroc, Le sultan du sud', ibid, no 10
    (October 1907), 367–8. The religious conflict is discussed in Maxwell,
    Lord of the Atlas, 100–2.
30 Clemenceau to Jonnart, Paris, 9 September 1907, as quoted in
    Auguste Terrier, 'La situation à la frontière Orano-moroccaine',
    Bulletin 17, no 11 (November 1907), 401–2. The entire Algero-
    Moroccan border policy of France was complex and was formulated
    in France to keep Morocco from claiming a complete delimitation.
    For the background to this problem see Anthony Reyner, 'Morocco's
    International Boundaries: A Factual Background', The Journal of
    Modern African Studies, 1 (September 1963), 313–26.
31 Jonnart to Pichon, Algiers, 27 August 1907, as quoted in Terrier, 'La
    situation', 401.
32 'Colonies françaises: Algérie', ibid, 18, no 1 (January 1908), 26.
33 'Pays indépendants: Maroc', ibid, no 2 (February 1908), 66, 68.
34 'Colonies françaises: Mauritanie', ibid, no 6 (June 1908), 221.
35 Auguste Terrier, 'Notre action en Mauritanie', ibid, no 9 (September
    1908), 303–4.
36 Laperrine to Etienne, Southern Oases Command, 24 September 1909,
    Etienne Correspondence, letter number 70.

37   Laperrine to Etienne, Southern Oases Command, 19 October 1909,
     ibid, letter number 71.
38   Pichon to Etienne, Paris, 10 November 1909, ibid, letter number 73.
39   'Pays indépendants: Maroc, le Maroc au parlement français', *Bulletin*
     18, no 3 (March 1908), 112.
40   Ibid, 113. For a good description of Abdel Aziz and conditions within
     Rabat in 1907 see letter from General Lyautey to Viscount Eugène-
     Melchoir de Vogüé, Rabat, 7 October 1907, as found in Hubert
     Lyautey, 'Lettres de Rabat (1907)', *Revue des deux mondes*, 64 (15 July
     1921), 380–3.
41   'Pays indépendants: Maroc, L'appel d'Abdel Aziz aux puissances',
     ibid, no 6 (June 1908), 228; Lyautey to Viscount Eugène-Melchoir
     de Vogüé, Rabat, 17 October 1907, Lyautey, *Lettres de Rabat*, 294–6.
42   Charles René-Leclerc, 'L'année administrative Morocaine en 1910',
     ibid, 12, no 3 (March 1911), 104.
43   'Comité du Maroc', ibid, 20, no 12 (December 1910), 383.

Chapter 12   THE TWILIGHT OF IMPERIALISM 1910–19
     (pages 158–70)
1   France, Chambre des Députés, *Exposé des Travaux durant la
     deuxième partie de la session ordinaire de 1911* (Paris: 1911).
2   Ibid, 196, 273.
3   France, Chambre des Députés, *Résumé générale des travaux legislatifs
     de la chambre des Députés pendant la Dixième legislature 1910–1914*
     (Paris: 1914), 283.
4   France, *Exposé des travaux* (1911), 286–9.
5   Eugène Etienne, 'L'oeuvre de la troisième république en Afrique
     occidentale', *Bulletin* 20, no 11 (November 1910), 329.
6   Ibid, 330–1.
7   This statement appears in a Preface written by Etienne to a book
     published under the patronage of the *Comité de l'Afrique française*.
     See Charles Mourey et Auguste Terrier, *L'expansion française et la
     formation territoriale* (Paris: 1910), 11.
8   Eugène Etienne, 'Discours 2ᵉ séance du 24 Decembre, 1910',
     Bulletin 21, no 1 (January 1911), 18.
9   Ibid, 16–17.
10   Robert de Caix, 'La crise morocaine', ibid, no 4 (April 1911), 133–4.
11   De Segonzac to Etienne, Fez, 25 May 1911, *Etienne Correspondence*,
     letter number 81.
12   Ibid.
13   Ibid.
14   During 1911 there were two cabinets: Ernst Monis and Joseph
     Caillaux. They were not overly friendly with the imperialists, however.
     In January 1912, Raymond Poincaré formed a cabinet and in 1913
     he became president of the Republic. Under his administration the
     expansionists were back in favour. Etienne became Minister of War,

for example, and Jonnart and others held important posts in the government.

15 General Dalbiez to Etienne, Tangier, 19 July 1911, *Etienne Correspondence*, letter number 75.

16 Ibid.

17 Robert de Caix, 'Les dernier développements de l'affaire moroccaine', *Bulletin* 21, no 6 (June 1911), 197.

18 Caillaux has written a very defensive set of memoirs; see Joseph Caillaux, *Mes mémoires*, 3 vols (Paris: 1942–5). See also Ima C. Barlow, *The Agadir Crisis* (Chapel Hill: 1940).

19 The Italian intervention in Libya is beyond the scope of this work. The invasion is well recorded in E. E. Evans-Pritchard, *The Sanusi of Cyrenaica* (London: 1954); Mahid Khadduri, *Modern Libya: A Study in Political Development* (Baltimore: 1963); William C. Askew, *Europe and the Italian Acquisition of Libya 1911–1912* (Durham, North Carolina: 1942).

20 Robert de Caix, 'La guerre italo-turque et la tripolitine', *Bulletin* 21, no 10 (October 1911), 326.

21 Jolly, *Dictionnaire des parlementaires*, 62.

22 Confer, *France and Algeria*, 74–6.

23 Robert de Caix, 'L'appel du Maroc', *Bulletin* 22, no 1 (January 1912), 3–4.

24 Saint-Aulaire, *Confessions*, 271. André Maurois in his biography does not mention the influence of Etienne on Lyautey's nomination. Maurois, *Lyautey*, 184–93.

25 Colonel Bulard to Etienne, Casablanca, 16 January 1912, *Etienne Correspondence*, letter number 77.

26 Eugène Etienne, 'Discours', *Bulletin* 22, no 4 (April 1912), 141–2.

27 René Normand to Etienne, Fez, 11 April 1912, *Etienne Correspondence*, letter number 86.

28 The massive home of the el Glaoua family in Marrakesh was open to many of the French officers and diplomats. It became a centre of collaborationist activity. Maxwell, *Lords of the Atlas*, 122–8.

29 'Pays indépendants: Maroc, les incidents de Marakesh', *Bulletin* 22, no 3 (March 1912), 113.

30 Normand to Etienne, Fez, 3 May 1912, *Etienne Correspondence*, letter number 87.

31 Jolly, *Dictionnaire des parlementaires*, 63–5. Etienne served as war minister through three separate cabinets: two Briand cabinets and the Barthou ministry.

32 Report from the Political office to Stephen Pichon, Paris, 30 July 1913, Great Britain, *Collected Documents*, 136–42.

33 France, *Résumé générale des Travaux*, 779–827.

34 Letter from Albert de Mun to Etienne, Paris, c June 1913, *Etienne Correspondence*, letter number 145.

35 Lyautey to Etienne, Fez, April 1913, as found in Pierre Lyautey,

ed, *Lyautey l'africain: textes et lettres du maréchal Lyautey*, I (Paris: 1953), 69.

36 Eugène Etienne, Directive number 1958—9.11, 'Limite du circle de Colomb Béchar', France, *Service historique de l'Armée*, Carton Algérie 19 (1911–18), Dossier 19.

37 Jolly, *Dictionnaire des parlementaires*, 66.

38 Gaillard to Etienne, Rabat, 24 June 1914, *Etienne Correspondncee*, letter number 96.

39 Galliéni to Etienne, Paris, 14 August 1914, ibid, letter number 89.

40 Galliéni to Etienne, Paris, 29 August 1914, ibid, letter number 90.

41 Lutaud to Etienne, Algiers, 16 February 1915, ibid, letter number 105.

42 Ibid.

43 Lutaud to Etienne, Algiers, 28 February 1915, ibid, letter number 108.

44 Lutaud to Etienne, Algiers, 28 February 1915, ibid, letter number 107.

Bibliography

ARCHIVAL SOURCES

Chamberlain, Joseph. *Joseph Chamberlain Papers*, University of Birmingham, Birmingham, England. Dossiers: JC 11/6; JC/57.

Etienne, Eugène. Eugène Etienne Correspondance, volume 24, 327, Nouvelle acquisition française, Bibliothèque nationale, Paris.

France, Archive Nationale, *Series F80, Algérie*, Paris. Cartons: 1684; 1686; 1687; 1688; 1689; 1690; 1693; 1695; 1696; 1697; 1698; 1709; 1710; 1711; 1715; 1727; 1729; 1733; 1744; 1773; 1784; 1785; 1816.

—— ex-Ministère de la France d'outre-mer, Correspondance politique, Paris. Series: Afrique II; Afrique III; Afrique IV; Afrique VI; Soudan VI.

—— Ministère des Affaires Etrangères, Archives diplomatique. *Correspondance politique*, Paris. Vols: Aden (1855–95) 113; Angleterre 898, 899, 900, 904, 905; Espange (1894) 924; Espange (1895) 925; Espange (1895) 929; Espange (1896) 928; Grand Bretagne—politique avec France (1897–8); Maroc 70, 72, 74; Zanzibar 19.

—— Service historique de l'Armée de Terre, Section d'outre-mer, Château de Vincennes (Val de Marne), Paris. Series Afrique occidentale française; Series Algérie; Series Algérie, Sahara 1904–7; Series Algérie, Troupes Sahariennes; Series Légion Etrangère; Series Maroc Amlet et Oudja; Series Maroc; Series Oran. (Over 200 cartons consulted.)

Great Britain, Public Records Office, *Foreign Office: Africa*, London. Cartons: Africa 403, 413, 416, and 633.

Mizon, Lieutenant de Vaisseau Louis Alexandre. Mizon Correspondance, volumes 10726, 10727, Nouvelle Acquisitions française, Bibliothèque nationale, Paris.

United States, Department of State. *Dispatches from the US Consular Officials in Algiers*, rolls 17–19. Washington: National Archives Microfilm Publications, 1961.

—— Department of State. *Dispatches from the United States Ministers to France 1789–1906*, rolls 103–7. Washington: National Archives Microfilm Publications, 1961.

—— Department of State. *Dispatches from the US Consular Officials in Tangier*, rolls 27–37. Washington: National Archives Microfilm Publications, 1962.

PRINTED AND MICROFILMED DOCUMENTS AND LETTERS

Bulow, Prince Bernhard von. *The Letters of Prince von Bulow 1903–1906*. Translated by Frederic Whyte (London: c 1930).

Cambon, Paul. *Correspondance 1870–1924*, 3 vols (Paris: 1924).

Deutschland. Auswartiges Amt. *Die Grosse Politik des Europeanishen Kabinette, 1871–1914*, vols 17, 18–1, 21–2, 39 (Berlin: 1924–7).

Duget, Edouard. *Les Députés et les Cahiers électoraux de 1889: Année parlementaire, Première Année* (Paris: 1889).

Etienne, Eugène. *Son oeuvre—Algérienne et politique 1881–1906*, 2 vols (Paris: 1907).

—— *Projet de loi ayant pour objet de l'exploitation du Chemin de Fer à Beni Ounif* (Paris: Chambre des Députés, document number 107, 8 June 1903).

—— *Projet de résolution ayant pour objet de créer un institut morocain* (Paris: Chambre des Députés, document number 1,893, 8 July 1903).

Ferry, Jules. *Lettres de Jules Ferry* (Paris: 1914).

France. Chambre des Deputés. *Exposé des travaux durant la deuxième partie de la session ordinaire de 1911* (Paris: 1911).

—— Chambre des Députés. *Résumé générale des travaux legislatifs de la Chambre des Députés pendant la Dixième legislature 1910–1914* (Paris: 1914).

—— Ministère des Affaires Etrangères. *Documents Diplomatiques Françaises*, 1ère Series, vols 1–12, 1929–51; 2ème Series, vols 1–12, 1930–54 (Paris: 1935–50).

—— Ministère des Affaires Etrangerès. *Rapport au Président de la République sur la situation de la Tunisie en 1897* (Paris: 1898).

—— Madame du Gast, Chargée de Mission du Maroc. *Le Maroc*

agricole: Rapport addressé au Ministre de l'Agriculture (Paris: 1908).

—— Service des Affaires indigènes. Résidence général de France à Tunis. *Historique des services des affaires indigènes de Tunis* (Bourg: 1931).

—— Ministère de la Guerre. Section technique des troupes coloniales. *Une étape de la conquête de l'Afrique equatoriale françasie 1908–12* (Paris: 1912).

Gooch, G. P., and Temperley, Harold. *British Documents on the Origins of the War 1898–1914*, vols 1–4 (London: 1927).

Great Britain, Cabinet Documents. *Committee for Imperial Defence 1880–1914*, Rolls 1–6 (London: 1965).

—— *Collected Diplomatic Documents Relating to the Outbreak of the War* (London: 1915).

—— Foreign Office. *Morocco: Correspondence Relative to the Conference Held at Madrid in 1880* (London: 1880).

Italia, Ministero degli Affairi Esteri. *I Documenti Diplomatici Italiani*, Terza serie 1–3 (Roma: 1962).

Jaurès, Jean. *Textes choisis: contre la guerre et la politique coloniale*, vol 1 (Paris: 1959).

Jolly, Jean. *Dictionnaire des parlementaires français*, vol 1 (Paris: 1960).

Lyautey, Hubert. *Paroles d'action, Madagascar-sud Oranais-Oran-Maroc (1900–1926)* (Paris: 1927).

—— *Vers le Maroc: lettres du Sud Oranais 1903–1906* (Paris: 1937).

Lyautey, Pierre, ed. *Lyautey l'africain: textes et lettres du maréchal Lyautey*, 4 vols (Paris: 1935–7).

Perham, Margery, and Bull, Mary, eds. *The Diaries of Lord Lugard: East Africa* (Evanston: 1959).

—— *The Diaries of Lord Lugard: Nigeria* (Evanston: 1963).

Rich, Norman, and Fisher, M. H., eds. *The Holstein Papers: Correspondence 1897–1909* (Cambridge: 1963).

MEMOIRS AND AUTOBIOGRAPHIES

Baden-Powell, Robert. *The Downfall of Premphe: A Diary of the Life with the Native Levy in Ashanti* (Philadelphia: 1896).

Barclay, Sir Thomas. *Thirty Years: Anglo-French Reminiscences 1876–1906* (Boston: 1914).

Barrere, Camille. 'Lettres à Delcassé', *La Revue du Paris*, April 1937, 721–63.

Blanchard, Marcel, ed. 'Correspondance de Félix Faure touchant les affaires coloniales 1882–1898', *Revue d'Histoire des Colonies*, 44 (1955), 133–85.

Caillaux, Joseph. *Mes Mémoires*, 3 vols (Paris: 1942–5).

Caix, de, Robert. *Fachoda: La France et l'Angleterre* (Paris: 1898).

Cambon, Paul. 'Lettres de Paul Cambon à Félix Faure', edited by René Dellet, *Revue d'histoire diplomatique*, 67 (1954), 189–201.

Chailley-Bert, Joseph. *Dix années de politique* (Paris: 1902).

—— 'Le ministère des colonies', *Revue des deux mondes*, 64 (April 1894), 908–24.

Cheusi, P. B. *Gambetta: Life and Letters*, translated by Violette Montagu (New York: 1910).

Cousins, W. E. *Madagascar of Today* (New York: 1895).

Crispi, Francesco. *The Memoirs of Francesco Crispi*, vols 2–3 (London: 1914).

Faure, Félix. 'Fachoda (1898)', edited by René Dellet, *Revue d' histoire diplomatique*, 69 (1955), 29–39.

Foureau, F. *Mission Saharienne Foureau-Lamy: d'Alger au Congo par le Tchad* (Paris: 1902).

Gelfand, Michael, ed. *Gubulawayo and Beyond: Letters and Journals of the Early Jesuit Missionaries to Zambesia 1879–1887* (New York: 1968).

Gentil, Louis. *Missions de Segonzac, dans le Bled es Siba: exploration au Maroc* (Paris: 1906).

Grey, Sir Edward. *Twenty-Five Years, 1892–1916*, 2 vols (New York: 1925).

Hanotaux, Gabriel. 'Carnets', edited by Gabriel Louis Jaray, *Revue des deux mondes*, 118 (April 1948), 385–403, 573–88.

Hardinge, Sir Charles. *A Diplomatist in the East* (London: 1928).

Joffre, Marshal. *The Personal Memoirs of Joffre, Field Marshal of the French Army*, translated by T. Bently Mott, 2 vols (New York: 1932).

Johnston, Alex. *The Life and Letters of Sir Harry Johnston* (London).

Johnston, Sir Harry. *The Story of My Life* (Indianapolis: 1923).

Lebon, André. 'La boucle du Niger 1896–1898', *Revue des deux mondes* (September 1900), 356–83.

—— 'La mission Marchand et la cabinet Méline', *Revue des deux mondes*, 70 (March 1900), 274–96.

Lefant, Capitaine Eugène. *Le Niger: voie ouverte à empire africain* (Paris: 1903).

Legand, Jean. *Le leçon de Fachoda* (Paris: 1899).

Lennox, Lady Algernon Gordon, ed. *The Diary of Lord Bertie of Thame 1914–1918*, 2 vols (London: 1924).

Loti, Pierre. *Au Maroc* (Paris: 1890).

Lucien, Hubert. *Politique Africaine—Maroc, Afrique occidentale, Algérie, Tchad, L'Effort étranger* (preface by Eugène Etienne) (Paris: 1904).

Lugard, Frederick D. *The Rise of Our East African Empire*, 2 vols (London: 1968).

Lyautey, Hubert. 'Lettres de Rabat (1907)', *Revue des deux mondes*, 64 (July 1921), 273–304.

Maistre, de, Charles. *A Travers l'afrique centrale, de Congo au Niger, 1892–1893* (Zug, Switzerland: 1970).

Mangin, Charles. 'Lettres de la mission Marchand', *Revue des deux mondes* (September 1931), 241–83.

Martinière, Henri de la. *Souvenirs du Maroc* (Paris: 1920).

Memier, M. A. 'Lettres du commandant Marchand à Guilaume Gandidier', *Revue française d'histoire outre-mer*, 45 (1958), 61–108.

Montiel, P. L. 'Contribution d'un vétéran à l'histoire coloniale', *La Revue de Paris*, XXX (1930), 97–131.

Paléologue, Maurice. *Au Quai d'Orsay de la veille de la Tourmente, journal 1913–1914* (Paris: 1947).

—— *The Turning Point: Three Critical Years, 1904–1906* (London: 1935).

Poincaré, Raymond. *Au service de la France: L'Europe sous les armes 1913*, vol 3 (Paris: 1926).

—— *The Memoirs of Raymond Poincaré, 1913–1914* (Garden City: 1928).

Portal, Sir Gerald. *The mission to Uganda* (London: 1894).

Porter, Commandant. *La question du Touat: Sahara Algérien* (Alger: 1891).

Pourvourville, Albert de. 'Les congrès coloniaux français', *La Nouvelle Revue*, 26 (January 1904), 225–9.

Rodd, Sir James Rennell. *Social and Diplomatic Memories*, vol 3 (London: 1925).

Saint-Aulaire, Comte de. *Confessions d'un vieux diplomate* (Paris: 1953).

Segonzac, Marquis de. *Au coeur de l'Atlas: Missions au Maroc 1904–1905* (Paris: 1910).

Sevin-Desplaces, Louis. 'La mission monteil et la politique de la France en Afrique du nord', *La Nouvelle Revue*, 81 (March 1893), 138–41.

—— 'La politique Franco-Africaine', *La Nouvelle Revue*, 84 (October 1893), 627–32.

Tardieu, André. *La Conférence d'Algeciras, histoire diplomatique de la crise morocaine* (Paris: 1908).

Villa-Urrutia, Marquis de Ramirez. *Paleque diplomatico: Recuerdos de un Embajador*, 2 vols (Madrid: 1923).

Woff, Theodore. *The Eve of 1914* (New York: 1936).

SECONDARY SOURCES

Ageron, Charles-Robert. *Les Algériens musulmans et la France 1871–1919*, 2 vols (Paris: 1968).

Anderson, Eugene N. *The First Moroccan Crisis 1904–1905* (Chicago: 1930).

Anderson-Morshead, A. E. M. *The History of the Universities' Mission to Central Africa, 1859–1898* (London: 1899).

Andrew, Christopher. *Théophile Delcassé and the Making of the Entente Cordiale: A Reappraisal of French Foreign Policy 1898–1905* (New York: 1968).

Askew, William C. *Europe and the Italian Acquisition of Libya 1911–1912* (Durham, North Carolina: 1942).

Barbour, Nevill. *A Survey of North West Africa (The Maghrib)* (New York: 1962).

Barlow, Ima C. *The Agadir Crisis* (Chapel Hill, North Carolina: 1940).

Baumont, Maurice. *L'essor industriel et l'impérialisme colonial 1878–1904*, 7: 18 (Paris: 1949).

Betts, Raymond F. *Assimilation and Association in French Colonial Theory 1890–1914* (New York: 1961).

Bocca, Geoffrey. *La Légion* (New York: 1965).

Bodley, R. V. C. *The Warrior Saint* (Boston: 1953).

Boncour, Joseph P. *Recollections of the Third Republic*, vol 1 (New York: 1957).

Brace, Richard M. *Morroco, Algeria, Tunisia* (Englewood Cliffs, N J: 1966).

Brogan, D. W. *The Development of Modern France*, 2 vols (New York: 1966).

Brunschwig, Henri. *Mythes et réalités de l'impérialisme colonial français 1870–1914* (Paris: 1961).

—— *L'avènement de l'Afrique noire de XIXᵉ siècle à nos jours* (Paris: 1963).

Caillé, Jacques, et Charles-Roux, François. *Missions diplomatiques françaises à Fes* (Paris: 1955).

Carrouges, Michel. *Soldier of the Spirit: The Life of Charles de Foucauld* (New York: 1956).

Chastenet, Jacques. *La république des républicains 1879–1893* (Paris: 1954).

—— *La republique triomphante 1893–1906* (Paris: 1955).

Cobban, Alfred. *A History of Modern France 1871–1962*, vol 3 (Baltimore: 1965).

Confer, Vincent. *France and Algeria: The Problem of Civil Reform 1870–1920* (Syracuse: 1966).

Cook, Arthur W. *Africa: Past and Present* (Totowa, NJ: 1965).

Cowles, Virginia. *The Kaiser* (New York: 1961).

Cragg, Kenneth. *The Call of the Minaret* (New York: 1962).

Craig, Gordon A. *From Bismarck to Adenauer: Aspects of German Statecraft* (New York: 1965).

Dardenne, Henriette. *Lumières sur l'affaires Dreyfus* (Paris: 1964).

Derfler, Leslie. *The Third French Republic 1870–1940* (New York: 1966).

Despois, Jean. *Pays d'outre mer: L'Afrique du Nord*, vol 1 (Paris: 1958).

Dubois, Marcel, et Terrier, Auguste. *Les colonies françaises: un siècle d'expansion coloniale* (Paris: 1901).

Evans-Pritchard, E. E. *The Sanusi of Cyrenaica* (London: 1949).

Fallot, Ernest. *La Solution française de la question du Maroc* (Paris: Delagrave, nd).

Friedjung, Heinrich. *Die Zeitalter des Imperialismus 1884–1914*, 3 vols (Berlin: 1922).

Girault, Arthur. *The Colonial Tariff of France* (Oxford: 1916).

Goldberg, Harvey. *The Life of Jean Jaurès* (Madison: 1962).

Grenville, J. A. S. *Lord Salisbury and Foreign Policy: The Close of the Nineteenth Century* (London: 1964).

Hance, William A., Kotschan, Vincent, and Peetrec, Richard. *Source Areas of Export Production in Tropical Africa* (New York: 1961).

Hanotaux, Gabriel, ed. *L'empire colonial français* (Paris: 1929).

Hartford-Battersby, Charles F. *Pilkington of Uganda* (New York: 1899).

Heggoy, Alf Andrew. 'The Colonial Policies of Gabriel Hanotaux in Africa, 1894–1898' (PhD dissertation, Duke University, 1963).

Huttenback, Robert A. *The British Imperial Experience* (New York: 1966).

Iiams, Thomas M. *Dreyfus, Diplomatists, and the Quai d'Orsay: Gabriel Hanotaux at the Quai d'Orsay 1894–1898* (Paris: 1962).

Jackson, J. H. *Clemenceau and the Third Republic* (London: 1946).

Johnston, Sir Harry. *A History of the Colonization of Africa by Alien Races* (Cambridge: 1930).

Judd, Denis. *Balfour and the British Empire, A Study in Imperial Evolution, 1874–1932* (New York).

Kanya-Forstner, A. S. *The Conquest of the Western Sudan: A Study in French Military Imperialism* (Cambridge: 1969).

Khadduri, Majid. *Modern Libya: A Study in Political Development* (Baltimore: 1963).

Lafore, Laurence. *The Long Fuse: An Interpretation of the Origins of World War I* (New York: 1965).

Langer, William L. *The Diplomacy of Imperialism 1890–1902* (2nd edn, New York: 1956).

—— *European Alliances and Alignments 1871–1890* (New York: 1950).

Lapsley, J. W. *The Life and Letters of Samuel Lapsley: Missionary to the Congo Valley and West Africa, 1866–1892* (Richmond: 1893).

Lavisse, Ernest. *Histoire de France contemporaine depuis la révolution jusqu'à la paix de 1919*, vol 13 (Paris: 1921).

Martel, André. *Les confins Saharo-tripolitai de la Tunisie 1881–1911*, 2 vols (Paris: 1965).

Maurois, André. *Lyautey* (New York: 1931).

Maurras, Charles. *Kiel et Tangier, le république française devant l'Europe 1895–1921* (Versailles: 1928).

Maxwell, Gavin. *The Lords of the Atlas: The Rise and Fall of the House of Glaoua 1893–1956* (New York: 1966).

Miège, Jean-Louis. *Le Maroc* (Paris: 1961).

Monger, George W. *The End of Isolation: British Foreign Policy 1900–1907* (London: 1963).

Montgelas, Count Max. *British Foreign Policy Under Sir Edward Grey* (New York: 1928).

Murphy, Agnes. *The Ideology of French Imperialism 1871–1891* (New York: 1968).

Newton, Lord P. C. *Lansdowne: A Biography* (London: 1929).

Nickerson, Jane Soames. *A Short History of North Africa* (New York: 1961).

Nord, Pierre. *Charles de Foucauld: français d'Afrique* (Paris: 1957).

Oliver, Roland, and Mathew, Gervase. *A History of East Africa* (Oxford: 1968).

Petit, Edouard. *Organisation des colonies françaises et des pays de protectorat*, 2 vols (Paris: 1894–5).

Porter, Charles W. *The Career of Théophile Delcassé* (Philadelphia: 1936).

Postgate, Raymond. *England Goes to Press* (New York: 1937).

Preminger, Marion M. *The Sands of Tamanrasset* (New York: 1963).

Priestly, Herbert D. *France Overseas: A Study of Modern Imperialism* (New York: 1938).

Ralston, David B. *The Army of the Republic* (Cambridge, Massachusetts: 1967).

Reclus, Maurice. *Grandeur de la troisième de Gambetta à Poincaré* (Paris: 1948).

—— *La Troisième république de 1870 à 1918* (Paris: 1945).

Renouvin, Pierre. *Histoire des relations internationales* (Paris: 1955).

—— *Politique extérieure de Théophile Delcassé 1898–1905* (Paris: 1954).

Roberts, Stephen H. *The History of French Colonial Policy, 1870–1925* (London: 1963).

Robinson, Ronald, and Gallagher, John. *Africa and the Victorians* (London: 1961).

Ronze, Raymond. *La question d'Afrique* (Paris: 1918).

Rouget, Fernand. *L'expansion coloniale au Congo français* (Paris: 1906).

Sanderson, George N. *England, Europe, and the Upper Nile 1882–1899* (Edinburgh: 1965).

Scham, Alan. *Lyautey in Morocco: Protectorate Politics, 1912–1925* (Berkeley: 1970).

Sieberg, Herward. *Eugène Etienne und die Franzosische Kolonial-politik 1887–1904* (Koln: 1968).

Smith, Wilfred C. *Islam in Modern History* (New York: 1957).

Stern, Jacques. *The French Colonies: Past and Future* (New York: 1944).

Taylor, A. J. P. *The Struggle for the Mastery of Europe, 1848–1914* (Oxford: 1954).

Tint, Herbert. *The Decline of French Patriotism 1870–1940* (London: 1966).

Tuchman, Barbara. *The Guns of August* (New York: 1962).

Villot, Roland. *Eugène Etienne* (Oran: 1951).

Webster, J. B. and A. A. Boahen. *A History of West Africa* (New York: 1967).

Wellard, James. *The Great Sahara* (New York: 1965).

Williams, Wythe. *The Tiger of France: Conversations with Clemenceau* (New York: 1949).

Wills, A. J. *The History of Central Africa* (Oxford: 1969).

Wright, Gordon. *France in Modern Times* (Chicago: 1966).

ARTICLES

Brunschwig, Henri. 'La parti colonial français', *Revue française d'histoire d'outre-mer*, 46 (1959), 49-83.

—— 'Colonisation française', *Revue historique*, 222 (July–September 1959), 133–56.

Cooke, James J. 'Madagascar and Zanzibar: A Case Study in African Colonial Conflict, 1894–1897', *African Studies Review*, XIII, 3 (December 1970), 435–43.

—— 'Rudyard Kipling in France: French Imperialist Authors and Literature', *Studies in English*, XI (Winter 1970), 69–82.

—— 'Lyautey and Etienne: The Soldier and the Politician in the Penetration of Morocco', *Military Affairs*, XXXVI, 1 (February 1972), 14–17.

'La frontière morocaine du Sud oranais', *La Nouvelle Revue*, 77 (August 1892), 830–7.

Heggoy, Alf A. 'The Origins of Algerian Nationalism in the Colony and in France', *Muslim World*, 58 (April 1968), 128–40.

Jeaugeon, R. 'Les sociétés d'exploitation au Congo et l'opinion française de 1890–1906', *Revue française d'histoire d'outre-mer*, XLVIII (1961).

Menier, M. A. 'La marche au Tchad de 1887 à 1891', *Bulletin de l'Institut des études centrafricaines*, NS 5 (1953), 5–18.

Renouvin, Pierre. 'Les origines de l'expédition de Fachoda', *Revue historique*, 22 (1948), 179–97.

Reyner, Anthony. 'Morocco's International Boundaries: A Factual Background', *The Journal of Modern African Studies*, 1 (September 1963), 313–26.

Stengers, Jan. 'Correspondance de Leopold II avec van Eetvelde', *Academie Royale des Sciences d'Outre-mer*, XXIV (1953), 474–505.

Sylvain, Fabre. 'Eugène Etienne', *Société de géographie et d' archéologie d'Oran* (1921), 97–103.

Valbert, George. 'Deux missions françaises dans le boucle du Niger', *Revue des deux mondes*, 107 (October 1891), 684–95.

de Vogüé, Eugène-Melchior. 'Les Indes noires: L'Europe et la France en Afrique', *Revue des deux mondes*, LX (November 1890), 49–92.

Wally, George de. 'L'Afrique obligatoire', *La Nouvelle Revue*, 75 (April 1892), 586–92.

PERIODICALS

Bulletin de l'Afrique française, 1895–1912.

La dépêche coloniale, 1900–10.

L'Illustration, 1880–1910.
La Nouvelle Revue, 1880–1910.
Revue Africaine, 1898–1910.
Revue des deux mondes, 1880–1910.

Acknowledgements

THERE ARE many people who aided me in the preparation of this manuscript. I am especially indebted to Dr Alf Heggoy, Professor of North African History, of the Department of History of the University of Georgia, for his help and guidance. I am also grateful to Professor Heggoy for his generous permission to consult his notes taken at the *Archive Nationale* (*Series F80, Algérie*), the *Ministère des Affaires Etrangères*, and *ex-Ministère de la France Outre-Mer*. I must also mention the help given to me by Drs Victor S. Mamatey, John Vogt, Joseph Berrigan, and Horace Montgomery of the University of Georgia, and also Drs William Strickland and Frederick E. Laurenzo of the University of Mississippi.

Dr Edouard Morot—Sir, Cultural Attaché of the French Embassy—must be thanked for the time he took in helping me obtain a grant for research in Paris. His letters of introduction to many of the archives proved to be invaluable. I would like to thank the director and staff of the Bibliothèque Nationale for their help in obtaining for me the correspondence of Eugène Etienne. Special thanks must be given to the excellent staff of the Bibliothèque Nationale for their aid in microfilming the Etienne and Mizon papers. I would like to add a special word of thanks to Colonel Sellier, Chef de la Section Outre-Mer, Service Historique de l'Armée de Terre, Château de Vincennes, and to Mlle Sueur, his secretary, for the great aid they gave in examining the many cartons of documents pertaining to Algeria, Morocco, the Sahara, French West Africa, and the French Foreign Legion. Without their excellent direction and help much information concerning the colonial expansion of France could not be included.

I would also like to thank Dr Vincent Confer of Syracuse University who gave his valuable time to answer some lengthy questions about Eugène Etienne as Minister of War. Three other people who deserve special credit for this manuscript are my wife, who helped read it and who has lived, for five years, with the ghosts of many French colonialists, Mrs Robert Crabtree, who typed a draft, and Mr Bobby Ratliff who typed the final draft.

University of Mississippi   J.J.C.

Index